GUILLERMINA
AND THE ROSE

*The story of a little girl who only
wanted to be wanted*

DON CUSH

PublishAmerica
Baltimore

Hardcover 9781462690411
Softcover 9781462683154
PUBLISHED BY PUBLISHAMERICA, LLLP
www.publishamerica.com
Baltimore

Printed in the United States of America

TABLE OF CONTENTS

PROLOGUE

This really started with the CEO of my computer corporation being asked at a press conference what his company was doing in the way of education.

He avoided giving a real answer thanks to his executive skills of looking like he'd replied, when he in truth did not. Yet, when he returned to corporative headquarters, he asked that question to the more responsible executive, my boss, who in turn asked me, his Technical Assistant. My reply was a shrug and a "Nothing."

That set the wheels in motion to where I ended up with a cart blanche expense account and five years to come up with the first way to use computers to teach children and prove they had learned from using them.

I thus started my worldwide, very expensive odyssey to answer the question first posed by the press.

However, halfway through the adventure, in an establishment where I was testing the capabilities of computers to teach, a little Mexican girl popped into my life and sent it helter-skelter, producing many more problems than just establishing the efficiency of educating via computers, which I was being paid to accomplish.

I am not an essayist, nor am I an author; however, I believe that I must reveal what I have experienced these past twenty-one years to all who are concerned with children and their environments. This chronicle describes the children of one world and the abhorrent conditions that they are subject to every day.

Although, my experience occurred in one country, these situations exist throughout the world. Furthermore, this narrative discusses such things as the relationships among the United States and Mexico, government agencies, big business, drugs, prostitution, and trafficking. So, please bear with me as I unfold the story from the start to finish, at least as much of it as I can remember.

In my opinion, it is a story that must be told even if it is to the detriment of many people and countries. In days gone by, many things have occurred in an attempt to obstruct the completion of this account. With the technology of this day and age, these situations should never take place. Maybe if this experience can help what has happened, and what is still happening, to cease or at least bring about an investigation with the authority to bring about corrections, then I have accomplished my purpose for exposing these circumstances.

These forgotten children of the worlds are pleading and begging for assistance in their plight for a better existence and life above and beyond the well-known cry for nourishment. Yet, so very few listen to their calls and cries for salvation beyond the bare necessities. Supplying food only solves one present problem. But is this the real answer to the dilemma? A vast majority of the people who lack nutrition and substance have a family that can help them. However, what about the children who have no one to turn for help and must face not only hunger, but also physical and sexual abuse, emotional neglect, and the knowledge that no one will ever come for them? The children who have no parents or family? Who have no one to turn to for comfort, so still they suffer? Who endeavors to assist them? These children are the forgotten ones, who have perpetually been last in the thoughts of mankind because they often don't have an adult to speak for them or to hold and comfort them.

In conclusion, should not "the last become first?"*

This is a treatise on one of those forgotten children who lived through many horrible occurrences. Her name is Guillermina, and her cry was actually, thankfully, heard. Once this lamentation was exposed, people of the world were prompt to rise to her assistance. But what about the other children who still live in the world from which Guillermina was released? Can we help them? What do we do? How do we do it?

I truly believe that if the good people of the world were to become aware of these circumstances under which these forgotten children live, they would quickly rise up, en masse, and these circumstances would be corrected. It would take time, of course. However, at least these trials that Guillermina has lived through, and other children are still living through today, might have a chance at coming to an end.

Why must salvation and assistance always be left to the common people? Why have governments and companies, who have known about such dire situations for many years and should have the responsibility for solving them, done nothing? Most of the time, in fact, they were responsible for the situations in the first place. Where were they? Where are they now? Why didn't they do something about it? Maybe this narrative will help to answer some of those questions, and to end the cycle of abuse and neglect.

THESE CHILDREN CRY OUT WITH OUTSTRETCHED ARMS
AND TEAR-FILLED EYES
INTO THE COLD AND EMPTY NIGHT
FOR ASSISTANCE AND DELIVERANCE.

IN RETURN,
THEY
HEAR NOTHING.

*the Bible

CHAPTER ONE

TIJUANA AND THE CASA

I suppose it all started when I was in San Diego on a trip. For some reason or another, the people whom I was suppose to meet called and canceled at the last minute. This now left me with the entire day free. With all this time on my hands, I wondered what to do. I had been to San Diego many times previously; therefore, sightseeing did not seem very interesting. I then remembered that it had been a long time since I had been to Mexico, and that the town of Tijuana is only a short seventeen miles from San Diego. I had not visited that town in several years. I started to wonder if Tijuana was still as wild as it was in the past. If so, it ought to be a fun place, now that I had time on my hands.

As I drove those short miles to Tijuana, many thoughts came back to me of those youthful days when I used to visit Tijuana. The things we did and said—those were the days! Days when we were so young and our troubles were so very few, although, they seemed large at the time. The drive seemed to take much longer than it actually did, as trips always do when you are going someplace (and for some reason, they always seem so short when you are returning). In those long minutes, I thought of many things, such as how lovely were the views of the highway that flew by my car window. Numerous things reminded me of previous trips; then again, many objects seemed new. As a whole, the drive was as I remembered it those many years ago. When I arrived, I exited the highway just prior to crossing the border so I could park my rental car. As was the case years ago, you ought never to take your car into Tijuana. That is, not if you wanted your car in one piece when you returned to the States.

The parking lots had not changed; they were the same as I remembered. The only difference was now they had automatic money collectors. There was still no pavement on the property, just a dusty lot with holes and bumps that could swallow your car if you did not drive slowly and carefully. I parked and got out. I made sure that the car was locked securely, as cars at border parking lots are always prime targets for burglarizing. I proceeded to the border on foot and crossed into Mexico. It was hot. But then again, it always seemed hot in Mexico during the day.

Once I had crossed the border, I stopped for a minute and looked towards Tijuana. There stood a new Mexico. The border crossing into Tijuana had completely changed on the Mexican side. Years ago, it was just a single dirt road with a rickety bridge going to Tijuana. The road was full of bumps and holes that threatened your car if you did not drive conscientiously. Only two cars could travel it at the same time, one going and one coming. Now in its place was a super six-lane paved highway. It was thoughtfully constructed, with elevated ramps and many lanes in both directions. It was a sight to behold. The course to Tijuana on the Mexican side of the border had become a modern compliment to technology and science.

The American side had not changed in any way. There were still the same amount of checkpoints for cars crossing the border, the same long line of cars waiting to be inspected, and the same loud, fresh voices of the American customs inspectors belittling those at the border waiting to be allowed into the world of milk and honey. This attitude from the inspectors had not changed, nor do I expect it ever will. The inspectors still had the same way of taking their time to search the cars as they did in the past. Not so much to scrutinize the crossing cars and people, which would be reasonable, but just to show their absolute authority by taking their sweet old time. Much of their time was spent leaving their booths and crossing to the other booths to drink coffee or just to pass the time talking to other inspectors while the cars waited. Who would dare say anything to them? One unfavorable word to them and you would have trouble like you would never believe, not to mention you most likely would not cross the border that day.

As I stood there, I saw one young Mexican being dragged from his car by two American Customs officers. I mean actually dragged, not just escorted. It seemed that the American guards had found something in his car and wanted to question him further on the subject. The young Mexican kept looking back at his wife and two adolescent children that were still in the car and saying something in Spanish that I did not really understand. A man standing next to me, who was also observing the scene, told me that the young Mexican was saying, "My family does not know what is going on, please let me explain to them." I do not know if that was what the young Mexican being dragged from the car really said, but, I do know what the inspectors were saying, and those words cannot be written here, as most of them were four letters. However, the words all added up to "No, you cannot." I have often wondered what happened to that young man and his family.

Later on in this story, I was to find out that these happenings were minor compared to what these Customs inspectors are really capable of doing to Mexicans and Americans, both adults and children. Even when the agents are proven guilty of a wrongdoing, there is never any real punishment given to them. The pathetic fact is that when you cross from America to Mexico and compare the way that the Mexican Customs officers (those backward, third world people!) are at the border, you find them to be always polite, chivalrous, and eager to help a tourist. Oh, how I wish sometimes that we, the Americans, could also be backward in these respects.

Such thoughts soon came to an end as the reality of where I was came swiftly to the front of my mind. I had to defend myself against the many people who were shoving and pushing on the streets. This seemed to be a way of life with the Mexican people. As I proceeded further into Mexico to secure a taxi for the short ride into the center of town, my reflection of Tijuana wandered to questions like whether or not the Blue Fox Cantina was still there. Were the streets on the main thoroughfare as dirty and crowded as they were back then? Did they now have pavement on the main streets as they do here at the border crossing?

Those and many other thoughts crossed my mind until I heard a voice say, "Anything for the orphans of Tijuana that live in The Casa?"

This swiftly checked my meditations. I looked to my left and there stood a young man. A collar signified that he was a member of the Catholic faith and he held a box to collect money. The container had pictures on its side of little children in a dirty street during a rainstorm. The water from the rain was running in heavy torrents down the street. The children were shown drinking from the street. They had no shoes and little clothing. It was a pitiful spectacle that would have turned the coldest of hearts.

Believing I was worldly, I asked for his credentials. He showed me a card from the Mexican and American governments that gave him permission to solicit on the streets. I did not know at that time that these cards were the easiest cards to obtain. In all truth, these cards meant absolutely nothing except that the person who possessed one had either a Mexican or American driver's license. It had nothing to do with what he was trying to sell or achieve. I reached into my billfold and gave him ten dollars, as the picture on the container really affected me.

Soon I was having a conversation with him and he told me many stories of the children and their problems in Mexico. He told me stories of poverty, abuse, and the lack of governmental funds to help these children. Their only support was obtained by contributions. But, to get on with the story, let me just end this section by saying that this discourse soon had me giving him a check for one hundred dollars and feeling bad that I could not have given him more.

I then proceeded to flag down a taxi, and tried in my very best Spanish (of which I knew very little at that time), to tell the driver to take me to the center of town. Soon I got the message across and I was on my way. Within two minutes, I was in the center of town and five dollars poorer. Behold, the center of town had changed. Gone were the dusty dirt roads that I remembered, and in their place were modern streets with pavement, traffic lights, and police all over the neighborhood. Every street seemed to have a policeman on it. It looked like a typical American town center, with the exception of the many police.

I started to walk in the direction of the Jaji Palace, which I remembered was at the east end of town. Years ago, that area was the best place to have fun. As I walked, the same shops seemed to be there as before, with what could have been the same shop owners, all trying to lure you into their shops to buy items that would only last until you started to use them. Usually this was after you returned home, many miles away, and could do nothing about it.

The day was hot, in fact, very hot. Soon I became tired on my walk to the Jaji Palace. Also, I could see that Tijuana was not the same wild town; law and order had taken over. The fun and adventure were gone. So I sought a place to sit and have a cool drink of something bottled. I was sure that the water situation had not changed in Mexico and I did not want to chance what happens to you when you drink their water. The place I found was on the main drag. It looked as if it was presentable and clean, so I sat down at one of their tables on the sidewalk. The place was crowded with Americans, each showing the others the prizes of the day that they thought they'd gotten at a bargain from the poor Mexican salesman. Little did they know who had really cheated whom. Like anything else in Mexico, I waited and waited until a man finally came and took my order. After you place your order, you wait again. The only thing is you wait a little longer than before the order was taken. I did not really mind as I had a lot of time on my hands and it was still early in the day.

During this wait, I had an opportunity to observe the people rushing to and fro. This was one of my favorite pastimes when I traveled. Also, I had the opportunity to observe the children who were constantly trying to sell you something as you sat there. It was morning, so these children should have been in school. However, due to the circumstances of the parents, these children were not permitted to go to school. In Mexico, there is no compulsory school age. It is up to the parents to decide when and if their children will attend school.

It was not just one or two young children that I saw, but twenty or thirty, or maybe even more. The children looked as if they hadn't had a bath in two to three months and their clothing was shoddy and dirty. Few of them were wearing shoes. Each had their own object to sell. Some sold Chiclets, some candy, and some just a flower. Whatever they sold, it did not cost much for the parents to buy, and the child sold it for quite a markup, anywhere from two to three times the actual cost. The Americans bought the items out of sheer pity for the child. I thought at the time, were these people who were buying the items really doing the child a favor? Or were they just encouraging the exploitation of the children by their parents? As I watched these transactions, I thought of how most American children complain that they don't have this or that and become upset when they have to clean their plate at dinnertime. After watching these hardworking children, I no longer felt sorry for that type of spoiled child.

The children that I was now watching were about six or seven, no older than ten. I very seldom saw children in their teens anywhere on the streets selling things, as they were usually working in the stores or doing other higher paying jobs. They were very seldom in the schools where they belonged. As I watched these children, I started to think of the young priest that I had spoken to at the gates of Tijuana and the orphanage that he supposedly represented, the "Casa." I thought that if I were to visit there, maybe I could get some answers to why these children were permitted to do these things, and also I could see how the children there were treated.

When I was not on vacation, I worked for an extremely large computer company. I was the assistant to a very fine man who had the responsibility of worldwide early education. My responsibility was to create and instruct others in the new ways to educate children with the use of computers. Thus, my concern for these children went far beyond just being a human being. The more I thought about the idea of visiting the Casa, the more I liked it. It could show me how education was carried out not only in the Casa, but maybe it could answer some questions that were starting to form in my mind about Mexico's educational process. As my assignment in the States was almost finished and my next assignment was to see how culture entered into the computer educational process around the world, I started to think that maybe Mexico could be the place to start the investigation of the effects of culture on computer education.

I finished my drink, which finally came, and paid the check. Then I left and went to the nearest taxi stand. Once there, I tried to explain to the driver that I wanted to go to the Casa. If anyone thinks trying to explain something as simple as that was easy, you have another guess coming. That little conversation took fifteen minutes and the help of three other taxi cab drivers and a passerby that spoke somewhat good English.

After that experience, I was on my way. Up hills and down hills, it seemed like we drove to the very edge of the world. Taxi drivers throughout the world are notorious for their driving abilities. In Mexico, only the strong of heart should ever desire to drive a taxi. First, the taxi itself is usually only one step from the junk yard. Then, you add in the drivers' capabilities, and each ride within a taxi is like taking your life in your hands. But finally, after one and a half hours and almost two heart attacks, we were going down a one-way goat path to the orphanage. I knew we were getting close because at the start of the goat path was a sign in Spanish that said something including orphanage, which is spelled in Spanish almost the same as it is in English.

During the ride down the path, I saw many young children playing. Their clothes were worse than what the children were wearing in the town. Again, very few, if any, had shoes. As we drove by, they were all screaming something in Spanish. The taxi cab driver explained in his broken English that they were saying "Please adopt me, American, please. Take me with you." I wondered, now, what I would see at the end of this road.

Soon I was at the house, if you could call it a house. It was sorely in need of repair. The doorways had very small doors if they had any at all. The roof was sagging and the grounds surrounding the house were unkempt and filthy. The driver sounded his horn a couple of times and soon a man came out and introduced himself to me as the director of the orphanage and asked if he could help me.

I asked, "Is this the Casa?"

He replied, "No, this is the orphanage of Saint Maria. The one you are looking for is nearer the center of town." I expressed my gratitude to him, gave him a donation for which he was very thankful, and, once again, I was on my way. Since it was a long drive, I was now wondering if we would ever make it back to Tijuana, let alone the Casa.

After a perilous ride, we arrived back at the taxi stand in Tijuana. I got out and paid him an arm and leg. By this time, I was half scared out of my wits from driving with him. So I decided that the best plan was to leave him and find another taxi driver who spoke some English, and then maybe I could reach the Casa in one piece. Soon I was on my way again and this time with a taxi driver who spoke fairly good English and had convinced me that he knew where my goal was.

The drive proceeded up many winding and dusty, unpaved roads that led into the suburbs of Tijuana. In approximately ten to fifteen minutes, I was standing in front of an immense parcel of land. The area was equal to about one normal city block and it was completely surrounded by a towering wall. The barrier was about twelve feet high and roughly two feet thick, with broken glass placed all along the top. I assumed it was to stop the inhabitants from leaving and to protect the people inside from intrusion from outsiders. Painted on the wall were the words that I had been seeking for the past three hours: "The Casa." I had finally arrived at my goal for the day.

The vicinity of the Casa was shabby and rundown. The houses that surrounded it had many broken windows. The broken panes were stuffed with rags or paper to keep the cold winter nights at bay. The unpaved streets were strewn with garbage and refuse. Garbage containers looked as if they had not been collected for many weeks as they were not only full but overflowing onto the streets. This made the refuge easy prey for the many wild street dogs that inhabited the town. In later years, I was to find out that I had arrived at what the residents of Tijuana call "the slums."

As we drove along this fortress, which was the only means of ingress or egress, I could see two colossal iron gates that looked as if only a giant could open or close them. Within these gates was a door to allow people to enter or exit without completely opening the immense gates. On top of these gates were spikes embedded closely together. I noticed that a peephole in these gates was the primary means of communication to the occupants on the inside. There was also a button by the side of the gates that I presumed was the method of summoning the inhabitants.

I pressed the button and was promptly rewarded by the door opening. A man appeared that I was soon to know as Felipe. He was a giant of a man. He must have stood seven feet tall and had arms of great length and strength. Although, he was 55 years of age, his hair was still black as the night, typical of most Mexicans. He wore a T-shirt and a pair of old worn blue jeans. His face was kindly yet showed an expression of not being the smartest man in the world.

"Is this the Casa?" I asked.

"Si," he replied.

I was happy; at last, I was there. I was quickly ushered inside the gates. Then Felipe shut the door behind me and quickly bolted it again, separating me from my driver. I had previously told him to wait until I came out if I was let into the orphanage. (Later, I learned never to do that in Mexico.) Once inside, Felipe said something to me in Spanish and then left me standing there in the courtyard to return to his duties.

As I stood there waiting, I was amazed at what I observed. I was standing in the courtyard of a Mexican hacienda. In the center was a huge statue of a Madre of the Order surrounded by a beautiful garden with a variety of well-kept flowers. The garden was completely weed-free and the soil was turned up and raked. The rest of the area was extremely clean and well-kept as well. On one side, there were huge steps leading to an old church. The other sides led to dwellings of some sort.

All the entrances of the buildings that faced the patio had flowers or plants in abundance. They too were as well-kept as the flowers surrounding the Madre's statue in the center of the square. It was as though I had entered into the Garden of Eden. I had never expected to see such a sight from what I had experienced at the previous orphanage. The outside environment of this paradise gave no hint to what one would find here. Yet, I puzzled at the fact that I neither saw nor heard children as I had at the other orphanage. I wondered where they were.

As I paused there gazing on this beautiful sight, I was soon confronted by a Madre, a Catholic Nun. She introduced herself as Madre Esmeralda; by her mannerisms, I could see that she was the Madre Superior of the Casa. She was about 59 years of age and stood about 5 feet 6 inches tall. Like many Mexicans, her body weight was extremely heavy in comparison to the average American. She wore the habit of her order. It was dark blue and light blue and reached to the ground with a tightly coupled collar at the neck. Her hair was raven black, much like Felipe's. It was pulled neatly to the back of her head and coiled into a bun. Her skin was much darker than Felipe's. I thought that this must have come from many long hours in the sun. Her face was weather-beaten, with piercing eyes. Her face had an expression that you would not expect to see on a nun: a look of tyranny, signifying a woman who could be extremely merciless and vindictive if she so desired. Her eyes gazed at me with mistrust and suspicion. I introduced myself as I handed her my business card.

She spoke absolutely no English. I could see she was asking why I was there and what I wanted just by the expression on her face. I tried to explain that I was interested in children and the children of Tijuana. In addition, I tried to explain that I had met one of the priests at the border soliciting for her Casa. I also hoped that I could obtain some answers to my questions about education in Mexico.

The conversation with the Madre was not going well until another woman came into the courtyard from one of the dwellings. Unlike the Madre, she wore no habit. Instead, she was dressed in blue jeans and wore a button-down shirt with the top two buttons undone. She was tall, slender, and approximately 48 years of age. Her hair was light brown and cut short, somewhat like a man's. Contrary to the Madre's hair, the woman's was fairly unkempt. Her kind and understanding face also was divergent from the Madre's. From first glance, you could see she was not of Mexican origin. Her skin was white and had no hint of the deep brown that accompanies someone of Mexican birth. She introduced herself as Estella and explained that she had been a volunteer worker at the Casa for the past ten years. She spoke perfect English and Spanish with an Irish brogue.

I was extremely happy to see her. I told her why I was there. She translated it into Spanish for the Madre. The Madre seemed happy and with haste asked if I wanted to see the Casa and how it operated. The Madre's expression had taken on a different appearance, one of kindness and understanding; although, as Estella translated the part about my encounter with the priest at the border, I could see the Madre's face turn white with anger and her eyes flashed with fire. The Madre's eyes were always gateways to her true feelings, as I was to learn in the years to come. I was eager to hear Estella's explanation as to why the Madre seemed to become so upset at that mention of the priest. After the translation, Estella turned to me and explained.

Estella told me, "The man at the border crossing does not represent the Casa, nor does he represent any other orphanages. He is a phony and she has tried to stop him and others like him many times before but there is no law to do so, as long as they have that 'card.'"

After receiving a short lecture on how foolish I was to give him money, I stopped payment on the check. Then, I replied to the offer to see the Casa with a quick and sure "Yes." So off we went to see what everyone sees when they ask to tour the Casa, with Estella accompanying us to translate.

As soon as we started, the Madre said something in Spanish in a loud voice and then out of nowhere the children appeared. The funny thing about it was that only boys appeared. The Casa was beautiful and well-kept, and the children seemed happy and content. The children, like the Madre, neither spoke nor understood a single word of English, not even "yes."

As I started to tour the area, I thought, what more could a child ask for except parents? The place was especially amazing when I remembered the children in the streets of Tijuana that I had seen earlier that day. The first section we started on the tour was of the children's play areas.

The play areas were divided. The boys had one area and the girls had another. Both were about the same size, 50 by 25 feet. The only difference between the two areas was that the boy's area was exposed to any visitor who entered the grounds. The girl's area, on the other hand, was in the back of the Casa. It was under the Madre's sleeping quarters, away from all visitors' sight. This play area could only be accessed by a narrow passageway. The only exception to the accessibility was a small stairway from the Madre's quarters to the girl's dormitory. This was the reason that the girls did not appear when Madre spoke previously.

We went to visit was the girls' play area first. To gain admittance into the area, you had to pass through two massive iron gates and a small narrow passageway about twenty feet long. One of the gates was at the entrance of the passage that faced the inner patio. The other was at the termination of the passage. In this passageway was a door to the sleeping quarters of the giant, Felipe.

I found out later that Felipe's prime mission at the Casa was to oversee and protect the girls. Any time that the girls went outside their play area, Felipe was close by to manage who communicated with them and what they uttered and expressed. Felipe was not a man to mislead and he did not enjoy any practical jokes played on him. His strength was beyond question. I was also to find this out later in the years to come. Now Felipe joined us at the gateway of the girls' area and proceeded with us on the rest of the tour, following behind at a respectable distance. At the end of the girl's area tour, he left us and returned to his duties.

As we entered into the girls' area, Estella explained that, "Permission to enter into the girls' play area was only obtained by Madre Esmeralda or an act of God." Into the second section, the girls' dormitory where they slept, permission was only granted by Madre Esmeralda. God was left out of the permission sequence at that point. And then, only if Felipe was available to accompany you.

The children's voices could be heard as we walked up the narrow passage that led to their play area. They were loud and girlish, as you would expect. However, as soon as we entered the area, a silence quickly descended and a feeling of discomfort came upon me. The younger children, the ones about three to five, came up to us with smiles. The older girls, the ones about six to twelve, stopped playing and were very aloof and standoffish. They gathered in a tight group at the farthest end of the play area and just stared. The stares were directed at Madre and Estella. The girls seemed to watch every movement that the women made, especially Estella's. They did not come near us unless Madre called one of them over. Then the rest would stand there with a concerned look at what was taking place as we talked to the child. The child that was called to us would walk slowly across the yard and then stand in front of Madre with her hands and arms held tightly at her side and with her head bowed so not to look at you. She would only speak if Madre asked her a question and then the answer was rapid and short, without ever raising her head or making eye contact.

During the entire time I was in the area, the older girls never approached us unless the Madre summoned one of them to present herself to us. If none were called, then they all stood in that tight group in the far end of the area. The eyes of the girls had a strange look in them. At the time, I could not seem to put my finger on why that look should be present in such young children. I had never seen such an expression before in children's faces in all the times I had visited schools in pursuit of my profession of child education. It bothered me but I said nothing. I thought maybe it was just me, and that I was not used to how Mexican children behaved and reacted when first encountering a strange and unknown person.

A rather large shelter was constructed at one end of their play area where they could go if the day became too hot to play in the exposed section. The only article in the area was a merry-go-round type object. Later, I was to see the same article in the boys' area. The boys' merry-go-round was in working condition but the girls' was not. Through all the years that I spent there, I never found an answer to why the girls' merry-go-round was broken and the boys' was not. The girls were always so gentle with their toys and the boys so rough. Broken toys were strewn all over each area. The girls' dolls were of a fourth generation hand-me-down type, along with broken skates and bikes that had been thrown away by their previous owners.

All the children were clean and well-kept. The girls in the area all appeared to be physically mature for their age. The younger ones seemed to play quite well with each other. There seemed to be a strange alliance between all the children. I thought at the time that the alliance came from what they all had in common: the want for nothing, strict obedience to the Madres, and the always-present hope that one day, someone would come and adopt them and then take them to live with a real family.

On my world travels, I have found that this hope is the utmost feeling in any child's mind in this situation. It is what really keeps them going and alive. The children will withstand anything as long as they can hope that one day someone will walk through that door and take them out of there. I think of all the people throughout the world that want to give this love and affection these children need. Then I think about how the countries place such obstacles and time limits to adopt a child that only Jesus could withstand and comply with them. Why are these countries so misunderstanding? Especially America—don't we realize that these children live on this faith of being adopted? Most will never fulfill their dream and will thereby go on to oblivion and nothingness in their later lives.

After leaving the girls' area, we proceeded to the boys' area. In that area, I felt no discomfort, as the boys acted as I thought typical boys should. Upon entering the area, all the children rushed up to us and spoke wildly in Spanish. Estella, who was still accompanying us, said, "They are asking who you are and if you came to adopt one of them? Also are you one of the rich Americans?"

The boys clung to our clothes trying to get your attention. They were so anxious to gain our attention that we had to hold onto our clothes or risk losing them. Madre said something to them in Spanish and they were quick to leave. However, they remained at a respectable distance, still trying to attract our attention.

At the end of each play area was the children's sleeping quarters. The boys' entrance was right off the play area. The girls' dormitory entrance was not the same. Although it was off the play area, the entrance to their sleeping quarters was only accessible by going through two more huge gates with strong locks and a short passageway. The Madre explained that in the evening, gates to the girl's play area and dormitory were locked and only Madre Esmeralda had the keys. For some reason, she seemed to be proud of all these gates and locks. This now made a total of four gates and locks to obtain entrance into the girl's sleeping quarters. The boys had only one gate to the play area and that had no lock. Passage through the girl's gates was the only way in or out of the girls' dormitory, with the exception of that small stairway into the Madre's sleeping area. Realizing this, I wondered about what would ever happen to those girls if there was a fire in the evening. I was worried that most of them would die trying to get out of there through that small stairway to the Madre's quarters.

Both sleeping areas were about 50 by 25 feet in size. There was no heat evident in either dormitory. The dormitories had about 20 small cots on either side of the room. On one end was the entrance to the bathroom. In that area there were eight showerheads of cold water in one rather large room. There were no hot water faucets or heating units evident in either bathroom. The toilets had no seats or seat covers, just the bowl itself. Nor was there any separation of toilets as you would see in a normal bathroom, especially a bathroom for girls. At the end of each bathroom was a basket to put the used toilet paper which was only secured by asking a Madre for some. When I asked about the basket, I was told that if you put the paper in the toilet it would clog it up and require expensive repairs; thus, the necessity for the basket.

Each cot had only a sheet, a thin blanket, and no pillow. At the end of each bed was a tiny cardboard shoebox in which each child kept his or her small amount of "treasures." These were the only items each child was allowed to possess and consider as their own. They were not allowed to have a toy that would not fit in their shoebox. All clothing was kept in one closet by the entrance to the bathroom. No child was permitted to have his or her own clothing. When it was time to get dressed in the morning, each child would stand in line after taking their cold shower and wait at the entrance to the closet. Then one of the Madres would hand out all the necessary clothing for each child for that day, starting with the underwear, as they wore nothing at night when in bed.

The walls were painted stucco white and were spotless. They contained no pictures or decorations. There were two windows on either end of the room. Both windows in the girl's area had heavy, thick bars on them, while the boys' windows had no bars. The ceilings were about twelve feet high and held the only lighting for the area, two light bulbs hanging from long electrical wires.

Along the way, the Madre, through Estella, explained that there were 139 children at the Casa. They ranged all the way from two days old to twelve years old with only five Madres to care for them. After twelve years old, they were transferred to some another Casa of the

Order on the other side of Tijuana. There they had the facilities to care for the older children.

The only shoddy locality I found was the boys' bathroom that was presently under renovation. Madre explained that the work had stopped due to the lack of funds. I offered to donate so the construction could be completed. The Madre accepted it gracefully and thanked me.

She often told me later that she thought the check would bounce and was quite surprised when it did not. She had too much experience with people giving her checks for donations after they had walked around and patted the children on the head. (Why do people do that? The children hated it so.) Then when she went to cash them, many of the checks were either stopped or not good. I don't believe that these people realize that donations are the only means of support for the Casa. The church and government give them no support, and the Madres' faith does not allow them to beg. Their only means of support is from contributions. Madre often explained, and I later witnessed, that most of this type of bad check writing came from the Americans who visited the Casa to pat the children on the head and give them lollipops and a couple of pesos. To this day Guillermina (Gigi) will never allow anyone to pat her head, for any reason.

Back in the main courtyard, we continued our tour by viewing one of the most beautiful small churches I had ever seen. It was built in the year 1640 and still had most of its decorations from back at that time. The church must have been built first, and then the rest of the Casa added at some later time. Once inside, the church was cold and damp. There were ten benches, five on each side, forming a small aisle down the center. I figured about 50 people could sit on one bench. The altar was beautiful and had many flowers on either side of it.

The Madre explained that at 4:00 a.m. each morning, the children would come for about an hour of prayers. On Sunday morning, it was for two hours. Prayers were done before each morning's work assignments. These assignments generally lasted one hour. Then at 6:00 a.m. they would have breakfast.

I asked, "What kind of assignments do they have?"

The Madre, as interpreted by Estella, said, "They scrub the bathroom and sleeping quarter's floors and walls, clean the toilets, empty the baskets at each end of the bathrooms, wash their clothes, and many other things."

The children quit their assignments only for breakfast and school. After breakfast, they were picked up again where they had left off and did not stop until 9:00 a.m. when they went to school. If no school was in session, then most of the day was used to complete these assignments, along with others that were passed out when they finished their first chores. The only exception was Saturday and Sunday, when visitors were permitted in the Casa for a couple of hours. Then the children were released from their tasks and allowed to associate with the American visitors.

After the church, we went to the dining room, which was on the other side of the main courtyard. There I found another well-kept and clean area. There were two long tables. Estella explained that one table was for the boys and the other was for the girls. This was the only time that the girls ever came in contact with the boys. At the end of each table was a seat for a Madre. Beside each of the long tables was a single long bench where the children sat as they ate. Food was served at the end of each table by the Madre. When the food was served, each child would pick up a spoon and soup bowl and line up by the Madre. They were not permitted to have forks or knives. (Estella added that the children knew nothing about the existence of these pieces of silverware.) Later I was to witness this feeding process many times and its aftermath. I still now dream about it sometimes and wake up in cold sweat thinking about how lucky most American children are.

We then proceeded to the kitchen. It was spotless, which was for a good reason. There were five small girls about six or seven years old on their hands and knees scrubbing the kitchen floor. Madre was quite proud of the cleanliness and commented on it as I watched these five children, who had no shoes and were only dressed in their thin panties, scrubbing the floor.

I replied, "Yes, it is something to be proud of." Estella got what I meant and I'm sure that the Madre did not. As Estella was translating my remarks, a small smile came over her face, acknowledging my slight sarcasm.

There was not much in the way of appliances in the kitchen. The stove was an old wood-burning stove from the early pioneering days with four places in which to cook the food. There was no refrigeration of any kind that I could see. The food was kept in the open until ready to be used by the children. I could see milk cans lined up by the wall. I opened one and it was full of foul-smelling milk. The water came from a hand pump that was installed by the sink. No purification of the water was evident.

"Where does the water come from?" I inquired.

Madre responded, "From a small underground reservoir in the Casa. When it rains, it is full. When it does not rain, then we have to buy the water from a man in a truck. Sometimes the Casa goes three or four days without water."

"Do the children drink this water straight from this reservoir?" I asked.

"Yes, we use the water for everything, including drinking," Madre replied, with a look that clearly asked what was so bad about that.

Yes, the kitchen was very clean. However, as far as modernization went, it looked like 1776. When the inspection of the kitchen done, the tour of the Casa was complete.

We then spent some more time talking about education, the plight of the Mexican children, and how people should be more concerned about children all over the world. The conversation was quite stimulating and almost moved me to tears as I listened to some of the stories of the children that were there at the Casa. One story in particular interested me about an eight-year-old girl named Maria. Madre said she had extremely good marks in public school but was limited, as the public schools in Mexico were not the greatest due to the extremely low salary paid to the teachers. Thus, these schools obtained only the lowest of the teaching profession. The good teachers went to teach in the private schools where the pay was much better.

I asked the Madre, "Are there any other schools in Tijuana that are better?"

Madre replied, "Yes, but they cost a lot of money."

"How much?" I questioned and the answer that I received was not very much when compared to American currency. So I volunteered to pay for this little girl, Maria, to go to the private school in Tijuana.

In Florida, I had donated enough money to a good Catholic school to provide a scholarship for a needy child. Likewise, my company had provided the school with computers for their computer room. So, I thought, why not do it here as well? This Mexican child could use the education of a private school just as much as a child in Florida. In fact, she needed it more. Estella disappeared and quickly returned with a short, chubby little girl with the ever-present head down and eyes focused on the floor.

Estella said, "This is Maria, she speaks no English. The other girls call her 'Chicky.' Say hello to Senor Roberto." The last bit, Estella told Maria in Spanish.

Maria responded in a gentle and quiet voice: "Hola." I responded likewise, but in English.

Maria was then informed I was going to send her to a private school. At that statement, Maria's head rose from the ever-present gaze on the floor and, with a rapid glance at me, her eyes opened wide and seemed to glow with anticipation. Then just as quickly as she raised her head and eyes, she immediately focused on the floor again.

Maria then said via Estella's translation, "Thank you."

Maria had that Mexican dark hair that hung to the middle of her back and big brown eyes. Her dress was rather worn but clean. She wore no socks, only sandals. Her skin was not so dark but a mixture of white and brown. Later, I was to learn that this color was known as "morena" and the color of a pure Mexican as "café." Maria's actions were that of a child who had no real inner feelings and only responded to the attitude of the person directing her. However, her face expressed much more than her words and actions could. There was a look of fear and distress on her young face. Estella escorted Maria back to the well-secured girls' play area and then returned.

Madre told me that she would make the arrangements for the child to go to the school and forward a letter to me as to exactly how much it would be and any other pertinent facts concerning the school. I agreed and then Madre and Estella accompanied me to the door of the Casa. As I left, the Madre thanked me for the contributions and what I was going to do for Maria.

Once outside the gates of the Casa, the driver was still waiting. I told him to take me to the border, as it was getting late. As we drove, I had a strange feeling that there was more to the Casa than met the eye. I wondered what it was. I could not shrug the feeling off even though I tried many times on the drive to the border. I finally calmed my thoughts by thinking, "You will never see those people again, so why get so upset?" With this thought, I finally was able to push the worry deep into my inner self.

When we arrived at the border, the driver told me the charge would be eighty dollars. He threatened to summon a Mexican policeman if I did not pay. As I could see one standing close by and I did not like the idea of spending time in a Mexican jail, grudgingly I paid the outlandish fee. I then crossed the border only after a few insulting remarks from the American customs officer. He implied that I was drunk because of my speech. Once he realized that I stuttered, he gracefully allowed me to return to my own country and my car in that dusty parking lot. From there, I went back to San Diego and my hotel, as it was very late and the next day I had to catch a plane back to Austin, Texas.

I had trouble sleeping that night due to the events of the day. The Casa was stuck deep in my mind for some reason, as was the plight of all those Mexican children. I had seen poverty in my world travels but never like there was in that area of Mexico. I wondered if this was just because it was a border town, and if the rest of Mexico was any better. What was the real story of the Casa? Why was Estella, a fairly good-looking woman, at the Casa for all those years and why did the girls stare at her like that when we were in their play area? Why did the little girl, Maria, act so scared and frightened? Why did the older girls stop playing and huddle so close together when we entered their play area? I soon drifted off to sleep with all these and many more thoughts rambling through my mind.

Little did I know that I was to find the answers to these questions and many more, much to my regret and disgust, as I continued my adventure into Hell. And little did I know that my adventure into Hell would also lead me to the most wonderful little girl in the world.

CHAPTER TWO

DOCTOR ADOLPH'S UNEXPECTED VISIT AND GUILLERMINA

I arrived back in my office in Texas the following day. It was a hot and sultry day. However, I don't think it could ever be as hot as it is in Mexico. With the lack of sleep that I'd had the night before and the hours I'd spent on the plane back from Mexico to Texas, I had time to think about my experiences in Tijuana the previous day. It was now bothering me to the point of anxiety and discomfort.

In the office, Tom, my boss, was anxious to hear what ensued at the meeting in San Diego. I told him that it never materialized, as they had to cancel for some reason or another. He then asked what I did that day, as he knew there were no flights out of San Diego until early the next morning.

I answered, "Nothing really, just took in the sights of Tijuana, as I hadn't been there for many years and I've seen San Diego a hundred times already. Although," I added to my statement, "I think I found a perfect place to start the project on how culture affects early education and how that in turn will affect computer and software design." I did not mention the odd feeling that I had about the Casa.

Tom said, "Swell, let's hear it."

Tom was a rather short and portly man in his late thirties. He had a rounded face with a mustache and a well-kept beard that made him look much older than he really was. His hair was still black and kept in a rather long fashion. I enjoyed looking into his eyes, as they were always filled with kindness and understanding. Tom loved his wife and family and, unlike most executives, he found the time to enjoy them.

One of Tom's good points was that he worried about other people. This was soon to be his downfall. (Why do people always take advantage of individuals like Tom?) Tom loved his job, did well for the company, and had great consideration and concern for the children of the world, as did the entire chain of upper management, all the way to the president at that time. It was an honor and privilege to work with and for such people.

I told Tom about the Casa in Tijuana and how the children and the Madres spoke no English and had very little contact with English-speaking people. This was just what we needed for our proposed project, as the outcome must be the results of our efforts and not from any assistance given by the outside environment. One of the main goals of the project was to study the use of a computer and software in the instruction of children and illiterate adults on how to speak either their own language or a different language, along with how to use computers in early education in a foreign country.

Tom said, "Sounds pretty good, why don't you get another opinion on your appraisal. Maybe try Dr. Adolph in New York? This should be right down his alley. He speaks Spanish as well as being an expert in his field of child development."

Now, Dr. Adolph was the Director of Psychiatry on Child Behavior and Development at the leading hospital in America. Furthermore, he instructed other psychiatrists throughout the world on new methods of psychiatry and updates in the field. Above and beyond that, his reputation as a child behavioral psychiatrist was known throughout the world. He happened to also be a consultant to our company on such matters.

At that time, our management team believed that before they produced a computer and software for a school or early education, both computer and software must be psychologically suitable for the purpose. This was in addition to the normal analysis that these items regularly received within the company. We had employed Dr. Adolph when we were developing the strategy and design for the computers and software that were just being introduced into American schools. I must also note that without help from him and other leading consultants in similar fields in early education, I do not think that our entry into the field of early computer education would have been as successful as it was.

I had worked with Dr. Adolph on this implementation of early computer education in America for about three years and found him to be well-justified in his reputation as a world leader in his field. He was a man in his mid-fifties with gray hair, average height, and a slender build. He had a gentle manner that put everyone at ease. You could see the compassion and understanding in his eyes. Although his livelihood was working with children, he had a great love for them above and beyond what his profession required. He was the type of man who would learn all about you on your first visit to his office without you realizing what took place. He just had a way of putting people at ease and drawing them out of their shell. When I was with him, I felt like I was constantly being psychoanalyzed, but could never prove it. He always denied it when I asked him if he was studying me.

After leaving Tom's office, I quickly placed a phone call to Dr. Adolph and explained what I thought I had found. He was quite interested and wanted to hear more about it. So we arranged a parley in San Diego for the following week to discuss the subject. In addition, we planned to visit the Casa so Dr. Adolph could analyze the situation firsthand.

Prior to the expected visit by Dr. Adolph, better known as 'Doc' to his friends, I had received the promised letter from Madre Esmeralda about the school particulars for Maria. The only subject that was a surprise was that Maria was going to be adopted. Therefore, she would not be eligible for the private school, as she would be leaving soon. Despite this setback, the Madre had a solution. In the Casa there was a second little girl that was just as bright as Maria. However, this child was not as outgoing as Maria. Her name, the Madre told me, was Guillermina.

The Madre then went on to explain a little more about Guillermina and some of her mannerisms. Guillermina spoke no English. The child was small for her age of eight, and was extremely thin. She was so thin that she had to constantly pull up her pants. "If she does not," the Madre wrote, "It looks as though they would fall off." Madre went on to write, "Unlike Maria, she is not popular with the other girls. In addition, the girls are always taking advantage of her to the point that the Madres have to tell the girls many times to stop." Madre thought this was due to Guillermina being shy and withdrawn.

Guillermina had been with the Casa since the age of two when police deposited her there after finding her on the streets of Tijuana. This is not an unusual thing in Mexico for certain classes of people. When a woman of these classes wants to leave a relationship, she just vanishes one evening without any warning, leaving the man with the children. If the child is too young to provide an income for him, the man will abandon it. With the exception of this class of people, Mexican families are usually a tightly knit group that give much respect and love to all its members. This Mexican family attachment is the greatest that I have ever seen in the world, with the exception of maybe the Chinese family.

Due to Guillermina's mannerisms, she was never presented to any of the people who came to the Casa to inquire about adoptions. The

Madre felt that Guillermina would never be considered for adoption. In the Madre's mind, this made the child a prime candidate for private school.

This letter aroused my curiosity about the Casa even further, especially concerning this one little girl named Guillermina. She seemed to be a very interesting child. In addition to finding a perfect spot for the culture project, I have now discovered a child that must be in some kind of psychological trouble if the things that the Madre wrote about her were true. To this day, I still retain that letter. I called the Madre that day and asked if she would be so kind as to see Dr. Adolph and myself the following week. This of course was done through Estella's translations. The Madre said that she would be happy to see both of us then.

The following week, I traveled to San Diego for my meeting with Dr. Adolph and met him in the lobby of the hotel. We exchanged salutations according to the Mexican custom. A Mexican's man greeting is where they embrace you with both arms and then hug you while at the same time slapping you hard on the back. Doc was okay, but when you greeted a man of great strength, you could hardly breathe or stand up after one of those "greetings."

We then went to a bar to have a drink and discuss the project and my thoughts on why the Casa would be an excellent location. During the conversation, I also mentioned the strange feeling that I had at the Casa and hoped that he could explain why after he visited there. He seemed to agree, but with the understanding that he would like to see the Casa and talk with the children and the Madres before reaching any final judgment on either topic. As we talked, I showed him the Madre's letter concerning Guillermina. This seemed to interest Doc even more than the project.

He said, "I cannot wait to see this Casa. It sounds as though you have not only found an ideal location for our project but many children in need of help as well." He further added, "When there is one like Guillermina, shy and withdrawn and the other things mentioned in the correspondence, it usually signifies many problems with the other children's development. Coupled with your feelings you have just discussed with me, it is important that we look into this situation."

As mentioned previously, the Doc was concerned with children's welfare worldwide and had done many charitable works to assist them. Doc transferred his deep interest for children's welfare, especially for the poor and downtrodden children of the world, to me. I never really had any sensation like that until I'd met and worked with him.

After our discussion, we were both tired, not only from the conversation but from the long plane ride as well. Doc was especially tired, as he had a three hour time change from New York to California. So we decided to get some sleep in order to get an early start to the Casa. Doc wanted to see as much of the routine of these children as possible in one day; plus, he wanted to arrive at an unexpected time. He was looking forward to talking to the children and the Madres. He had the advantage over me of being a fluent Spanish speaker.

Bright and early the next morning, we were on our way to the Casa in Tijuana. The sights were the same as last week, but, to Doc, who had never been to Tijuana, they were all new. Upon arriving at the border, I decided to take our rental car across rather than use the more expensive taxicabs. As we crossed, the American border officials were impolite and downright rude, as usual.

When we reached the Casa, we were admitted by Felipe, and greeted by the Madre and Estella. They were surprised to see us so early, as we were not expected until nine that morning. The first thing I asked Doc to do after he was properly introduced was to ask why the American border guards were so unfriendly, as Doc could now do the translating due to his command of the language.

The Madre explained why they were so unfriendly and why the rest of the Mexican people felt the same way—at least the Mexicans who did not depend upon American tourist trade. The week before, a couple of nine-year-old children were playing by the border and started to throw rocks at an American guard. The guard ordered them to stop. Later, he claimed that he told them many times, but to no avail. So, he took out his magnum pistol and shot one of the children in the head. The child died instantly.

The Mexican papers carried the entire story. Yet, not one word of it was printed in any American paper. Further adding insult to injury, when the guard was brought in front of his superiors for judgment, the findings were that he acted in self-defense and no punishment was administered. The only action taken was to transfer the guard to some other crossing point in Tijuana for his own protection.

The Madre went on to explain that this was not the first time these American border guards had done things like that. They were always causing difficult situations between the Mexican people and the Americans. She continued her dissertation on this subject, citing other crimes that these guards had committed. Some of these things would make your hair stand on end. I believe that due to the poor pay and the type of job, the people who are attracted to this sort of employment leave a lot to be desired. This sort of thing does not endear the American in the hearts of the Mexicans. I like to think that the other nations would not condone these actions in Mexico either, if they were to be reported in their periodicals.

When we arrived at about 6:50 in the morning, the Madre invited us to breakfast. We thanked her for her kindness and accepted, as both of us had very little to eat that morning due to our early start. We were escorted to the side of the courtyard where the dining rooms were for both the children and the Madres. The Madres who were not at the children's tables ate in a separate dining room that was off the children's dining area. To enter the Madres' dining room, you had to pass through the children's area.

As we were crossing through the children's section on the way to the Madre's dining region, we saw the children eating. Doc and I both stopped simultaneously as though we'd walked into an invisible wall. All the children were there, both boys and girls from about five to eleven years of age. They were all lined up in a row with the boys at the end of one long table and the girls at another. Both tables were made of wood and were similar to picnic tables. Neither had any tablecloths or coverings of any kind, just the bare wood. Both groups of children had their plates, glasses, and spoons in their hands waiting to be served. As Estella had pointed out in my previous visit, none of the children had knives or forks. The Madres were at one end of each table to serve the food.

The walls here were painted a bland white, much like the walls of the children's dormitories. Also like the dormitories, nothing hung on the walls. The floor was just the bare cold tile with no carpeting or rugs to protect against the chill. The walls and floor were spotlessly clean and obviously washed each day. This was one of the children's chores before school. This was done before eating and then again after eating. The room had three windows that faced the inner courtyard. Two or three of the windowpanes were broken.

Unlike most children's eating areas, there was a deathly silence that hung over the room. There was no laughter or giggles from the girls and no loud noises or shouting from the boys that you would expect from a group of young children. There was just silence and an expression of concern and hunger on every child's face.

The children and the Madres all looked at us with surprise that anyone other than themselves would be up at such an ungodly hour. The children's hair was unkempt and in a tangled mass for the most part. It was a far cry from what I had seen on my last visit. Most of the children did not have any shoes on and were dressed in very little clothing for the weather. What they did have, no American child would ever wear. As I stood there, I thought about how cold it must be to walk on these floors with no shoes. Their clothing was ripped and threadbare. Both Doc and I were wearing our heavy jackets, as the mornings in Mexico at this time of year were very cold. The children's faces looked tired, pale, and gray. Their entire appearance had taken on a completely different countenance since last week.

I thought, "My God, am I in the same location I was last week? It cannot be. I do not remember any children like these being here last week. What had changed? Am I now seeing the real Casa? Is there more to see like this? What will I see? How can children be like this? Do the children accept this as being right?"

As we paused there, two women came from the kitchen with large pots of frijoles (mashed beans) and placed them on the end of each of the tables where the Madres were waiting. In each of the pots was a serving ladle. The two women then vanished back into the kitchen and promptly returned with two large pitchers containing hot, unpasteurized milk and two plates of tortillas. These too were placed at the end of each table in front of the Madres.

The serving now began. Each child would stand in front of the Madre with his or her plate and glass outstretched, waiting to be served. The portions of food that were placed on their plates and glasses would not even feed a fly. When the portions of frijoles, milk, and one tortilla were gratefully received by each child, they would curtsey and thank the Madre. Then the children proceeded to their gender-appointed table and sat down at their assigned position on a single bench. Finally, the children were allowed to consume their meager portions of food.

Even though each child had a spoon, few of the children used them. They mostly used their hands to scoop up the food and eagerly place it into their mouth. They ate as if it was to be their last meal. If any of the food was to drop to the floor, they would quickly bend over and scoop it up with their fingers and eat it anyway. Nothing went unwanted.

As the serving continued, the tables filled until the long benches were completely overflowing with children. Each child would quickly eat their own meager allotment of food and then commence looking at the child next to them or across the table. If any child was to hesitate in eating their portion of victuals, the other children at the table would seize the food and eat it themselves.

The children had to eat within a certain amount of time; if they did not finish within the allotted time, the food was taken away. This time limited forced the children to eat fast. One girl in the middle of the table was eating too fast and vomited her meal onto the table. Upon seeing this, the Madre at the end of the table directed the child to eat what she had expelled. The expression on the girl's face as she was fulfilling the Madre's order was one of utter disgust.

Doc and I looked at each other and were also disgusted. Madre Esmeralda, upon seeing this and the expressions on our faces, issued an order to the Madre that Doc translated as "Madre, why did you tell the child to do such an awful thing. I will see you after in my room." The Madre at the table looked at Madre Esmeralda in absolute surprise but was quick to obey. However, no one stopped the child from completing her task.

During this feeding process, the tables soon became a nightmare to behold. When the children finished their plate, they would lift it to their mouth and lick the dish clean. The children would then look around to see if any other child did not do so. Any dish that still had food on it was snatched up and licked clean as well.

The Madres did not eat at the tables to which they were assigned. They were only there to keep law and order. While the children were eating, the Madres did nothing to stop or to correct a child who stole another child's food or drink. To them, this seemed to be proper. The only time that they took action was when a child left their appointed position at the table without permission. There were no excuses for leaving the table except to leave the dining room when finished eating. This was done only after the Madre gave them permission to do so.

When each child finished eating, if you could call it that, the children would then raise their hand for permission to leave the table. They then went to the other end of the table from where the Madre sat and placed their spoon, glass, and dish into a large container that contained soap and cold water. Washing their dishes consisted of placing their hands in the cold water and then wiping their hand across the plate, in the glass, and on the spoon. Once this was finished, they put their utensils on a table near the door to the courtyard. Upon doing that, they immediately left the room to finish their early morning assignments prior to leaving for school.

For years to come, I could not enter this dining room during mealtimes. I would avoid the entire process if I could help it. Observing this "feeding process" always made me dreadfully ill.

I broke our silence as Doc and I stood there analyzing what was in front of us. I looked at Doc and requested him to ask the Madre which one was Guillermina, whom the Madre wrote to me about. This he promptly translated and the Madre pointed to a girl at the far end of the girls' table.

The letter, which I received from the Madre, did not do justice to the misfortune of this child. She was a little girl about eight or nine years old. While she was not the youngest child at the table, she was the smallest. She was the skinniest and frailest child that I have ever seen in my travels. She wore a blue dress that was obviously too small for her. While she was sitting, the dress was up around her hips, leaving her legs exposed to the bottom of her underwear. The top of the dress lacked the first two buttons, exposing part of her upper body, along with her legs, to the cold, early morning air. Like most of the other girls at the table, she had no shoes. I couldn't imagine how cold she must be.

We watched the child as she ate. Both her elbows were on the table and the plate was in her hands as she licked it clean. Her hair was not like the other children's. Hers was sort of a light brown. It hung down to about the middle of her back, much like Maria's had. Part of it was hanging across her shoulders and the rest was hanging down her back, but it all wound up in a tangled disarray. I thought it would take a week to comb it into some semblance of order.

Her face was lean and shallow and her cheekbones protruded exceedingly due to this facial distortion. Her teeth were crooked. The face was not that of a typical Mexican; it lacked the heavy thick lips and the broad nose. It was the face of a Caucasian. The only thing that identified her as a Mexican was the light brown skin of a Moreno Mexican, but even lighter. Her Bambi brown eyes were sunk deep in their sockets and were accompanied by large black bags under them. Her eyes held a world of sorrow and affliction. The arms and wrists showing past her short sleeves were so thin that the bones there could be counted with ease from a distance. Her legs were so thin that I would be surprised if they could hold up her body had it been one pound heavier. She looked up, as did the rest of the children, when the Madre pointed, and then kept one eye on us and the other on her dish.

Children of this background tend to be deeply concerned that you are talking about them. Therefore, they try to listen intently to what you are saying. I have observed this phenomenon in many other establishments similar to this. The child psychologists that I have been with at these houses have never been able to answer why they act this way, except that they have a deeply rooted paranoia complex for some reason or another. To this day, Guillermina still possesses that paranoid trait. When I ask her why she does it, all she does is shrug her shoulders and says, "I don't know why, I just do."

Guillermina's section of the table was unlike the other children's. Her area did not possess the disorder and jumble that the other girls' spaces had. Hers was neat and tidy. As we watched, the boys did not seem to worry about their appearance. However, the girls seemed greatly concerned, as each girl was trying to straighten their hair and dress into a somewhat presentable manner. Guillermina was also trying to fix her hair but the more she tried to straighten it, the more it seemed to become tangled. She was also trying to pull her dress down over her knees but it just would not cooperate since it was three sizes too small. I had to laugh to myself, as she was trying so hard to become presentable. The expression on her face as she was performing these feats was that of utter despair and complete embarrassment. I felt so sorry for her. She was trying so very hard.

The Madre broke the complexity of my thoughts and said, "Would you like to meet her?"

I replied, "No, maybe afterwards, I was just curious, as your letter was so intriguing about this little girl. I had to see what she looked like. Now I can see what you meant by holding up her pants or they would fall down." I added, "Do they make pants that small at the waist here in Mexico?"

The Madre laughed and so did Doc and I. This laughter really disturbed the children, especially the girls, as now they thought we were laughing at one of them or maybe at them all. They all immediately looked away with sorrowful expressions on their faces. I never did that again in the Casa or any other similar place once I learned that such laughter causes great emotional distress for the children.

One of the results of my time spent at the Casa was to discover that this and other incidents cause great stress and anxiety in these children.

Circumstances that we would really consider nothing of concern will cause them distress. This is a section of society that very few people really see. They visit and feel sorry for the children so the visitors pass out lollipops along with a nice pat on the head. The children hate that pat so very much but dare not say anything. Then the people leave and think they have done something worthwhile for the children. In truth, most of the visitors have done great psychological harm to each and every child that they came in contact with that day.

It is not only the average person who arrives and causes these dilemmas; it is also those studying social work and spending the summer there to do research. Most of them do more harm than the ordinary visitor because they believe that they have all the facts from reading a book or listening to a lecture. But above all, the real harm that they do is from the time spent there. Each of these college kids seems to seek out a child and give that child special attention. They create a bond similar to that of the family that these children want so badly. Then what do these college kids do? At the end of two or three months, they leave, never to return. Psychologically, where does that leave the orphan child, who was just befriended, when her new friend, the social worker or student, leaves?

The students that I have been with at the completion of their field research always seem to say, "I have learned a considerable amount that was never instructed nor written about in any books."

My response to those people is "Great for you and your research, but do you realize what you have done to the children while you were experimenting with their real lives?"

They always reply, "Yes, now I do, but, I did not understand before; I'm sorry…"

"'Sorry' is almost good enough for me. However, "I don't know if those children would really accept 'sorry,'" is my answer to these kinds of statements.

Then when these students graduate, they very seldom return to this type of situation because they know what awaits them and they desire no part of it. In fact, most of them return to their universities and change their planned degree to something other than social work. Therefore, many of the ones who do graduate with a degree in social work have no experience in such conditions. However, they are the ones who dictate what is valid and what is inappropriate for those establishments like the Casa. How can they do it properly and accurately, without the necessary background?

You must be very solicitous with every action or word that you use with these children. You cannot presume to do what you would with your own children or children who have not lived in this setting. These children are very sensitive to every word and motion. They are constantly watching you for unacceptable signs or conduct. They will never state anything to forewarn you that you are performing inappropriate actions or words. It is you who must analyze the situation and be constantly on your guard.

I have often wished that all of these people would stay away from the Casa and just send money. Money is what the Casa needs to care for these children, not visits that only make the visitor feel good about himself or herself. Also, I wish that these summer "experiences" would stop. The college students should stay away from these types of children until at least the students graduate from the institutions of higher learning and are ready to spend some genuine time with the children, say three or four years. Only then can they actually help the children and not just themselves.

The Mexican universities do not allow this experimenting. It is only the American universities that appear to be proud to offer such "training" courses to their students. There are also quite a number of high schools that offer the same "experience" to show the children of affluent parents how lucky they are in comparison to these orphans. If I were able to terminate anything, I hope I could stop these high schools from sending their young children to locations similar to the Casa. But I would be hard pressed to do so, because at the end of these children's stay (some of them no older then the children at the Casa), the high school always gives a hefty donation to the Casa.

I could continue this rant all day, but I must continue my story. Maybe then you will understand my sensitivity on this subject. Although, let me finish by emphasizing that these children are very real. They have feelings way and above the wants and feelings of other children not in surroundings like this. They breathe, eat, bleed, and show the children of those affluent parents how they suffer like other children, but in so many more ways. The average child wants this or that. These children live under unbelievable restraints and desire only to have a family, and nothing else. They want to be loved and to love in return more so than any other child that was born into a natural family. Their wants cannot adequately be explained by my mere words written here.

Once more, my thoughts about the eating process were interrupted by Madre saying, "If you don't mind, we should go to the dining room, as breakfast is almost over and the help has other chores to do."

I answered, "By all means, let's go."

Madre then led us through the children's section and into the separate dining area of the Madres and staff. It was like a different world. There stood a dining room equal to any that you would find in an average American home. Pictures of saints, including Saint Esmeralda, the patron saint of Mexico, were displayed on the walls. There was even a rather large mirror on one of the walls. Everything was well dusted and clean. The walls were painted a pale pink and, like the walls in the children's area, spotlessly clean. Against one wall, a china closet stood beside a serving buffet. In a corner of the room was a large bottle of drinking water in a stand like you would see in a corporate office. This was pure water, not like the other water used throughout the Casa for the children to drink.

The table was long and had a beautiful Irish linen tablecloth. In the center of the table was a beautiful flower arrangement. The dishes were made of china and there was a full complement of silver placed in proper order around each plate. The glasses were not crystal, but pretty close to it. There was a chair for each place setting, along with a larger chair at the end of the table. This was where Madre Esmeralda sat, as she was the Madre Superior. At each of the chairs was a nun, who had stood when the Madre entered the room. All the nuns looked similar to the Madre Superior with the same robes and their hair pulled neatly to the back of their head and tied in a tight bun. The one similarity to the children's area was the deathly silence that filled the room.

We waited until Madre Esmeralda took her seat at the end of the table in the grand chair before we too sat down along with the other Madres. The Madre introduced us to the other Madres at the table and explained each of their functions at the Casa. Each had many jobs to fulfill along with going to church most of the time. After their tasks were completed, there must be little time left, I thought, for interaction with the children.

Our breakfast consisted of coffee, fresh orange juice, eggs, bacon, ham, and toast. This meal was a far cry from the food I saw being bestowed on the children in the other dining room. During the meal, Doc asked many questions in Spanish and seemed quite pleased with the responses he received from the nuns.

In a short time, breakfast was over and all the participants waited for Madre Esmeralda to leave before departing themselves. Doc and I left with Madre Esmeralda to start the tour of the Casa. Doc was very anxious to inspect it when they were not really expecting us to be there. He hoped to catch them off guard as we did during the breakfast feeding of the children. Doc did not leave the Madre's side from the time he was introduced to her until we left. He told me afterwards that he had wanted to make sure that the Madre did not issue any orders that could conceal the actual happenings at the Casa. To do so, Madre would have to speak in Spanish and she knew that the Doc spoke and understood Spanish.

CHAPTER THREE

CASA OFF GUARD AND MEETING WITH GUILLERMINA

Doc and the Madre walked side by side as they exited the dining area. I walked slightly behind them so they did not feel obliged to speak in English. This way, I could still hear they were talking, although I did not know what they were saying. I could always ask Doc afterwards or during their talk what they were saying if their faces indicated concern or happiness. I did not want to be left entirely out of the tour; I might want to ask some questions if new ones arose since the last visit.

As we walked from the dining room, we saw one of the girls cleaning the steps on her hands and knees. She looked about seven years old and was dressed as she had been for eating except her dress was now pulled up above knees. I assume this was done to keep it dry and not to get the dress any more soiled then it already was, although, it did not seem to help. As we went by, she did not pay attention to us. She just went about with her labor. Beside her was a pail of cold water with soap and every so often the little girl would immerse the brush into the bucket for more soap. She looked very cold but it did not seem to bother her as she went about her chore on those stairs.

Once outside and down the stairs, we were in the central courtyard. Doc said something to Madre in Spanish. Then he turned to me and said "I asked her to start the tour in the children's dormitory." He added, unbeknownst to Madre, "This way we can see how the children slept last night and in what kind of circumstances."

"Sounds good to me," I replied.

It was about 7:00 in the morning when we started our adventure of inspecting the Casa. The weather was still cold enough to see our breath as we exhaled. We walked down the vine-covered arbor that bound the inner patio until we reached the passage way to the girls' dormitory and play area. If I was not certain of our location, I was quickly assured once we passed the open iron gate used to seal the entrance to the girls' quarters and started up the passageway. Felipe, the giant, appeared and blocked our way. Upon seeing Madre Esmeralda, he quickly stepped aside and gave us a greeting as we passed.

Now, instead of the three of us on the tour, there were four. I quickly joined Madre's side and no longer walked slightly behind the group. I felt that discretion was the better part of valor, since Felipe was now walking behind us. Once through the passageway and the other gate, we stood in the recreation portion of the girls' area.

It was alive with activity. Four little girls about eight or nine years old were on their hands and knees scrubbing the concrete floor. These children were like the one we saw as we exited the dining room. With brushes in hand and a pail close by, they were busily cleaning the entire area. As with the other child, they also had their skirts above their knees in an attempt to protect the garment. They looked very cold; however, they all went about their tasks without ever looking up as we walked around the play area.

This behavior was characteristic of most of the children at the Casa, as I was to find out. As the years passed during my visits to the Casa, I realized that the children there would never look you straight in the eye or face no matter what you did to encourage it. They would either look down to the ground or to the side when you spoke to them. They would also turn away from visual contact when they discovered that you were looking at them. The only exception was when a Madre or Estella spoke to them. Then they would look at them, but never anyone else.

The recreation area was very clean. The only task remaining was cleaning the floor, which the girls were already doing. "The walls were done earlier in the morning, before breakfast," Madre said as we hesitated there, gazing at the children and the area.

From there, we entered through the other two gates that barred entrance to the children's actual sleeping area. This prompted Felipe to close any distance that he might have had between us. Now he was almost breathing down our necks, causing me to walk closer to Doc. I kept glancing back at him in case I might jounce him unintentionally and provoke him.

Once inside the sleeping area, we could see that all the beds had been moved to one end of the room and about nine children, approximately eight or nine years old, were down on their hands and knees scrubbing *that* floor. At one end of the room a Madre stood, keeping a diligent eye on the children's activities. As we watched, we could see the children take a quick glance upward every so often to see if the Madre was looking at them.

Doc said something to Madre as we paused there that caused Madre to look concerned. Afterwards, Doc recounted to me that he had asked her if the age of the child doing the work made any difference to the cleanliness of the room. Doc was being "cute," which was rather unlike Doc. But I noticed by this time, Doc was really getting disturbed at what he had observed since his arrival at the Casa. Doc had requested to visit the Casa to determine if it was the right locality for the educational undertaking that we wanted to do. Now it appeared that Doc was also attempting to psychoanalyze the children and their care. I was interested to hear what he might announce when we were finished at the Casa later this day and driving back to the hotel.

We now proceeded into the bathroom and once again, there were little girls cleaning. Some were cleaning inside the toilet bowels with rags and others were in the shower stall doing the same. Madre pointed at one of the little girls who was scrubbing the toilets and said, "There's Guillermina. Would you like to meet her now?"

I replied "Okay," as I thought that this would at least take her away from this 'task' for a short duration.

I quickly realized that I had made the wrong decision. When Madre asked her to approach, I could tell by her expression she was ashamed that anyone had seen her performing such a chore. Guillermina approached Madre immediately, dropping her rag by the privy.

Madre said in Spanish, "Guillermina, this is Doctor Adolph and Dr. Nielsen. Dr. Nielsen is the man who wants to send you to the private school. What do you say?"

Guillermina looked at Madre and then quickly dropped her head and stared at the floor. After a brief hesitation, she turned to us and said in Spanish, "How do you do?" Guillermina could not speak a word of English.

This was the first time that I had seen her close up. I thought I had viewed a pitiful sight previously when I saw her in the dining room. I was horrified at what I now gazed upon, without the distance between us. The child was so thin that a strong wind could blow her away. Her hair was still a tangled mess of I don't know what. Her legs were even flimsier then I saw in the dining area. Her feet were bare and wet and her clenched face showed that a great amount of cold was within her body. The expression in her eyes was considerably older than that of an eight-year-old child. She gave the impression of a girl who has seen and felt considerable pain for a child of that age. Her expression was one of destitution, and showed the lack of love and understanding. Her actions were that of a child who had neither received anything nor wanted anything. Her expression was that of an automatic "thing," an automated human being. She was a robot that did what she was told, never questioning, wanting, or expecting anything.

I looked at Doc with an expression of absolute disbelief. This was the first time that I had ever seen any of the children really up close during this unexpected tour. I have never forgotten how that little girl looked or the expression on her face. I constantly think, "How could any child reach that age and not have experienced the joy of being alive?" Guillermina did not show any emotion as she stood there, looking at the floor.

Thank God Doc was trained in these matters and had seen conditions like this frequently, even though I had not. He clutched my hand and gave it a tight squeeze, unbeknownst to Madre. He knew I was about to say something that I would regret later. He was right. I was about to say something that would have gotten us cast out of the Casa and forbidden to return.

By this time, I was succumbing to what I had been observing all morning. Maybe I could disregard my sensitiveness if there were only one child involved, but every child that I saw was in a similar condition. I never dreamt that things like this could ever happen to children. I could maybe accept these things occurring to more seasoned adults, but never to a child. I was ready to say just what was on my mind; however, that would not have been too tactful if I wanted to have the Casa's participation in our project.

By this time, I was hell-bent to do something to assist these children. I did not know what yet, but it was going to be something above and beyond the project. I thought, "Are these people who run these places or animals? Don't they have any feelings at all? Don't they see what is happening?" Numerous other thoughts came to mind. I could hardly wait to talk to Doc alone on that trip back to the hotel.

The Madre broke my contemplation by saying something in Spanish to Guillermina. Before Doc could translate it, the child responded to the Madre's words by turning and speaking to me in Spanish. Doc translated as she was speaking them. The words went something like this, if I remember, "Madre told me that I was chosen to go to the private school and I am happy that it was me. Please accept my many thanks and may God bless you." She sounded as if she was a parrot, uttering what she was instructed to say.

I asked Doc to inform her that it was an honor to send such a bright child as the Madre told she was to the private school. I also added that I had faith that she would do well there. With those words, a small smile emerged on her face, turning her expression into one of pride and delight. Doc's face mellowed a little, as we both then realized what a few kind words said to one of these children could do.

I asked the Madre if Guillermina could accompany us on the rest of the tour. I hoped to save her from the dreadful task of the toilet bowls at least for that day. The Madre consented, so Guillermina joined us as we continued on the jaunt. Guillermina looked very cold as she walked. Her dress was still wet from cleaning of the toilets, she wasn't wearing shoes, and the ground was very cold. I felt so sorry for her. I could tell from Doc's face that he felt the same way.

The entire expedition followed the Madre back to the central courtyard. At this point, Felipe left us and returned to his duties. I breathed a sigh of relief over his withdrawal from the tour. I returned to my previous position in the back of the progression. Doc was no longer walking with just the Madre. Guillermina walked on one side of Doc and the Madre was on the other. Doc was now talking more to Guillermina than to the Madre. I could see that the Madre was becoming disconcerted at this new event; however, Doc seemed to be managing the situation sufficiently so I kept out of it. After all, he was the psychiatrist, not me. I just hoped that he knew what he was doing.

Guillermina would say something to Doc in response to Doc's statement or question, but after each reply, she would look at Madre for approval. Her answers were short. She never said anything unless Doc said something first. However, every so often Guillermina would smile and then Doc would. Madre Esmeralda never smiled, only the child and Doc. It appeared that Doc and Guillermina were having a wonderful time talking to each other. I wished that I knew what they were taking about because every so often, both of them would turn around and look at me and then smile or laugh. I was almost becoming paranoid.

The desire to talk to Doc alone became the driving thought in my mind at this point. I was interested in what Doc's reflections were about the Casa and other matters. However, my main goal now was to find out what he and the child were saying. I don't think anyone desired to speak Spanish more than I did that day.

After the girls' quarters, we went to the boys' area. As I had previously written, this area was exposed for all to see, unlike the hidden and guarded girls' area. It was at one end of the courtyard. The boys were all out in the yard and did not seem to be working as the girls were. They were all playing.

I asked the Madre, "Who cleans the boys' area?" The answer was that when the girls were finished with their area, they did the boys' location. She also added that the boys were moved to the girls' area while the girls cleaned theirs. I thought it was a bit unfair to the girls that they had to do the boys' area also; but in Mexico, it's a man's country. I was starting to see why the girls were so worn down and frail. They did all the work at the Casa. The boys and the Madres hardly did anything. The girls' lives were to go from one job to the next, only to be interrupted by the short time at school and to eat.

During the years that followed, I learned that the older girls' work was also interrupted for other tasks outside the confines of the Casa. Even going to school did not give the girls much of a break. In Mexico, the school hours are broken into two sections: one in the morning and one in the afternoon. The boys all went in the morning with half the girls. The rest of the girls went in the afternoon. This way some of the girls were always available to work.

Doc asked, "What time do the girls go to bed in the evening?"

The Madre responded, "At 9:00 or when they have finished all their appointed chores."

Doc was translating everything without being asked now. He could see that I was upset over this whole situation and wanted to be sure that I understood everything that was being said when he spoke to the Madre. This way, I would not be left out of the conversation if I wanted to say something. I suppose this was one of his many psychological tricks he realized he had to use on me.

From the boys' area, we went to the kitchen and once again, as in my previous visit, it was spotless, because there were five little girls cleaning it. Once more, an appointed Madre was just standing around overseeing the children as they did their chores.

I learned afterward that on Saturdays and Sundays, when visitors were present, the girls did not work all day. They "only" worked until noon when the visitors were expected. At that time, the boys and younger girls were properly dressed and granted permission to play. The older girls were not at the Casa at that time; they had work to do on the outside. Each of the children who were permitted to interact with the visitors was taught how to smile and act towards guests. This way the Madre was certain to receive a couple of dollars from the rich Americans.

We then proceeded to the room where the babies were kept. This too was spotless for the same reason: the overworked girls. There were rows upon rows of cribs with a baby in each one. I must have counted at least 45 babies in the room. Their care was being administered by four Madres. Doc was allowed to examine two of the infants at will. He proclaimed, "These babies are in very good health. I expect it is from all the care that they receive. I congratulate you, Madre Esmeralda, on the perfection of *these* children."

Through the tour, Guillermina and Doc strengthened their confidence in each other through conversation. I could observe them becoming more friendly and comfortable with each other. The smiles on Guillermina's face were present now more than when we first started talking with her. The Madre also seemed to have accepted sharing her time with Guillermina now more than she did originally.

During the visit to the babies' quarters, Doc let Guillermina hold one of them. Guillermina's eyes lit up like a Christmas tree. She held the baby properly and spoke softly to it in Spanish. When the baby smiled at her, Guillermina's expression clearly showed her delight. Doc told me that while she was doing this, she had said that it was the first time she had ever held a baby. She had asked Doc if she was doing it properly, as she'd only seen it done in magazines. Most children would say "as they did with their doll." This was not the case with the children of the Casa, as they had no dolls with which to play.

I could see so much love in Guillermina's eyes as she held the baby. I do not think any mother could have held a baby more tenderly and lovingly than Guillermina did in that instant. When she looked down on the baby with her big Bambi brown eyes and cooed to it, your heart almost broke. How could you love so much when you yourself had never experienced it? It was a sight to make the tears come to your eyes. In all truthfulness, they started to come to my eyes. Doc saw it and once more squeezed my hand but this time said nothing. Then he looked at me with a kind, understanding expression that Doc always had when you were perplexed and needed encouragement. With Doc's intervention, I quickly recomposed myself before Madre observed my condition.

With the inspection of the babies' quarters, the tour was completed. We then returned to the courtyard and Doc and I bid goodbye to Guillermina at the gates to the girls' area. Doc promised to return and maybe take her outside the colossal walls of the Casa, her sole cosmos, for an ice cream or something. He gave his promise to the child only after first securing permission from the Madre. Madre told Doc that no one had ever said that to Guillermina previously. She warned him to be careful to only say it if he meant it, as she would look forward to it and place great importance on the pledge. With that promise to return and take her out of the Casa, she expressed her pleasure with a great smile. Then she skipped up the long passageway to the girls' area. It was a skip that I was to come to know was only used when she was extremely happy and excited.

Doc and I both watched her vanish at the end of the long passageway into her microscopic universe. Just prior to turning the corner and disappearing from view, she turned, waved, and coupled with a majestic smile, said in Spanish, "God bless you all and hasta la vista."

I asked Doc, "What is the difference between 'Adios' and what she just said?"

Doc replied with a sort of frog in his throat, "'Adios' means goodbye but 'hasta la vista' means 'see you soon.'"

I wondered what was going through Doc's mind as he watched her round the corner and fade from sight. Now that we were alone with the Madre, Doc asked her, "Do you have any objections to the placement of computers in the Casa to assist the children in their school work?"

Madre was quick to reply, "Yes, I do not know anything about them. But what I have heard is that they deprive the children of the ability to think for themselves."

Doc responded, "That is a common belief and has been open to much debate. I just asked, as you seem to be quite knowledgeable about world events. Thank you for your opinion."

He left it at that and did not pursue it any further. Later, Doc told me that the Madre was a very opinionated woman and that was not the time to advance the subject any further. We would not be able to change her mind until she got to know us better. He further added, "A Mexican's greatest attribute is that they take time and never dash into anything. Things must be discussed many times before they are willing to accept a change of outlook. Plus, they must get to know you and trust you. Mexicans and Americans view time differently; to a Mexican, tomorrow never seems to come."

After thanking her for her opinion, Doc said, "Hasta la vista" to the Madre and thanked her very much for the tour. Madre told us that she was honored to have such a great man come and visit her. Because of this, she was more than pleased to show us the actual Casa and its workings on a day other than Saturday or Sunday. She also added that she would appreciate any suggestions on how to have the Casa operate in a better fashion.

Doc looked at me with an expression that said, "Don't you say a word, I'll answer for us." Doc replied to the Madre's request with a statement that went something like this, "Madre, the efficiency of this Casa and your role in supervising it is beyond words. And one day God will reward you for what you are doing to [note: not 'for'] those little children." I got the implied and arguably more sinister message; however, it was quite evident that the Madre did not.

She answered promptly, "Thank you, and you and Dr. Nielsen are always welcome any time you wish, regardless of the prescribed visiting hours. Mi Casa es su Casa."

All three of us strolled to the large iron gates that thwarted people from entering and children from defecting. The Madre removed a massive key from her costume and unlocked the door that was inside the gates. She then accompanied us to our car, which was parked outside. Before leaving, we once again thanked the Madre for her time and kindness and promised to return shortly.

She replied, "That will be a very fine thing, and I will look forward to it."

We started our journey back to the border. As we turned the corner of the dirt street, we both waved goodbye to the Madre from our open car windows. I was driving, as Doc was not the greatest driver of all time. I had found that out in England when he had persisted in driving on the wrong side of the road. During the drive back to the border and then to the hotel, I was overflowing with questions. The only dilemma I had was where to start. After reassessing it all in my mind, I settled on the conversations between Doc and Guillermina.

I asked, "What were you and Guillermina talking about? All you two kept doing was laughing and smiling and then looking at me. Did I have my tie on wrong or something?"

Doc responded with sort of a chuckle, "No your tie was on okay but your long hair was all over the place and your nose was dripping from the cold. The child asked me if all Americans scientists have long hair and big noses like you. I told her, 'No, only the funny ones.'"

"Some pal you are! Okay, what else? There was more than that."

"She was asking if you really would send her to that school and if you were not just saying it. I satisfied her by remarking 'He rarely says something he does not mean. I absolutely believe he will do it.' So," Doc pronounced, looking at me with a stern expression, "You'd better go through with it." Doc then queried me, "Bob, did you notice the care given to the babies versus the care given to the older children?"

"Yes," I answered. "What are you trying to imply?"

"Nothing. It just struck me funny, that's all. You would think that they would all get the same type treatment and care."

That statement of Doc's puzzled me as Doc very seldom wasted words. Something was on Doc's mind. To push it further would be useless since Doc was the kind of guy that would clam up once he used the word 'nothing.' So, I just let it go and put it in the back of my mind.

By the end of the day, I had decided that I would do more for this child, Guillermina, than just send her to school. Compassion, or call it what you will, took complete control of my thoughts. Of all the children that I saw that day, she was the worst off. Yet, she accepted her position as last in the Casa and last in the world.

CHAPTER FOUR

THE BORDER CROSSING

The biggest adventure you can have prior to the border crossing is trying to miss as many of the large potholes as possible with the car. These holes were substantially larger than the ones in the parking lot on the American side of the border. I wondered if we would reach China if we were to fall into one.

Doc was unusually quiet on the drive. Something was obviously bothering him. I asked him a couple of times what was wrong. He just looked at me with a blank expression and replied, "Nothing, there is just something about the Casa that I cannot put my finger on. Above and beyond the treatment of the older children, I mean."

Until Doc figures out what he's thinking so that it sounds correct in his mind, he will not discuss the matter with anyone. Thus, Doc was not talking too much. Instead, he was busy writing in his notebook. He always does that after we have completed anything, so that he can accurately remember things. Then when he wrote his report, it would be as complete as possible. Doc was a very methodical individual and his reports were a sight to behold. They were always flawless and precise in every small detail.

I finally broke the stillness and asked, "All right, what else went on between you and Guillermina? You must have said more than that.

You two were talking up a storm when we were walking all over the place."

Doc stopped writing and looked up at me. He smiled and answered, "The main thing she was talking about beside the school was you and McDonald's hamburgers."

I said, "Well, at least I was in good company. What did I have to do with a Big Mac?"

Doc replied, "Nothing, but those were the two things that she really wanted to know about. Bob, you have to realize that this little girl knows nothing about the outside world except for what she has been allowed to see on television, and even that is closely supervised. Most of the other girls have someone who visits them every so often, or sees people on Saturday or Sunday. Guillermina has none of that."

Doc continued to discuss the child. "Furthermore, due to her appearance, she has been kept out of sight when visitors are there. As Madre said, 'Guillermina's appearance would cause embarrassment to the Casa.' She also said that she has tried to put weight on the child but to no avail. I asked her if she had taken Guillermina to a doctor and Madre said, 'No, because she is not sick.' I ended the conversation on that subject and just told Madre 'Well, I'm quite sure you will work it out.'"

Doc shook his head sadly and continued, "Bob, the trouble with the child is that she likely has so many different parasites in her body, I don't think you could count them all in a year. You are the first person to show any interest in her and to allow her to ask questions about what goes on outside the walls of the Casa. A Big Mac to you might be an everyday occurrence. To her, it's a dream that will never come true. She never said that she would like one; all she wanted to know was what they were really like. 'Have' is a word that is not in their vocabulary. They are constantly told and exposed to the philosophy of not to want and not to have."

"As far as the Big Mac went, I answered her question with 'Maybe one day Dr. Nielsen would bring you one when he comes to visit you.' I also cleared that with the Madre before I said it, and she pleasantly said, 'Okay.' As far as you were concerned, Guillermina wanted to know who you were. Where did you come from? What did you do? Are you an American? Were you in the Army? Questions like that. She wants very much to know all about you. Don't you want to know about her?"

"Yes," I quickly replied.

Doc continued, "So, why should she be any different than you? The trouble is that she has no way to ask you due to her inability to speak English and yours to speak Spanish."

Doc seemed a bit upset so I said nothing more and allowed him return to his writings. My concern went back to the potholes and getting to the border. Eventually, we were back on the main roads. Finding my way back to the main road always felt like an accomplishment to me. I always got lost on the back roads that led to and from the Casa in the years to follow.

Shortly after reaching the main road, we arrived at the border crossing. The number of cars waiting to cross was beyond belief. They must have stretched for at least two miles. I really do not know how many miles it was but we waited in line for three and a half hours until we reached the border crossing station.

It was now mid-afternoon and the sun was at its highest. It was one of those very torrid Mexican days. I would say it was about 98 degrees. Many of the cars in the line had their hoods open, indicating that their automobiles had overheated. However, this overheating did not stop them from progressing in the line, as all the occupants of an affected car would push it when the line moved. This was done so they would not lose their place in the line. Most of the automobiles in Mexico are not of the latest vintage. Some of the cars would fit the standards of antique cars in America. The difference between our antique cars and the Mexicans' older cars is that ours are a showpiece for exhibition and pride of ownership. The Mexicans' cars are a necessity for life and travel, and they have little money to keep their cars in any reliable working order.

As I approached the border, I could see there were about 15 or 20 crossing stations. However, only four of them were open to the crossing cars. All the rest were closed, which had produced the extremely long lines. I could see many idle American customs agents talking to each other on the other side of the border stations. There must have been about 15 of them all in a group. They were all just standing there and having a good old time while the people trying to cross suffered in the heat.

When we finally reached the station, the agent asked, "Are you U.S. citizens?"

We both replied, "Yes."

He then looked at Doc and said, "You look as if you are a Mexican. May I see some ID from you?", Doc was part Mexican and he looked it. Doc promptly produced his passport. The agent took the passport and studied the picture within. He then commented, "You travel a lot, don't you?"

Doc responded, "My profession requires travel."

Then the agent warned, "Don't get sassy with me, Mexican."

Doc said, "Who's getting sassy?"

I turned to Doc and in a low voice said, "Now you've done it. For being a brain, sometimes I have to wonder about you."

In the same low voice, Doc replied, "During my early childhood, I lived in a border town and I acquired an utter dislike for those people and just right now, for one of the few times in my life, I forgot myself. I'm sorry."

I was about to reply but our low conversation was broken by the agent interrupting in a rather mean voice, "The picture of you in this passport does not look like you." We were then commanded to cross the border and stop in an enclosed area on the other side. We followed the orders and when we arrived at the appointed section, there were about twenty other cars there and only two agents. Each agent was talking to the occupants of a car. The other cars were waiting for their turn. Once more we sat and waited. We waited for about one hour until it was our turn to be investigated.

When our turn came, an agent asked for Doc's ID. Once more he showed his passport. The agent took it and immediately disappeared into a small building at one end of the area. Now we waited again, but this time for only 15 minutes. The agent returned with another man who looked as if he was the agent's superior. This man asked Doc to step out of the car and me along with him. They then promptly proceeded to dismantle the car, piece by piece. The seats were tossed to the side, tires came off, headlights were removed, the trunk was pulled apart, and so forth. I inquired what they were doing and why. The reply was absolute silence. I must have asked the question about six times. Finally, I gave up and just watched the holocaust that was taking place to my rented car.

After about an hour of this, the agent turned to us and said, "Okay, you can go."

"What about the car?" I asked.

He roughly answered, "What about it?"

I said, "Who is going to put it back together?"

With a smirk, he replied, "It looks like you have a job to do."

I then asked if I could borrow some of their tools to put it back together. The answer was a short "No." I then proceeded to ask if I could leave the area and buy some tools.

He graciously said, "Yes, you are free to go anywhere, anytime." I thanked him for his kindness and proceeded to leave the area to purchase the required tools for the two-hour job of putting my car in a somewhat workable condition to get back to the hotel.

As the two agents left, they were laughing. The chief went back to the little house at one end of the area. The other went to the next car in line. They seemed to gain a great deal of enjoyment from this kind of treatment.

When I returned from purchasing the tools, I started for the little building into which the chief had disappeared to give him a piece of my mind. By this time, I was furious. Doc stopped me and said "Bob, it won't do any good. Let's put the car back together and get back to the hotel."

Still angry, I asked, "Are you going to let them get away with this?"

With a little smile on his face, he quickly replied, "It won't do any good and all it will accomplish is to take more of our time. Who knows what they will do if you go in there and get all upset?"

I agreed and turned back to help the number one psychiatrist in America put the car back into a somewhat presentable fashion for travel. As I was doing this, I said, "I wonder what Hertz is going to say when we get back?" We both sort of laughed and then went about the business of making a car again out of the junk heap that the agents had left behind for us. And we were not the only ones doing it; all the cars in front of us were having to do the same thing.

It was now about 7:50 in the evening. Neither one of us said anything during the 20 minute drive from the border crossing to the hotel. I was openly disturbed over the whole incident but old Doc just went back to his writings and looked as calm and collected as he always did. It was as if nothing had even happened.

CHAPTER FIVE

PLAN OF ACTION

When we arrived back at the hotel, we returned the car back to Hertz along with a dissertation for why the car was as it was. They accepted our explanation and then supplied us with a bill that included the expected time and materials needed to make the car presentable to other customers.

With that dreaded affair over, the both of us immediately went to the bar. I wanted to drown my thoughts and the Doc wanted to discuss what took place today at the Casa, but not the border crossing. To my knowledge, Doc has never mentioned that border crossing incident to me or anyone else.

Doc opened the discussion with a remark that he was interested in whatever took place at the Casa where the company and I would be involved. He wanted to be part of it even if he had to pay for it himself. He also stated, "You have been asking me what is bothering me. Well, here is what I have so far. I believe that there is a lot more happening at the Casa than meets the eye. The things that we saw today, such as the absolute care of those babies. By contrast, the expressions on most of the children's faces, especially the older ones, were that of concealment."

He was very concerned about the children and wanted to discover just what had caused this expression of concealment. That seemed to bother him a great deal although it was not his job as far as the company was concerned. Even though it was not his job, Doc was a man who had much compassion and love for all children worldwide.

I asked him what he meant by concealment. He responded, "Concealment is when a child is old enough to express feelings of their inner self through the expressions on their face. As a baby, you express yourself by way of crying. Each and every mother in the world, after they have been with their newborn infant for a couple of weeks, becomes sensitive to the types of crying that their child uses. Some cries are for food, some for pain, some for attention, and so forth. The action of expressing your inner self continues as you grow older. It does not cease. The only difference at a later age is that sometime you cry but most of the time you express these feelings on your face and mainly through your eyes. Haven't you ever heard the old saying 'The eyes are the gateway to the soul?'"

I replied, "Yes, but I never really understood the full meaning of it."

Doc continued, "The older you become, the more you are able to control these qualities of inner self expression. But, a child from two to eleven has not yet really learned how to control them to any great extent."

"Mothers obtain this 'sensitivity' to their child's inner self though constant association with the baby. Doctors in my profession gain it through education and hone it through the vast amount of people that they interview throughout their professional career. You might not see it, but I did. There is something that each child at that orphanage wants to say beyond being hungry and cold. However, they are too afraid or ashamed to disclose it to anyone for some reason. Thus, it becomes that expression of concealment. Do you understand now?" he asked.

"Yes, somewhat," I replied. Later I was to find that his concerns were well placed. The only problem was that they did not extend far enough.

With that out of the way, I now ordered a drink and quickly downed it. Then I ordered one more at double strength since I could see that Doc was about to launch into one of his infamous all-night sessions. When you have traveled with Doc as long as I, you quickly learned to recognize one of these events. These all-night sessions consisted of Doc starting at the first page of his notes and proceeding to the last page. As I said before, Doc recorded every little detail in those notes. Thus, the time required to review them usually took anywhere from six to ten hours. These sessions were his manner of reviewing his notes to insure their accuracy while the events were still fresh in everyone's mind. The only times he ever did this was when he was very concerned about the events that took place and he wanted to make sure that he did not miss anything. Usually he did not review them with anyone prior to his final report. This would be only the second time he ever did this with me prior to his final report.

First of all, Doc thought that starting a computer project at the Casa was a splendid idea. Not only could we learn what part culture plays in either helping or hindering early computer education, it could also provide us with the necessary knowledge as to what extent parents and the environment play a role in this new method of computer instruction. Most of all, it would give us a perfect place to try our new method for learning a second language via computer, as these children had no contact whatsoever with any other language but Spanish. In his opinion, this set up would show if the computer or the surroundings had a greater influence on acquiring a second language and to what extent the parents and the association with speakers of the second language have on the learning process of a child.

Doc then sat back and asked for a cigarette. He would smoke only when he was deeply perturbed over something. As he lit the cigarette and started to blow the smoke out, he said, "Well, Bob, let's start with what you think happened today and we will take it from there."

The ball was in my park, so I began to speak. "Well, to summarize everything today, it was an eye shocker. I never thought I would see what we did. I don't know if we should really get involved. But, that's my company hat talking. If I were to put on my personal hat, then I would say let's get involved and as fast as possible. There's a lot of work that could be done to educate those children and to improve their way of living. To think that children could exist that way and really show no emotion about it is something I don't fully understand. I would very much like to find out why they would accept such an existence so willingly. In addition, your remarks on concealment have really got me interested in finding out what the hell you're talking about…"

Doc interrupted me and said, "Bob, there's a lot that you have to understand about Mexico before you jump to any conclusions. It is not that I am sticking up for the Casa. Yes, there are many problems there, but we will discuss those later. For now, let me explain one thing and if we are permitted to proceed with the project, I hope you will come to comprehend what I am about to say."

Doc took a breath and continued, "You are judging the children there and their care based on children in America. Remember, you are not in America; you are in Mexico. Things are different there in relation to America in many ways. What you saw today was one of them. Yes, the normal things I saw there today were bad in your eyes. However, in relation to a Mexican's eyes, they are not too bad when you think of the other children throughout Mexico. At least these children have some food, some clothing. As bad as things were, they still had them. Plus, they also had a roof over their head. Mexico is trying very hard to change, but it takes time. Remember Rome was not created in a single day. So from that aspect, life at the Casa is fairly acceptable to the children and the Mexicans. Think of your visits to India, Africa, and other third world countries. Were there not things like you saw today present there? Yet you never said anything about those things like you did about what you saw today..."

I now interrupted Doc and countered, "Yes, they were as bad but I never got personally involved with any of it."

Doc snapped angrily back, "Oh, you have to be personally involved to feel the anguish of the children?"

With that statement, Doc won the discussion. I did not know what to say except to reply in a low and embarrassed voice, "My God, you are right. It is because I actually got involved here and spoke to the people and children. Does that really make that much difference in a person's thinking for situations like this?"

Doc replied, "Yes, Bob, this is a common problem among the people of this earth. It is not only you; about 99% of the people feel and act the same way. It's like shutting your mind to what your eyes see if you do not communicate or personally associate with the problem or situation." Doc then ended his well-meant reprimand as he said, "Well, enough of that, let's continue with your perception of today's events at the Casa and if we should use their facilities in the project."

I promptly continued with my observations of the day's events. I was ashamed of my last remarks and wanted to get off the subject as quickly as possible. "To continue," I said, "I believe it is an ideal location for the second language project as I said previously. This way we can combine our findings here with the results that we will be receiving from the bilingual school in Boston under the supervision of my university, MIT."

For the past two years in Boston, we had been experimenting with a new way of teaching a language to children through the use of a computer. The only problem that we had was in determining how much the children learned from the computer versus what they learned at home from their English/Spanish speaking parents. Also, there was the issue of what they acquired from their totally English speaking environment and friends. We'd had many heated debates about the subject.

"Here at the Casa," I continued, "there is no association with the English speaking nationality. The only exceptions are the brief visits on Saturday and Sunday with a few visitors. Even then, they do not speak much to the children. The Madres and all the help speak no other language but Spanish, with the exception of Estella. The children only speak Spanish to each other. The Casa is so far out of the way of the mainstream of Tijuana that the schools only bother to teach Spanish to the children. Yes, it is ideal for the project."

"Also, with their schools being so far out of the way, they do not attract the best teachers. This would also allow us to analyze the early educational computer learning philosophy with the kids and how their pure Mexican culture affects the results and teaching methods that we have obtained so far in the American schools. In all aspects, I would vote let's go."

"Good," replied Doc, "my sentiments exactly. I think we could not have found a better spot for the project. You really stumbled into it when you discovered that place. And to think it all started with a phony priest. The one big problem that we now have and must resolve is that Madre Esmeralda does not want computers there. But I think we can handle that. Mexicans do not like to make decisions quickly, as I had mentioned before. Time must be taken to talk to them about anything, especially something that they do not know anything about. And they really know nothing about computers. What they do know is only what uneducated people have told them, such as what we heard today. 'They rob the thinking of a child.' Do you remember Madre saying that when we asked about computers there?"

I nodded.

Then Doc advised, "Although, before you bring the subject up again, you must first win Madre's confidence or else your words will have no value to her. This is another Mexican trait. I briefly discussed it earlier and you will quickly come to understand it if you spend much time in Mexico. Until they genuinely know and trust you, they will very seldom listen to you with two ears. A Mexican's favorite expression is "Si" and then they will leave it at that and will do nothing about what you thought they had agreed to do. Don't ever let Madre get to that level with you, or else we will never place computers in the Casa."

Doc continued with this line of advice. "I would suggest that you and I, especially you, spend as much time in the Casa as possible before we bring the subject of computers up again. You made a good start when you volunteered to send Guillermina to that school. We can use that as an excuse for being there frequently. This will not arouse the suspicions of Madre. Also we could help in the way of contributions to the Casa on our own behalf. With that aspect of contributions, count me in for whatever you feel that they should have when you spend some time there," Doc said. "But, be careful of Madre; she's a shrewd old bird and not to be taken lightly. Do not try to rush her decisions on those computers. Although I've only known Madre a short time, I am quite sure that once she gets to know you, she will bring the subject of computers up again on her own. The seed that I planted when I mentioned computers to her will grow. She's that type of a person."

After listening to Doc, I responded, "With these things in mind, I think the next step would be to go back to the office and tell Tom, my boss, that I agree with you fully and we should start right now. The only problem is explaining to Tom that it will take some diplomacy on your part first to win the confidence of Madre before the project can actually proceed. This way, you will be honest with him up front. He'll understand that the results will not be as fast as when we did the American study in just two years. I anticipate about four years before anything worthwhile will come out of the Casa. That is, if we are successful with placing the computers in the Casa in the first place."

Doc agreed with my assessment and added, "In addition, this time will allow us to discover what is really going on at the Casa. I am quite sure that what it is will affect any results we will receive from the project. Therefore, it almost becomes a necessity that we find out what they are hiding. Do not be surprised at what you find."

With that, I stopped him cold in his oration and asked, "Pray, tell what you mean by that little gem? 'Do not be surprised at what you find.' What are you expecting me to find? You have been at that 'what you will find' all day with me and I still don't know what you are talking about. Do you plan to let me in on it?"

"Not right now because the issue is still a bit cloudy in my mind, as I said before, and I'm not really sure yet what I think. Therefore, it is better for you if you do not know until I have clarified my thoughts more carefully. Okay?"

Doc had never before done this to me. He and I had always talked things over down to the last detail. This time he would not even let me see his notes that he had taken during the day.

Now my mind was really going wild with thoughts. He had been at these innuendoes all day. What did he see that I did not? Was it only in their eyes that he saw it or was there something else? Was there something that Guillermina said that he was not telling me? Was it something that Madre said during their walk and inspection? Was it something that he saw or heard in the children's or the Madres' dining area? What was this concern that he had over the babies' room? These and many other speculations raced through my mind.

With our discussion out of the way, we calmly had one more drink. At least, Doc was calm; he'd gotten out what was on his mind to some extent. However, he'd left me with my own worries. What the hell was I getting myself into here?

For the rest of the evening, Doc told me about more things that Guillermina said on their walk, his observations about the sleeping arrangements and the dining setup for both the children and the Madres, and other things. It was just small talk as he went through those secret notes of his. This went on for the better part of the night, since Doc could not sleep and just wanted to relax. It was now 2:00 a.m.

When we finally went back to our rooms, it was 4:00. As I was entering my room, he said, "Keep me informed of what is happening. I want to be involved as much as my practice will allow me."

The next day, Doc and I parted at the airport. He went on his way to New York and me to Texas. The plane arrived back in Austin at 10:00 in the morning. You could guess what I did throughout the entire flight. That's right: I slept and slept and slept

CHAPTER SIX

PERMISSION GRANTED*

When I arrived at the office the next morning, Tom was there to meet me. "Hi, did you and Doc have a successful trip? What does he think about the place? Does Doc think that it is worth placing the project in the Casa? What did you all do?" Tom spouted out questions.

I laughed and uttered, "Easy, one at a time. In answer to your first question, the answer is that Doc fell in love with the place. For your second question, Doc is all for putting the project in the Casa. For your last question, what did we do? We visited there at an early hour. Doc wanted to see what really went on from the time they got up in the morning. This was so he would know what condition the child's mind would be and its willingness to accept the computer when it comes time to sit in front of them. Also, by this early visit, he could learn more about the psychological aspect of the children early in the morning in relation to schooling. Plus there was a lot more things that had to do with the environment of the Casa."

"What do you mean 'in relation to schooling'?" replied Tom.

"How do I know? Doc tried to explain it to me but it went over my head. You know how he is with those big words. But all in all, Doc proposed that we should go ahead with it since we could learn a lot about the effects of culture and other aspects on learning in third world countries using this approach."

Tom responded, "Good, let's go into my office and see what we need to set up down there."

I figured that this was not the time to explain that there was going to be a lot of groundwork needed first with the Madre before the computers could actually be established and a school started in the Casa. The time to do that was in his office over a cup of coffee. So off we went to the office. I was wondering how Tom would take to the idea of spending time and money educating the Madres about computers and convincing them that computers would not harm their children's thinking or interfere with the running of the Casa.

Tom sat back in his chair and asked, "Well, what do we ship first?"

I looked at him meekly and said, "Me, and that's all for the time being."

"I expect you will explain that remark?" was Tom's reply as he leaned forward again.

"Well, it goes like this," I began. "The Madres have a problem. They have never seen a computer. Therefore, they know absolutely nothing about them. What they *think* they know is that computers would deprive the children of their thinking process. They believe that the computer would think for the child, thus, causing the child to lose that ability. Now, according to Doc, you cannot change a Mexican nun's mind in a couple of days."

Since Tom still seemed to be listening, I continued. "First, they have to learn to trust us and the computers. I contemplate that little job would take about five to six months. Even though it might take that long to get them to accept computers, I can use that time to start the children on the manual part of 'The Speech Learning Section' of the project. I think that the Madres will accept that." I sat back and waited for the explosion.

Much to my surprise, Tom asked, "Do you have faith that you can accomplish their acceptance of the computers in that short a time frame and not just be wasting our time and money there?"

"I believe so," I declared confidently to Tom's question.

"Well, your decisions usually have been good in the past. So let's lay in a plan to do this. Then I'll take it higher up to the CEO for approval." Tom was always one to make a quick appraisal of a situation and then, just as rapidly, make a judgment.

I walked out of his office and returned to my own. There I sat trying to come up with the plan that he requested. I also had to open up all my mail, which had been gathering dust. I hadn't looked at it for a couple of months. Even as I was flipping through my correspondence, my mind was on what had taken place over the last couple of weeks.

All I did was to take a trip to Tijuana for a few pleasant hours of relaxation due to a business meeting being canceled. Suddenly, I was planning on being in that region for a couple of years. I'd expected to be in some exotic foreign country to work on the 'computer culture' program for a period of time. In all truth, I was thinking of some place like Tahiti or Italy, places like that. Those localities have a nice ring to them. They were places that you could do some traveling and sightseeing afterhours and on the weekends.

Not only would I be in Tijuana, but I would be in the poorest part of the town. At least I could have picked one of those rich Mexican private schools where they have nice lunchrooms and food to eat that you did not have to worry about. Also the children in such a place would have been in a better position to learn, thereby allowing me to accomplish my task in a shorter period of time. The children at that type of school would have the time to devote to the computers and not have to work in their house, as the children of the Casa had to do. Likewise, I would not have to spend my time convincing the director of the school about the advantages of a computer.

How did I get into this? Why did I select the Casa? I am a man who usually does not get involved with the schools that I have experimented with. So why now did I want so very much to work at the Casa, in the poorest of all environments? And why did the children there look so scared and frightened? Would those things hinder my findings on how culture affects early computer education? After all, that is all I was paid to discover. So, why was I thinking about something other than computers and education for the first time in my life?

These were the thoughts racing through my consciousness instead of thoughts on how to do the job and 'laying in a plan,' as Tom had told me to do. Laying in a plan was what I had done in the past when I was about to start a new project. Now I was not even thinking about how many computers we would need there or how many children we should use. All I could see were the children of the Casa with no shoes, dirty faces, tangled hair, and that ever-present look of hunger and cold. I had seen all of that before in the streets of India, Pakistan, Africa, and other countries. It had never really bothered me before, not to any great extent. I would see the poor children there and continue walking on my way to my fine hotel and then eat a good meal. However, now it felt so different.

All my life, my mind had been trained to think logically. That logic said to examine the facts as quickly as possible and then present an answer. You should never become personally involved as this will taint your thinking. In most cases, by having this 'tainted' mind, you will present an incorrect solution to whatever problem that you are trying to solve.

It was driving me mad. The word "mad" struck a chord. I knew now what I would do. I would call up Doc in New York and have him tell me why I was thinking so illogically. He'd known me for a long time and had been on many assignments with me. Also, he was the number one shrink in the U.S. Who would be more capable to answer 'why' than he?

I reached for the phone and promptly called good old Doc. I got lucky and he was not too busy to speak to me. I explained to him what my problem was and asked him, "Why am I thinking like this when I have never done so before?"

Doc answered, "Well, Bob, don't worry. It's a normal thing to be concerned about people."

Frustrated, I said, "Are you trying to be funny, because I'm serious. It really bothers me to think this way. My mind should be on the project, not those kids."

Doc sighed. "No, I'm not trying to be funny. I'm deadly earnest. This is one of the biggest problems that intellects like you have. You very seldom get involved with people. Unless they are on your thinking level and you consider them a peer, you do not take the time to think about them as a person. Even then, all you do is to talk about the intelligentsia and never about the ordinary people. You all live in your own small world. Very seldom do any of you come out of it. Something mind-shocking is the only commodity that seems to bring you people out of this world to join the rest of us. Then it must be explained to you, because you guys just don't understand it. Once it is made clear to you by someone whom you respect, you are fast to grasp the dilemma. What you experienced at the Casa is just the shock that you needed. At last you have developed a sensitivity to people rather than your beloved computers that you are always talking and dreaming about day and night. You are becoming human like the rest of us."

"After those insulting remarks, I expect you will go deeper into them," I responded a little irritably.

He said, "I plan to, if you would stop interrupting me. Bob, most of your life has been about computers. You never have given yourself the time to look around you to see the beauty that the love of a human being can be. You have lived in that small world that I spoke about earlier."

Doc was getting warmed up on the subject. "Now, for the first time, you have taken that time with that little girl, Guillermina. That's what's bothering you; you don't have an answer for that little girl. With no answer or anticipated resolution, your mind is running amok. You don't know how to deal with a human problem, just those hard and fast facts that you have always lived by all these years. What you're finding out is that there is often a 'gray' area. Everything is not just yes or no or in black and white like the world in which you and your friends tend to live."

"It is not all the other children in the Casa," Doc continued. "For you it is just that one, Guillermina. With her, even you took the time to talk. You have never done that before this orphanage. You always let me do any talking with a child. This time all the circumstances were present. I was there, she was there, the Madre was bugging you, and you were upset over the way that the children were being treated, especially Guillermina. I could go on but it would take many hours to explain it to you."

"Please, just accept that your thoughts are good and normal. Do not worry you are not going off the deep end. Maybe you're just coming back from the deep end. Just go on thinking the way you were; there is nothing wrong with it. Knowing you, you will soon place your thoughts in the proper order. You will solve the problem and also present a damn good plan for our project, along with helping the children of the Casa, I expect, in many other ways than just their education."

I was quiet for a moment and then said, "Thanks. I do not necessarily like what you had to say. I never thought of myself that way, but I guess I am. Somehow I will change and join the human race. I believe I have missed a lot of living and many of the joys of life."

Doc very softly replied, "Yes, Bob, you have."

With that, I said my goodbyes and hung up the phone. I was feeling much better. All I wanted to do now was to put that plan into place, give it to Tom, and have it approved. Then, as fast as possible, I could return to the Casa.

That night I worked all through the evening to complete the draft. I did it and it was a good one. I then gave it to Tom. Within two days, he had it approved and I was on my way back to the Casa. I was off on an adventure never to be forgotten, an adventure that would be the most detestable and the most beautiful that I would ever experience.

I left the office that night with a sensation that I'd never had before when I was about to start a new project, a feeling of being alive and free. For too many years, I had felt bored with life and all that it had to offer. I could hardly wait for tomorrow and the trip to Tijuana, with my new outlook on life and people.

* I think I'd better explain to anyone reading this that in this moment of time, 1970, when these escapades were taking place, no one had ever thought about putting computers into a school but my company. It was about eight years before the first public computer school was in place and that was because of the results received from the first computer school in the Casa and our efforts in Boston.

CHAPTER SEVEN

WE START

Needless to say, I had yet another restless night. The recent events invaded my thoughts as I tried to sleep. I dreamt of what Doc had said, about what I would do when I arrived at the Casa, what I would say to Madre Esmeralda, and topics in the same theme. Above all that little girl, Guillermina, kept popping up throughout the night in my dreams. What Doc had said must have really made an impression on not only my conscience but also my id. I really was considering people for the first time in my life. Still, I had no idea why this particular child had made such an impression on me.

My alarm was set for 4:50 a.m. so I could be ready for my 6:30 a.m. flight. The alarm never had a chance to ring; I had been up and fully awake since 3:00 a.m. I just could not sleep any more. So at 5:00 a.m., I had my coffee and then went to the airport. Airports are always such a lonely place at that hour. I waited until the airlines opened at six to pick up my ticket and boarding pass. Soon I was in the air. The next stop was San Diego, then Tijuana.

As I walked through the San Diego airport to the car rental office, I actually noticed people for the first time. In fact, while I was flying there, I surprised myself by talking to one of the stewardesses on the plane. This was a first for me. I had never really spoken to anyone on a plane or looked at the people as I proceeded through an airport. For most purposes, I had been a loner since my childhood.

Once I had the car, I was on my way. It didn't take long to reach the border. I crossed over and started to drive toward the Casa. My concerns from the previous night were still running through my mind. What would I say about why I was there? What would Guillermina be doing? Would she remember me? Would the Madre be upset because I returned so soon? It had only been a week since Doc and I had been there.

I decided to go into town first and stop at a restaurant to have a drink and a sandwich. This would give me time to collect my thoughts on what to say. It was almost lunchtime, anyway. I went to the same restaurant where I first had the notion to call on the Casa. I decided to sit inside rather than outside to avoid all those little children who seem ever present at the sidewalk tables in Tijuana. While I noticed them before as more of an intellectual concern, now the condition in which these children must be living really upset me. I felt for them as I had never really felt previously. Before it bothered me because as a "civilized" man, it was supposed to bother me; now, it really did. Guess good old Doc was right when he said, "Your outlook on life has now taken on a new perspective." I was a changed man.

As I settled into my meal, I used the time to compose a reason for my early return to the Casa. I decided the reason would be that I wanted to see if my check for the boys' washroom had cleared the bank or if there were any problems cashing the check in Tijuana. After that, I would discuss the company's ideas for teaching the children foreign languages and to see if I could use some of the children to try the concept. Depending on how well the ideas were received, I would have to take it from there. I did not want to plan too far in advance. I did not know the Madre or her culture that well, so I really had no concept of how she would react to my request.

After lunch was finished, I was once more in my car heading for the Casa. I drove through those old back roads and their increasingly familiar ruts. By the time I arrived at the Casa, the shiny new rented car was looking as if it hadn't been washed in ten years. I was almost embarrassed by its condition. As I drove, I thought, "Bob, you were always so sure of yourself before this. Why do you have this sensation of uncertainty now? Get a grip on yourself." With that, I recomposed myself mentally just as I arrived at the iron gates of the Casa.

Not long after I rang the bell, the giant Felipe opened the door. He said something in Mexican and waved me inside the complex. All of a sudden, a new fear grasped me. What would happen if Estella was not here? I would not be able to communicate with the Madre. Estella was the only one at the Casa who knew both Spanish and English.

Felipe disappeared and I was left standing alone in the inner courtyard. Soon Madre Esmeralda appeared from the far end of the courtyard and came straight toward me. Much to my peace of mind, right beside her was Estella.

We exchanged greetings and Estella said, "When the Madre heard that you were here, she sent for me immediately to translate. She was worried that something was wrong. You have genuinely impressed her and she likes you." With that sentence, my mind was put at ease. Now, I felt assured that she would be attentive to me.

The Madre asked me into a little sitting room on one side of the courtyard. As we walked toward there, Estella talked to me about Guillermina. "She has done nothing except talk about your and Doc Adolph's visit. I have never seen the child so happy before," she said. "She is also very excited about going to the new school and going outside the Casa for an ice cream sundae. I had to explain to her what a 'sundae' was. Then she really was excited as she never had ice cream before, no less a sundae, but had heard how good it was and she also wanted to know how it tasted."

"The other children said, 'Dr. Nielsen will never return, as they never do.' Guillermina would reply, 'He said he would and I believe him.' She would defend you, although the look on her face did not express as much confidence as her words," pronounced Estella.

We soon arrived at the little room. It had one couch, two easy chairs, end tables, and a coffee table in front of the couch. On the walls hung pictures of the founder of the Order of Nuns and other holy pictures. A very pretty rug was on the floor and flowers were all over the place.

Estella exclaimed, "You are something special. She only entertains in this room when you're a special guest. Oh, by the way, your check cleared the bank. We are now finishing the boys' bathroom. Would you like to see it afterward?"

"Sure," I said. Then I continued via Estella as a translator. "Madre, I went to my office in Texas. I told my superiors about your wonderful Casa and the way you take care of your children. I then requested if I could start a project on teaching your children to speak English. The office said that it was great with them if you said okay. So, is it possible that I might do that?"

As Estella was translating my question, I watched the expression on the Madre's face. When Estella's rendering was finished, the Madre replied rather hastily to Estella's words. I was worried because, as Estella was conveying my words to the Madre, the expression on the Madre's face was not too encouraging. Much to my surprise, when Estella relayed what the Madre had just spoken in reply, the answer was pleasant. "Yes, she would be honored and pleased to have you do so but first she must see how you expect to do it."

Estella then added, "The Madre asked me to inquire if you would join her and the other nuns for lunch.

Even though I had already eaten, I said, "Yes, I would like that very much." So off we went to the nuns' dining room. As we were walking toward the dining area, I asked if the children were eating now.

Estella answered, "No, they eat a bit later today." I was so happy to hear that as I did not want to watch that process again, and I had to pass the children's dining area on the way to the nuns' dining room.

Upon arriving at the nuns' area, I was greeted by the other nuns who were already there. We promptly took our seats. As on my previous visit, I was seated next to Madre Esmeralda.

After we settled down at the table, I proceeded to discuss the forthcoming speech and language project. During one of the lulls in the conversation, the Madre told me she had contacted the school that Guillermina would be attending next year. Proudly, she announced, "The school would be happy to accept Guillermina next term."

This gave me an opening to ask, "How is she?"

The Madre answered, "Very well, would you like to see her again?"

"If it is possible, yes, I really would."

The Madre motioned toward one of the nuns. After a brief discussion, the nun promptly disappeared. A short while later, the nun returned with Guillermina by the hand.

Guillermina was dressed in a blue dress that looked as if it was newer. Her hair was fairly well combed although it appeared as if it had been done in a hurry. In addition, I could see that two or three buttons on the back of the dress were not buttoned. It was as if the dress had been hastily placed upon her. She was even wearing shoes. Although the shoes had holes in them, they were still something of a prize to Guillermina. She was one of the few girls that had shoes to wear on special occasions. She looked very pretty compared to how I had last seen her.

Once in the dining room, Guillermina curtsied to Madre Esmeralda. Then she swiftly approached me and gave me a little kiss on the side of my face. After that little kiss, Guillermina returned to her place in the doorway.

I was soon to learn that in Mexico, when a little girl greets you or leaves after they have met you once, they will always greet you with that customary kiss. It is a practice that goes far back in time. I think it is a charming tradition. Soon I looked forward to it. Whenever I saw a child a second time, I would always bend down for the required kiss.

Guillermina now stood in the doorway with her head down, looking at the floor. She did manage to look at me once and muster up a small smile when the Madre was not looking. However, after braving that, she promptly lowered her head again. The Madre said something. Then Guillermina spoke words in Mexican that started Estella translating as the child spoke.

"Senor Nielsen, it is a great honor to have you return to the Casa. I have been looking forward to it so very much. Will you be able to stay with us for any amount of time?"

I replied, "Yes, I will be staying for a little while. Would you like that?" As I was speaking through Estella, I was also looking at the Madre for her consent. I could see by the expression on her face that there was no problem.

Guillermina also looked at the Madre, who nodded her approval. Then Guillermina replied to the question with a smile. "Yes, I would like that very much." After the girl answered, the Madre motioned for the nun that brought her to have the child return to whatever she had previously been doing. Guillermina said, "Goodbye." She gave me the customary goodbye kiss and then left with the nun. As she was leaving, she turned her head in my direction and gave me a huge smile and wave with her small hand. Then she disappeared through the doorway and out of view.

The Madre said, "She has to leave now because their lunch will soon be starting. After lunch, she has to get ready for school. During your stay here, there will be many opportunities to speak with her."

I responded, "Good, I would like that, thank you."

As we were eating, I asked when I might start with the children on the speech project.

Estella asked the Madre. Then after some words back and forth between the two, Estella looked at me and said, "The Madre said, 'anytime you want as your explanation during lunch of what you wanted to do was very meritorious.'" Estella then asked, "How many children would you want to start with and how old?"

I answered, "About twelve girls between the ages of seven to twelve Then we would add the boys after three or four weeks."

Estella translated to the Madre and then replied, "The Madre will have them ready by tomorrow at nine in the morning. The only thing is that she wants to know how you plan on adding the boys to the class. This is because the boys are not allowed to associate with the girls."

"I will consult with her first when it is time to add them," I responded, "if that is all right with the Madre."

"No problem," Margaret answered.

We then went back to eating. All I did was think, "*Well, you are on your way. You are about to start.*" I wondered where this would all lead.

This was the first position I had where the children actually lived and went to school in the same place.

The Madre had an appointment with someone so she said her goodbyes early. She told Estella to stay with me and requested that I stop by her office to see her again before I left. I was interested in seeing what improvements my money had provided, so off Estella and I went to inspect the boys' bathroom.

Upon entering, it appeared as if it was a completely different room. The tile was back in place, the showers were working, and two more toilets had been installed. There were still no seat covers but the other changes made a huge difference. There were some men there installing lights. This would now make four lights in the room rather than the two that were there previously.

When the inspection was complete, Estella asked me if there was anything else that I would wish to do or see. "No, the only thing I need now is to find a hotel in Tijuana." I wanted to remain in Mexico and not face the border with its long lines and rude custom guards, so I added, "If you could direct me to a nice hotel, it would make my stay more pleasant and longer. The time saved from going back and forth to a hotel in San Diego, I could spend here."

Estella recommended the Hotel Lucerna. She told me that this was the hotel that the President of Mexico stayed in when he visited Tijuana. I figured that if it was good enough for him, then it ought to be good enough for me. I asked Estella how to get there. She removed a piece of paper from her pocket and drew an accurate map of the way to the hotel. We then went to say goodbye to the Madre and thank her for the meal.

Just as I was leaving, the boys and girls were going to lunch. I turned to watch the procession. Much to my surprise, Guillermina, whom I had not seen in the line, suddenly came rushing toward me at full speed. She jumped into my arms and said, via Estella's translation, "The Madre said that I could say goodbye and I love you." This exclamation was followed by a big hug and a kiss on the cheek.

I looked at Estella. She looked at me and said, "Looks like you have a real start to a beautiful friendship; cherish it well."

I responded to Guillermina, "I love you too." After I set her down, she promptly ran back to the end of the line and disappeared into the dining room. However, just before vanishing, she pivoted, looked at me, and smiled as she did earlier when she was leaving the Madre's dining room, along with a wave goodbye. Then she faded from sight into the room that I despised so very much, the children's dining area.

With that au revoir, I could hardly keep the tears from my eyes. I said my goodbyes quickly and got into my car. There I could wipe my eyes without being seen. Tears were a new experience for me as I was always taught by my father that men do not cry. Therefore, I was never allowed to do so during my childhood. This concept of not crying had stayed with me until that moment.

CHAPTER EIGHT

THE FIRST CLASS AND MEETING THE GIRLS

I followed Estella's instructions to the hotel to a T. It was in the better part of the city, a Mexican part of the town that Americans seldom see. As I entered the driveway, I saw that I was in front of a beautiful hotel. It was divided into two parts. The front was seven stories high and resembled an apartment house. The back was like a beach cabana style with the suites surrounding a sparkling clean Olympic-sized pool. The entire hotel was designed in a Mexican architectural style. I never thought I would ever see anything like this in Tijuana.

As the years rolled by during my stay in that town, I was to learn that I was not only wrong about my concepts of hotels, but about the entire town. Tijuana had really changed. The houses and people had changed beyond my wildest thoughts. The shopping plazas on the outskirts of the town were where the real Mexicans did their shopping. Very few, if any, Americans ever went there, for it was not by the main part of town where the tourists visit.

Tijuana had joined the rest of the world, although you would never know it if you were to stay only in the old section, where most Americans visit. The new section, however, was exquisite. The main part of Tijuana was still somewhat like it was long ago with the exceptions of the streets being paved. This old part still remained what the "Gringos" have come to see and expect.

I parked my car in the hotel lot and unloaded my bags. A bellboy was quick to secure them and bring them into the lobby. I registered with some complications because the hotel catered to Mexicans, not Americans. Therefore, the necessity of the employees to speak English was nonexistent. Eventually, they ushered me to a poolside cabana suite.

The accommodations were excellent. The room was clean, tidy, and well-maintained, unlike some hotels in which I have stayed during my travels to third world countries. This hotel I enjoyed very much. The living room had all the furniture required for such a room and a TV. The bedroom had a king sized bed and all the fixtures were tasteful. There was a door in the bedroom that led to my own private bricked-in patio, where there were a couple of chairs and a table. The accommodations were better than the ones I had in San Diego. Plus, they were half the price.

It looked like my stay in Tijuana was going to be more agreeable than I had thought. I had visions of being in some contemptible hotel with the usual bugs crawling all over the room. I had been in many of those before during my travels to third world countries. Those hotels always gave me the shudders. In Puerto Rico, I had even stayed in a hotel that had a sign on the door that read: "Please do not shoot holes in the wall."

I unpacked and then picked up the phone for room service. That was a mistake. Once more I was reminded that this stopping place was for Mexicans and not English speaking people. I did finally manage to order a Coke. It was not what I really wanted, but during my world travels, I had learned that if everything else fails, someone will always understand the word "Coca Cola" when you are thirsty.

My Coke soon arrived and I settled down to figure out my next move. Tomorrow, I would arrive at the Casa at nine to start the speech project. I inspected all the handheld computers that I had brought with me to make sure that they were in good working order. I hoped to use them in class tomorrow. These computers did not look like computers; they looked more like toys. Therefore, I hoped they would get the Madre's approval. She was really dead set against computers in the Casa.

I collected my notes into one package. Everything was set for the big day tomorrow. I had never been this nervous before starting a project. What had gotten into me? Doc was too far away to call. Anyway, how would I even place the call? Everyone in the hotel spoke Spanish.

Soon the nervousness feeling passed and I was my old self again. I finished my drink and decided to take a walk around the beautiful hotel. I seemed to be an oddity as all the people watched me as I wandered about. I suppose it was because I was a "Gringo" infringing on their place. Later, I was to find that my assumption was correct. However, the resentment only lasted for a short duration. They soon accepted me as one of them due to my association with the Madres and Guillermina. When my tour of the area was complete, I returned to my room and retired for the evening.

The next morning I was up bright and early. I went to breakfast at seven. The food was very good, much better than I had tasted in some places in America. This opinion was only reached after I had figured out what to order from the menu. Once again, it was all in Spanish. One thing saved me: "hot cakes" and "coffee" are spelled the same in both languages. All I had to do was point to them on the menu when the waiter appeared.

I finished breakfast about 8:50 and then set forth to the parking lot. My car was still there with all four tires in place. In Mexico, when you leave your car some place unattended, you never know if it will be

there when you return or if it will still be in working order. I entered
the car and I was on my course to the Casa.

Immediately upon arriving, I rang the bell to gain entrance. Instead
of the door opening within the huge gates as Felipe stood guard, I
was pleasantly surprised to find the gates themselves being opened
for me. Felipe stood on one side and waved me and the car inside the
compound. Once inside, he then directed me to one side of the inner
grounds to park the car.

Soon Madre Esmeralda appeared with trusty Estella at her side.
After greeting me, Estella said, "The Madre thought because you
might be here for some time today, the car would be safer on the inside
of the walls rather than on the outside." After I thanked the Madre
for her thoughtfulness, Estella continued. "The Madre cannot be with
you today as she has other duties to do. She did give me a list of the
girls that will be participating in your project. They are all waiting and
anxious to start." I looked at the list. I quickly spied who I was looking
for among the names. The fourth name down was Guillermina. I
smiled.

Estella looked at me and said, "Yes, she is there." She then smiled
and asked, "Ready to start?"

I retrieved the handheld computers from my car along with my
notes and off we went to a small classroom on the second floor, where
three windows faced the courtyard. At one end of the room was a
blackboard and fourteen chairs. I was greeted by twelve little voices
that said, "Good morning Teacher Nielsen." The girls were all standing
quietly beside their desks.

What struck me as I entered the room was the absolute silence. It
was completely unlike other classes of children that I had witnessed
in the past. In those classes, when there was no supervision, there
was pandemonium and chaos. These children stood there waiting for

Estella and me in quiet order. They were then instructed to sit down by Estella. Once in their seats, they folded their hands looked down at the desks almost in unison. It was kind of spooky. Also, all the girls were dressed the same. They wore white blouses and red shorts with knee-length white socks. Each girl had her hair in a single, neat ponytail.

I started to look for Guillermina but Estella beat me to it. She whispered in my ear, "In the front row by your desk. She was there at 8:45 this morning. She implored the Madre if she could come early just to get that seat. As I said before, you have become something special to her."

I looked at Guillermina and I could see that she was looking at me with one raised eye. I winked at her. She winked back at me and then immediately returned the attention of both eyes to her hands on the desk.

I decided that this would be one thing that I was going to change once I was accepted at the Casa. I wanted to defy the Madre and say, "When I walk in that room I expect to see pandemonium and chaos. In addition, I'd like to see more talking and giggling, as little girls do."

Estella then went about introducing each girl one by one. The first was Maria, age eleven. She was the one that I had been told was going to be adopted soon. Second was Maria Celer, also age eleven. She had long hair and was rather big boned and muscular. I was to learn that she was the strongest of all the girls and, thereby, the accepted boss, although Maria was the brains. Next was Blanca, age ten. She was rather on the stout side and had the longest hair of all the girls.

Then came Carmela, age eight. Other than Guillermina, she was the shortest one in the class. Her body appeared very frail, almost as bad as Guillermina's. She was a constant companion of Guillermina. Elizabeth was next. She was ten years old. Elizabeth was very pretty and of average build and size for a girl of that age. I have never known

Elizabeth in all my years at the Casa not to smile. She very seldom talked but she always had a smile. She was also a constant companion of Guillermina.

Suzanna was next; her age was eleven. Suzanna was the tallest of all the girls. She was also the one who had the hardest time learning. Lorannea stood up before Suzanna even sat down. She introduced herself without any help from Estella. Lorannea was ten. She had teeth that protruded quite far from her mouth. Lorannea was always the one who arrived first and did the most talking.

Estella then introduced Catalina, age ten. Catalina was of average height. Her skin was very dark in comparison to the other girls in the class. Altagracia was short but not as short as Carmela. She was nine. Vanassa and Rosio Rere were twins. Both had the big brown eyes that are so typical of the Spanish race. They were ten.

"Last, but not least, is Guillermina," Estella said with a smile. "Her I do not have to introduce. I am quite sure that you are in possession of the facts regarding her."

Guillermina stood up rather fast and smiled at me. Then with a turn of her body, she faced the other children in the class and said not a thing to them but just gave a big smile. Afterwards, she sat down with a vainglorious look on her face as if to announce, "I told you he would reappear."

All of the children were quite pretty. Yet, one characteristic was similar in all the children, with the exception of Guillermina. They were all very well developed for children of those preteen ages. I had been instructing preteen girls for years. In a typical class, there might have been one or two girls who looked like they were fourteen or fifteen judging by their physical appearance, but never the entire class except one. I thought it strange at the time; however, I soon forgot about it after the initial observation.

Estella sat in one of the chairs in the room and I then proceeded to provide each girl with a handheld computer. When turned on, these computers showed a picture of an object. After supplying the person with the illustration, the computer asked the person what it is. The student would type in the answer, and if correct, it pronounced the word in English and allowed you to continue to the next example. If incorrect, it requested you enter a new word. After the second attempt, the computer would furnish the accurate answer verbally.

Accompanying the minicomputer was a booklet with illustration that corresponded to the image presented on the computer. Under the picture in the pamphlet were three words of what the object might be. Two of the words were erroneous and one was accurate.

The children quickly learned how to operate the machines and proceeded to learn to speak and spell the word on the computer in English. This continued for about two hours. While at first they were anxious about the new class, all the girls were soon laughing and having a wonderful time with their new "toys."

By eleven, we had finished with the first session. Everyone, including myself, was pleased with the outcome. Most of the girls were speaking many words in English that they had learned. Some were even speaking sentences. Guillermina was learning extremely fast.

The girls did not want to leave at the appointed time. We had to physically remove the computers from each child because they did not want to give them up so soon. Madre Esmeralda had sat in on the last part of the class. When she saw their reluctance, the Madre stood up and requested the children to do as they were instructed and leave. Upon hearing the Madre, they quickly submitted to my request. The Madre asked Estella to tell me that she liked what she saw and heard very much. She then invited me to join them all for lunch if I so desired.

The girls left the classroom as quietly as I had found them. Guillermina was the last to leave. Upon leaving she looked up at me, smiled, and gave a little wave goodbye with her tiny hand.

During lunch, we talked about how I thought the class went. Madre Esmeralda was very impressed with the "toys" that we were using. She told all the other Madres how these toys would talk to the children in English. She had never seen anything like it. She even told them how she had held one and it talked to her.

"It even said my name!" she announced to all assembled in the room with great vanity. Then she added, "Senor Nielsen has now received my permission to enter the girls' quarters without interference." After she announced that little detail, she looked at me and smiled.

I was taken by surprise. I asked Estella to have the Madre to repeat her last sentence in case Estella had misinterpreted the statement. Estella responded, "She and I spoke about granting such permission as we were walking to the dining room. The Madre feels that if you are going to teach the girls, then you must have access to them without having to find her all the time to receive permission to communicate with them. She feels that this will let you and the girls have a better meeting of minds, and thus produce better and faster results."

I never ceased to marvel at the wisdom of this uneducated woman as the years passed. After all, she had hardly finished the fourth grade when she entered the order of nuns. Yet she had more understanding of children and life than most people with a college degree.

Estella continued, "I have been in the Casa for quite a few years and the Madre has granted that liberty to very few. Not only to very few, but it was only after knowing those people for a year or two. She has granted you the permission after only a few short visits. Believe me, she most hold you in great esteem."

I looked at the Madre and thanked her very much for bestowing such a great privilege upon me.

She nodded her head in recognition of my thanks. Then she continued on with her story of the talking toys. She mentioned how she had the only Casa in all of Mexico with such things, and that the other Casas would be envious of her. She could hardly wait to call the Madre General, Madre Maria, in Mexico City that evening and tell her of the events of the day. She was proud as she recounted the day's events, and how enraptured the children were with the class and Senor Nielsen.

CHAPTER NINE

GETTING TO KNOW GUILLERMINA

Upon the completion of lunch, the Madre, Estella, and I left the dining room for the inner patio. Once outside, the Madre asked, via Estella, if I wanted to stay a little longer.

I responded, "Yes, I would like that very much."

With that, the Madre started telling me how their water supply was not sufficient for the Casa's needs. She recalled my comments from my first visit. When we had toured the kitchen, I had asked a lot of questions about the water supply. Now that she felt she knew me better, she was willing to explain further.

She said, "In Tijuana, as it is in all of Mexico, water is a precious commodity not to be wasted. In Tijuana and similar towns, there is not a central source for water. Each house is on its own to provide water." (Water wells are unheard of in these towns. I have never figured out why in the years that I spent at the Casa. There must be a reason for the lack of these wells.)

She continued, "The only way for us to have water is when it rains. The water is captured from the roof or gutters in the streets. Then it flows into large reservoirs that lie beneath the houses. From there, it is pumped to the house for our use. We do not filter it on the way to the house. The only purification done is at each water tap in the house if you are rich enough to afford such filtration. Very few of the people have this equipment due to the expense. Therefore, the water in each of these houses is not suitable to drink. The people who do not have this cleansing equipment and want to have pure water must buy large bottles of drinking water from the stores. If you have none of this, then you use the water as is from the reservoir. We are not a rich Casa." She looked frustrated as she told me this, but continued.

"If it has not rained for some time and your reservoir is not large enough, you must then buy water from the trucks. The drivers obtain the water from the river. Thus, each house must have extremely large-capacity reservoirs for rainwater or else pay these people to deliver water."

The Madre then brought me over to a small hole in the ground at one end of the inner courtyard. The walls of this hole had no retainers other than the earth from which it had been dug. She told me, "This is all we have to hold the water for all the things that require water in the Casa. I am always buying water from the trucks. If I did not do this, the children and the Casa would have no water." She also added that there were times when she did not have the money for the water trucks. At those times, the children have to do without a bath for about one or two weeks and the Madre was forced to buy water in bottles for the children to drink after a couple of days.

In my mind, this told me that the children drank the water straight from the Casa's reservoir, since there was not any purification equipment on any of the water taps in the entire Casa. The part that I thought peculiar, as I stood there listening to her, was that in the nuns' dining room there was a permanent water holder. In this holder was a large water bottle. So the nuns only drank good water, yet they would have the children drink the unpurified water. All the outer signs said that the nuns cared for the children. Yet, they allowed them to drink impure water. It seemed paradoxical to me at the time, and I once again became unsettled thinking that there was more to the Casa than met the eye.

"If only we had the money to construct a larger reservoir for water, then the children would not do without," the Madre continued as she interrupted my meditation. At that point, I volunteered to furnish the money to construct such a water reservoir for the children.

The Madre thanked me and said through Estella, "It is such a pleasant turn of events that you were brought to Our Casa. It must have been a gift from God." She then kissed me on my cheek and, with her callused hand, blessed me with the sign of the cross. Continuing, she asked, "Would you care to see Guillermina? Estella has told me that you two seem to be getting along very well with each other. Guillermina really needs someone, as she is such an unwanted and lonely child."

"That would be very nice. Yes, I would like to see her. I am starting to take a great liking to her," I answered her query. After my response, she asked Estella to fetch Guillermina.

Soon Estella reappeared with Guillermina. The child kissed the Madre on the cheek then looked at me. Estella said, "She is waiting for you to bend over so she can kiss you too." For a moment, I had forgotten the custom. Once reminded, I quickly bent over and she then kissed my cheek as well.

The Madre stated, "Guillermina, you, Senor Nielsen, and Estella can go to our visitor's living room for the rest of the time you have left before school and talk. Would you like that?"

She eagerly responded, by way of Estella, "Yes, I would like that very much."

After the Madre excused herself to go about her many tasks of running the Casa, Estella took Guillermina by the hand and we walked to the Madre's little living room. As we walked to the room, Guillermina kept looking behind her to see if I was still there since I was walking behind them and not beside them.

Once there, Estella and Guillermina sat on the couch and I chose one of the easy chairs. Guillermina's feet never touched the floor. She sat there looking at me with her hands folded on her lap. I was quite surprised that she was looking directly at me. The behavior of constantly looking down seemed to be only present when one of the nuns was there or about to be there. I wondered why that was so.

Estella said to me, "What would you like to ask her?"

Soon I said, "Ask her if there is anything she might want."

Estella did not translate that question but answered it herself. "The girls are taught to want nothing thereby never to be disappointed. However, see those shoes she has on? They are two sizes too small. The tops on the side have broken loose from the soles. Every time it rains, she always has wet feet due to the rips in her shoes. So maybe you could buy her a pair of new shoes. She has never had new shoes. I'm quite sure that she would like to have a new pair. Do you want me to ask her?"

"By all means," I replied as I looked at the child's shoes. They had such wide rips on the side that you could see the socks that she wore. As I looked at her shoes, Guillermina saw the direction of my gaze and promptly tried to put one shoe over the other to cover how tattered they were. She was very embarrassed that I was looking at them. I quickly stopped my visual inspection so not to embarrass her any further.

Estella turned to Guillermina and said something to her in Spanish. Halfway through the conversation, Guillermina's face lit up and a big smile appeared; I assumed that Estella had gotten to the part where Guillermina was going to have new shoes. When Estella was finished, Guillermina started talking. I just sat there and listened. I had no idea what they were saying. Both of them looked very pleased as this dialogue was taking place. However, most of the time, Guillermina had a puzzled expression on her face.

After ten minutes or so, they stopped talking. I did not know Spanish but I was wondering why it took so long to ask about a new pair of shoes. Estella looked at me and said, "Guillermina has never been taken shopping. This will be her first time outside the Casa's walls so she was asking me all sorts of questions about shopping. She did not know what the words "shopping" and "buying" meant. I had to explain them. Once I did that, it opened up to many more questions. 'Where do you do this? How do you do it? What are shops? How do you buy?'"

At this point, I interrupted Estella. "My God, you mean to tell me that she did not know what the words 'buy' and 'shopping' meant?" Estella looked at me and then gave me my first lesson of the many I was to learn about the children of the Casa.

"Bob. May I call you Bob?"

"Yes, by all means do," I replied.

"Bob," she resumed, "you are a very intelligent person. On the other hand, intelligence does not always correspond to human life. These children here have been cloistered here for most of their lives. Nearly all of them have been here from their infancy. These children know nothing of the world outside these walls. They seldom leave the Casa, if ever. Some do not leave until they are eighteen. The Madres do not have time to talk to them, as they are always busy with their many tasks. Nor do they watch TV or read many magazines or newspapers."

"As far as money goes, these children only know what one peso is. If you have never been to a shop, why should you know what one was? I could go on with other examples but I'm sure you understand the point I am trying to make."

"Bob, just remember this when you deal with these children: they will not know the simplest of things that any normal child outside these walls of two or three years of age would know. At that age, the children really only know by doing. But what have these children ever done? They wake up in the morning. They go to church after working. Then they stop for food before going back to work. During school months, it is school, back to work, eat, and then sleep. Then the next day, the process starts all over again. The only exceptions to this routine is a short time on Saturday and Sunday when the visitors come to the Casa to pat the children on the head and give them lollipops."

"To these children, time stands still. In truth, they know nothing of time. They have no conception of time. Ask Guille what time it is. She will tell you that she does not know. She knows nothing about the watch you wear. To her that is a foreign object. Ask her what month, day, or year it is and she will tell you that she does not know. In all truth, she most likely will ask you what those words mean. They only tell time by the sun coming up and the sun going down. The time in between is not set by minutes or hours, as our time is, but by what the Madre tells them and the work they have to do. Bob, these children have no tomorrow, they have only today."

"If you are going to continue your association with Guillermina, then you must realize these things. Be patient with her and her questions. Some—probably most—of her queries will be those of a one or two year old who is first learning what life is all about and what her surroundings outside these walls will be like. I expect that when she ventures from the Casa for the first few times she will be scared and frightened. Those will be important events in developing her trust. You will need patience and understanding, as this is when you will either win her or lose her."

I sat there listening to Estella in complete discomposure. I had never expected to run into this situation with an eight-year-old child. I was at the Casa to do a project, not take on a little girl and her problems. Yet this child had drawn me to her. There was something about Guillermina that made me feel like life was worth living again.

My past had not been pleasant. I had two failed marriages that had produced two children, both of whom turned out to be proverbial "bad seeds" that I wanted nothing to do with. So life to me at that time was a meaningless thing. I had gone to almost every part of the world and had lived and eaten in the best places. I no longer owned big houses as I had in the past when I had a family. I now resided in a small one-bedroom apartment in the middle of Texas. I no longer attended parties or any other function unless forced to by work. Basically, I had become a hermit. I had learned by this time to live alone.

Many times I sat in my small apartment and pondered what to do next, or if I should do anything at all. I had the ability and money to go where I wanted, whenever I wanted. Yet, there was nowhere to go and nothing to do that I had not already done. Life was meaningless.

My conversations with Doc on this subject of Guillermina and a new life had allowed me to drop the defenses that I had constructed after my bad experiences with my own children. With those dismissed, I was now able to feel like life was important again.

I realized that I should have seen what Estella was saying when I had met Guillermina previously. Doc also tried to tell me this in his own fashion when we sat in the hotel talking that evening after we had visited the Casa. He was not so straightforward as Estella. This, I expect, was due to his training as a psychiatrist. Doc knew of my past and had helped me to get through my struggles with my last child.

I looked at Estella and responded, "Thank you, I will take your advice and cherish it. From what you said, I expect that Guillermina would like to go shopping for some shoes?"

"Yes, in a half hour she will be starting school and will not be finished until five this evening," Estella answered. "I will ask the Madre if we could do it tomorrow in the morning after your English class. The way that the Madre likes you, I do not see that we will have any problems in securing her permission."

As we were talking, I could see that Guillermina was wondering what was happening. After I finished, she asked Estella what we were discussing. Estella explained and then asked Guillermina if she had any questions that she would like to ask me. They talked a while and soon Estella looked at me and said, "She has many questions that she would like to ask you. The most important one is 'When will she learn to speak English so she can talk to you all the time without having to have words translated.'"

"Soon, I hope," I responded. I too wanted to ask many questions.

With that, Guillermina smiled and asked Estella if she could give me a kiss and a big hug. She also asked if I would mind if she called me "Papa" and if I would call her "Guille," pronounced Gee-jee.

Estella looked at her and said, "The kiss and the hug are all right. However, about calling Dr. Nielsen 'Papa,' we not only have to ask Dr. Nielsen for permission, but Madre Esmeralda also." Estella explained, "These children have only one desire and that is to have a family and a home. The desire to call someone 'Papa' is very strong within them as they call the nuns 'Madre,' the word for mother. So, in a funny way, that desire to call someone 'mother' is fulfilled. Now, on the other hand, they have no one to call 'Papa.' This they want to do very much. Then, in their mind, they will have a mother and a father, and thus a family. Would you mind if she called you that?"

"Of course not; I would love it. It has been a long time since someone called me that and meant it."

With that translation and explanation completed, Guillermina left the couch and came over to where I was sitting. She then gave me the biggest hug I had ever had. As she was doing that, she kept saying the same short phrase in Spanish over and over again. I look at Estella and silently asked, "What is she saying?"

In a low cracking voice, as she tried to hold back tears, Estella answered, "She is saying 'I love you papa. I love you papa. I love you papa.'"

I was already hugging the child but now that I knew what she was saying, I hugged her with all the might that I thought a little girl of eight could stand. I had to try my damnedest to keep the water that flowed from my eyes from soaking her. Before we broke the embrace, I recomposed myself. Then I just held her at arm's length and said, "Soon, we will be talking to each other."

At that instant in time, I knew what I was going to do with the rest of my life. There was nothing on this earth that would stop me from setting that child free from this place and having her as my daughter. I had never seen such love and affection from any child. Maybe God did send me to the Casa as the Madre said. However, if he did, it was not so much for the help of the Casa but for the release of this little girl and myself from the bondage and torment of our pasts.

Logically, I knew I needed to raise a little girl again as much as I needed to have a hole in my head. However, there was something about this little girl that cried out for a life other than what she now had.

It was soon time for school. We all left the little room and started across the inner courtyard toward my car. Guille was now not only holding Estella's hand but mine also, and very tightly. As we were heading towards my car, we met the Madre, who was crossing the courtyard at the same time. She asked us how our visit went.

Estella said, "Very well, in fact, extremely well. Guille asked if she could call Senor Nielsen 'Papa.' I said we would have to ask you along with Senor Nielsen." I looked at the Madre and indicated that it was okay with me.

The Madre replied, "If it's all right with Senor Nielsen, then it's all right with me."

Guille looked at me for approval. I smiled, nodded, and answered, "As I said to Estella before, Madre, I would love it."

Estella translated and then Guille hugged the Madre and gave her a kiss. Without delay, she turned to me and said, "Papa, Papa," along with another big hug and kiss. The Madre and Estella looked at each other and smiled.

Estella then asked the Madre if Guille, herself, and I could go shopping tomorrow before school and buy Guille some shoes and other things that she needed. The Madre swiftly responded with a big grin, "Yes, that would be nice but I think you would have more time if you went on Saturday." Upon hearing that, Guille gave the Madre and me one more hug and kiss.

We soon arrived at my car. I said, "Goodbye," to all and bent over for a kiss from Guille. She not only this time gave me the customary farewell kiss but hugged me very tightly as well. I got into the car and Felipe opened the gates to the outside world.

I started to drive out when Guille ran up to the car. She looked at me and said the first real phrase in Spanish that I was to ever learn: "Yo ama usted, Padre" ("I love you, Papa"). With that, I said the same phrase to Guille in my very poor Spanish and drove my car past those huge iron gates to my world beyond them. It nearly broke my heart to leave that little eight-year-old girl standing by the gates as she waved and repeated the same phase over and over again, "I love you papa, I love you papa," until I rounded the dusty corner and faded from her view and could hear her no more.

By this time, my throat was completely choked up and I could hardly swallow. Tears were once more flowing from my eyes. The tears were so severe that once I rounded the corner where Guille could not see me, I had to pull over to the side of the road to wipe my eyes before I could continue driving without impairing my vision.

My life had started over again. There was now someone for whom I could care, someone who made life worth living. Here was a child who did not want anything but love and affection. She was so unlike my bad seeds, who wanted everything but gave nothing in return. My own two children, whom I helped rear, had left me with a feeling that no child on this earth was worthwhile, not even my own. I now wandered the world seeking what I could do to prevent other children from turning out as mine did. I had been doing this for five years.

But to be able to hold a child like Guillermina, who was unwanted and wanted nothing, produced a feeling within me that was beyond my pitiful words or expressions. Even now, as I write this, my eyes water and my vision blurs as I remember driving down that dusty road that day, away from the Casa and Guillermina.

CHAPTER TEN

GUILLE'S FIRST TRIP OUTSIDE THE WALLS

I drove back to the Hotel Lucerna that evening with great difficulty. My eyes were constantly watering. I kept thinking of Guille and the life she must have led prior to the Casa and the life she was living now in the Casa. Who were her parents? When did she come to the Casa? Where did she live when she was with her parents? Why did she always lower her head when she talks? Why did she and the other girls always speak in a whisper? Why did she never really laugh? What would she be like when I took her shopping for the first time? Would she be afraid and frightened like Estella said? These and a thousand more thoughts ran through my mind during that drive.

By the time I arrived back at the hotel, I had regained my composure. The only problem was that my eyes were still a little red and I had a hard time swallowing. I wondered what the bellboy thought as he opened my car door. I tried to avoid his gaze. I guess I was not too successful, however, because he asked, "Is there anything wrong, Senor Nielsen?" in very poor English.

I replied in my own poor Spanish, "No, I'm perfectly all right, thanks anyway."

I entered the hotel and went straight to my room to put water on my face. I hoped it would eliminate some of the red from my eyes before I went to the pool for a swim and to have a drink. In a short time, I thought my eyes were presentable and I was ready to leave my room and descend to the pool.

Once there, I noticed that I was not alone at the poolside. There were many Mexican families there enjoying themselves. Funny, this was the first time in many years that I noticed that there are families in the world. I found a seat by the pool, sat down, and ordered my drink. As I waited for it, I looked around.

There were an abundance of little children in the pool and playing nearby. I thought about how they were enjoying themselves, being free and never even realizing it. Because they were free and living with a family, they were learning simple things each day. They learned what money was, how to shop, what movies are, and how to use a phone. What is time? What is a day, week, month, or a year? They were able to absorb these things just from being around their family every day.

Until now, I never really realized how much a child learns about life just by being part of a family and the everyday occurrences they encounter. Yet, there are little children right in the midst of us who know nothing of these ordinary incidents that these children here at the pool took for granted. I thought about how lucky they were, these children at the pool and others like them around the world, as I watched them romp and play.

One of the children, a girl about Guillermina's age, slipped and fell while I watched. It was a small fall, one that would have been nothing to an older child. Yet, to a small child, it was frightening. This child started to cry and run to her parents. Upon reaching her father, he picked her up and whispered, I expected, whatever all fathers would say in similar circumstances. She promptly stopped her tears. How fortunate are these children to have someone to run to when they fall or have problems.

Guille and the Casa's children had none of that. They must keep all of those normal childhood perturbations within themselves. God, what a situation that must be for them. Every child yearns for attention from an early age. How did Guille and the other children contrive to receive this necessity from the busy Madres? What must that do to them psychologically when things happen, such as what I had just witnessed when the little child ran to her father crying. The children at the Casa have no way to acquire the essential and necessary tenderness that a child requires. How do they feel, standing there with a child's pain and no one to comfort them? What hell must they be going through during these early years of life? How will it affect them as they grow into adulthood? What did Guille do in those sorts of circumstances?

Soon I finished my drink, forced such thoughts from my consciousness, and went for a swim. When I completed my swim, I decided to go to my room to freshen up before dinner. While I was in the elevator, a young family got on as well. They had two small children who were playing and talking to their father. Once more, I thought about how lucky they were. The elevator soon arrived at my floor. I left and proceeded to my room. There I rested for a short while before getting dressed for dinner. I had decided to eat in the hotel's restaurant, as the food was pretty good. The service was good as well. This was unusual in Mexico.

Arriving at the restaurant, I was greeted by the captain, who seated me and presented me with a menu, again in Spanish. I looked for something on the menu that was expressed the same way in English. Finding nothing, I just pointed to some item on the menu that did not look too scary when the waiter came for my order.

I tarried a short while for the food. As I waited, I noticed the abundance of families in the restaurant. After a short wait, the food arrived and I tasted it. It was excellent. I took a second mouthful but suddenly could not swallow it. Once again, I was thinking of the children at the Casa who were now having dinner, especially Guille. Their dinner consisted of warm milk and cookies in that hellhole that they called the children's dining room.

I tried again to eat and just was not able. I pushed the food away and ordered a couple of drinks. I thought that at least this would help me sleep tonight. I did not want to have any more trouble sleeping since I had to be up early for the children's lessons at the Casa. It would be the second day of speech school. When I finished, I left the restaurant and went to my room. The drinks did not help. I still had a restless night of sleep. The day's happenings created strange dreams.

The next thing I remembered was the phone ringing. It was my wakeup call that I had left last night just before retiring. I quickly got up and then shaved and showered. It was now seven thirty and I did not want to be late for school and Guille. I arrived at the restaurant and only had time for coffee and orange juice. Then I left for the Casa in my car.

As I drove through the increasingly familiar back roads of Tijuana towards the Casa, I was wondering what Saturday was going to be like. How would Guille react to being in a car? Had she ever even been in a car? What would she do when she saw the shopping plaza? Would she know what to ask the salespeople? These and many more thoughts were going through my mind again as I passed the gates of the Casa that the giant Felipe had just opened. The time was now 8:57 in the morning.

I proceeded to the same spot that I had parked in yesterday. Estella was waiting for me there. When I got out of the car, she said, "The girls are all waiting for you in the classroom. They were starting to think you were not going to come."

I look up at the window of the classroom and I could see one child peering out the window; it was Guille. Her face clearly showed her anxiety.

"Guille," Estella continued, "wanted to meet you here also but I said we would have to ask you if that was all right first."

I said, "I would like that very much."

Estella replied, "Then tomorrow she will greet you here also."

We then proceeded across the yard and up the stairs to the classroom. Upon entering, I saw all the girls were dressed in the same fashion as they had been the day before. They greeted me with "Good morning, Teacher Nielsen." That is, all the girls but one.

When the rest of the girls' greeting was complete, Guille said in an extremely loud voice, "Good morning, Papa," and produced a small smile as she said it.

I replied, "Good morning, girls." Then I turned and said, "Good morning, Guille."

With that, she turned around and looked at the other girls with an expression of "I have a Papa and you don't, Ha ha!" She sat throughout the entire class with a great look of pride on her face. It was hard not to smile at her.

The class was unusually noisy. The girls were whispering among themselves. I looked at Estella to see if she knew what was going on.

She said, "What it is, is that all day yesterday, Guille told them that you were her new papa and on Saturday you were going to take her outside the walls to shop for new things. Also, she was explaining to them what I told her yesterday about what shopping was. They did not believe her. They are trying to have someone ask you if that was the truth. They are all afraid to question you as you might get mad and tell the Madre. Then they would be in trouble."

I asked to Estella to translate what I was about to say and hoped that it would put that thought to bed in their minds. "Girls, Saturday, Guille and I are going shopping in the Plaza for new clothes and shoes. Maybe next time, Guille might ask one of you girls to come with her. But for now, let's get to work on the English, okay?" As Estella was translating it to the girls, I could see Guille's face light up like a Christmas tree. She was almost smirking, as if to say, "I told you so."

After the translation, Estella said, "You have just made Guille, who was one of the most unpopular girls in the Casa, the most popular."

I replied, "I thought that would be the effect it would have. I am happy it was so."

We now settled down and completed the second day of English class. The girls were learning fast. By the end of the second day, they understood many English words and were using them correctly in sentences. Guille was very quick at learning English. In fact, she was always the first to answer a question I might have for the class. I finally had to tell her to give the other children a chance at answering.

It was soon eleven o'clock. The girls did not want leave. Before long, the Madre was there and told them to leave as lunch would be ready and they had work to do before their regular school. She also told Guille that she did not have to go. She could stay with her newfound papa. This she did and we spent the rest of the day learning more English. In a short time, she and I were exchanging small words and sentences in English.

The day passed quickly and soon I had to leave. Guille and Estella saw me to the great iron gates that lead to the outside. Guille embraced me, along with the kiss I had now come to cherish. Then she said, "Goodbye, Papa." I left and returned to the hotel.

The night went by quickly and before I knew it, the next day was there. The big day. The day that Guille and I were to go shopping. I swiftly got dressed and ate some food at the restaurant. I did not eat much, as I was too excited about the upcoming day's events with Guille. Shortly, I was on my way to the Casa.

Upon arriving, Guille and Estella were waiting at my usual parking space within the walls. Guille ran to the car and hugged and kissed me as I descended. I returned both the hug and kiss. Estella stood there and smiled.

Then Guille said in English, "Good morning, Papa, how are you?"

The conversation was interrupted by the appearance of the Madre, who told Guille to go and put on her Sunday dress. This she did at a fast run. Halfway across the yard, she stopped and ran back to me and gave me the expected goodbye kiss that she had forgotten in her anxiety to get dressed. She then once more raced across the yard and vanished into the passageway to the girls' area.

The Madre looked at me and asked, "Would you like a Coke or something while you are waiting?"

I replied, "I would like that very much." With that, she and Estella led me to the nuns' dining area, where the Cokes were kept behind lock and key. They were only allowed to the Madres.

Soon Guille reappeared at the doorway to the nuns' dining room. The Madre nodded permission for Guille to join us. This she did straightaway, going to the Madre first to bestow the customary kiss on the cheek. After that, she came to me and bestowed a similar kiss. Then she remained at my side. She was dressed in a white dress with a red ribbon at her waist. The dress was about two sizes too big for her. She wore the same shoes from yesterday, with the same big rips down the sides.

The Madre said to her, "Be a good girl and listen to Senor Nielsen and Estella today when you shop." The Madre then blessed her with the sign of the cross, gave her a small kiss on the cheek, and told her to go.

Guille returned the kiss, smiled, and returned to my side. I got up and she grasped my hand. The both of us then looked at the Madre for approval of this action. This she gave with a nod of her head and a small smile.

We all left for the car. The Madre remained behind, as she had more work to do in the kitchen. As we proceeded to the car, Guille was jumping up and down and skipping her funny, excited skip. Guille raised one leg and touched it with the same hand in the back. Then when that leg was once again on the ground, she would do the similar thing to the other leg and hand. This she would do very fast, thus producing a skip-hop action. I could likewise tell she was happy by how hard she was squeezing my hand.

When we arrived at the car, all the girls of the class were standing there. Estella told me that the Madre had given permission for them to see Guille off on her shopping spree. Guille opened the car door and smiled at the girls with much gusto. She was so very proud. She promptly got into the front seat of the car and sat down, as graceful as the queen of England would do as she was getting into her carriage. Estella got into the back seat. Guille then looked out the window at the girls, who were standing there looking at her as if she was a princess. Guille was eating up every minute of it, and talking to them in Spanish at a high rate of speed. Whatever she was saying was receiving many smiles from the children by the car.

Felipe opened the gate and we were on our way to the marvels of the world outside the Casa. The drive to the plaza was rather short. As we went, Guille asked all sorts of questions of what this and that were, both what she saw in the car and outside of it. Her head would turn left, right, and then she would turn around to see something that she liked but did not get the opportunity to see the first time as we passed it. Some of the things that amazed her were traffic signals. The other things were car washes, gasoline stations, high-rise hotels, buses that carried people, smoke coming out of tailpipes, and most everything else that she saw. One of her favorite things to look at were the dogs in the street. She wanted me to stop the car so she could pet them. She was (and still is) very infatuated with dogs.

Guille had never been in a car before, only in the back of a pickup truck that the Casa used to drive the children to and from school and every so often to the park. Guille was fascinated by the electric seats and windows. She kept playing with them, making them go back and forth and up and down. Beyond the windows and seats, there were many questions about what various items were in the car. Estella was constantly explaining this and that to Guille, to the point of almost frustration.

When we turned the final corner and the plaza came into view, Guille's eyes opened as wide as I have ever seen. She quickly asked, "What are all those buildings over there?"

I said through Estella, "That is where we are going. That is the shopping plaza."

She exclaimed, "It's so very big. I never thought it was going to be that big. Look at all the people there. What are they doing?"

I replied, "They are shopping just like you and I are going to do now." With that, I pulled into the plaza's parking lot.

Guille, by this time, was turning all around again in the car to see everything. She just could not be made to stay still no matter what Estella or I said. She was dumbfounded beyond words by what she was now beholding for the first time in her life.

I got out of the car and went around to open Guille's door since she had not yet mastered the art of opening it. She got out and stood there, just looking all around her. On her face was an expression of fear.

I said to her in a low, comforting voice, "Don't be afraid. There is nothing here that can hurt you."

She really did not know what I said but just the way I said it, she understood what I meant and with that she sort of collected herself and took me by the hand. If I had thought she had held it firmly at the Casa, you should have felt how tight she was holding now. The palm of her hand was wet from perspiration created by the anxiety and fear. When Estella got out, Guille went for her hand also.

She stood in the middle of us not saying a word, just looking at all the cars in the plaza's parking lot and the people rushing here and there. The Plaza in Tijuana was much like the average American shopping plaza. This plaza was outdoors, as most are in Mexico. Many of the shops in these plazas are the same as ours: Sears, J.C. Penny, and Montgomery Ward. Then there are the Mexican owned department stores such as Liverpool, Commercial Mexicana, Castle de Oro, and Dorians, just to name a few.

I don't think there was anything that I could have wanted that could not be purchased at the Tijuana plaza, which only catered to Mexicans. The salespeople spoke nothing but Spanish and wanted nothing to do with the foreigners. The Americans had the old part of town, the run down streets, the dirty roads, the bargaining salespeople, and so forth. They were the things that the Americans wanted and expected to see in Mexico. Here, in this plaza, there was none of that.

Guille by now was squeezing the blood out of my hand. Estella kept bending down trying to comfort her. She would tell her, "See the other girls? They are not scared, why should you be? Papa and I are with you. Papa will not let anything hurt you." The words really did not do much to comfort her. She was out and out petrified of everything around her. Guille's eyes scanned the area. Her head was always in motion. We finally arrived at the point where you cross from the parking lot to the plaza. Guille stepped into the busy street without even looking. Estella and I both simultaneously pulled her out of the street before one of the oncoming cars could hit her.

Estella announced, "Bob, you have to remember she knows nothing of the danger of cars, no less crossing a street."

After she gave her warning, she bent down and spoke to Guille. Guille then looked both ways in the street before she started to cross again. Once across the street, we were at the gateway to the plaza. I was starting to become worried myself. What else will take place today that might put the child's life in danger or cause fear? I had never been in a spot like this before with a preteen child. What must I do to watch her? Thank goodness that Estella was with us. I had wanted her for only for translation. However, now I wanted her for advice, to make sure everything would go right.

We finally arrived at a shoe store. As we stood there, Guille kept looking at all the shoes in the window. Estella explained that Guille was supposed to look in the window and pick ones she liked. Then we would go in the store and ask them for the shoes she selected. They would ask her size and then disappear into the back room to find the shoes she wanted. After they brought them out, she could try them on to see if she really liked them when they were on her feet.

Guille did not reply. She just kept staring at all the shoes in the window. She was speechless. Estella laughed and said that Guille had never seen so many shoes in her entire life. Estella soon just said, "These look nice," as she pointed to a pair in the window. "Guille, do you like them?"

Guille whispered, "Si," and then we all went to the store. We sat down and a woman came over and asked in Spanish if she could help us. Estella replied and both of them went to the window where Estella indicated the shoes that she thought Guille would like. They returned and, as we had said to Guille earlier, the woman then disappeared into the back of the store for the shoes.

Guille was looking around at the other girls trying on shoes. Much to my surprise, she then bent down and took her shoes off before the woman returned. Once they were off her feet, she put them behind her to hide the fact that they were all ripped. She was embarrassed. From the instant that she put them behind her, I did not see them again all day until I arrived back at the Casa. There she asked Estella and me if she could throw them away. She did so with great enthusiasm. By her request, I had to accompany her as she did so.

The woman returned with the new shoes and helped Guille put them on her feet. Watching it was comical, as Guille did not know what the woman was doing when she reached down and tried to put the shoes on her. Guille quickly removed her feet from the woman's reach, as she must have thought they were in the way or something.

Estella finally said, "Guille, leave your feet on the floor. The woman only wants to help you put the shoes on."

At that point, Guille returned her feet to within the woman's reach. Soon the shoes were on and Guille was walking around the store looking at the shoes. She was mimicking the other girls in the store that were doing the same thing, though she only did that after she managed to take her old shoes from behind her and secretively give them to Estella to hide from view.

While we were there, Estella suggested that we buy her some tennis shoes as well. Then she would have shoes for school and shoes for play. I thought that was a good idea so we did just that. Guille looked at Estella and me when she was told that she was going to get tennis shoes. She had seen them on some children at school but really did not know what they were. She tried them on and started walking in them all around the store. After all, she was now a pro at buying shoes. She returned to us after her great stroll and said she like them.

After we left the shoe store, Estella mentioned that Guille only had two dresses, one for school and one for Sunday. She suggested buying her a couple of new ones. We walked to Dorians to buy the dresses, and I noticed that Guille would walk with her head down when not looking at the stores. She was starting to realize that she was not like the other girls in the plaza. I felt for her with all my heart as we walked. I now held her hand very tightly so as to reassure her everything was okay. One of the stores we passed was a doll shop. There she asked if we could to stop and look into the window. We stopped and Guille pressed her face hard against the window and stared at everything on display.

Estella said to her, "Maybe next time we can go in? Because right now we are running out of time, okay?" Guille nodded with great delight and approval.

We continued our walk to the department store. Soon we were there and in the front door. If you think Guille's eyes were wide open at the shoe store, you should have seen them now. She stood there looking all about her. People were all over the place. Each counter had many different items for sale. Guille looked at Estella for an explanation. Estella tried to make it clear why there were different counters and why there were items on each counter. Have you ever tried to explain the function of a department store to someone who has no idea of what the concept of "buying" is? It was a unique experience.

Once inside the doors, we inquired where the little girls' dresses were. They told us on the third floor. Being on the third floor necessitated using the escalator, and Guille had no idea what that was. We tried to explain they were moving stairs but until she saw them, she still did not know what we meant.

As we moved towards the center of the store where the "moving stairs" were, Guille constantly looked at everything she saw. She was shocked to see little girls in pants. "Madre says it is evil for a girl to wear pants. Only boys wear those," Guille announced through Estella.

Women with cosmetics on their faces also amazed her. We stopped so many times that I was wondering if we were ever going to reach the third floor by the end of the day, let alone in time to buy some dresses for her.

When we finally arrived at the escalator, Guille saw it and quickly proclaimed that there was no way she was going on that. They were the "makings of the devil," because stairs do not move unless the devil was doing it, even she knew that.

Estella and I tried to talk to her and explain that it would not hurt her. The results were the same; no way was she going on those devil stairs. I finally had to pick her up and then step onto the escalator with her in my arms, kicking and screaming at the top of her lungs. The people around us were staring. I expected the police at any moment due to me being an American and the little poorly dressed child a Mexican. Coupled with the fact that we were in a Mexican store and I was the only Caucasian besides Estella, I had cause to worry.

Soon a crowd gathered and the women were looking and the men were saying something to me in Spanish and trying to grab me. Estella came over and explained to them in Spanish that the child was okay. The little girl was only afraid of the "moving stairs" and we had to go to the third floor to buy her dresses. At this explanation, the crowd backed away a little and the men let go of my arm. Everyone just watched to see if Margret could settle her down, which she did somewhat.

Mexicans have a great love of children, way beyond most nationalities, and are fast to protect any injustice that they feel is being done to them. The action that was taking place with Guille really did not look good for me in the eyes of all the other passing Mexican people who were standing there watch this show Guille was putting on. I was quite scared.

By the time we got to the third floor, Guille had calmed down somewhat. She was no longer screaming, just kicking to get down and grab Estella's hand. The only friend she had now was Estella. I was on the outs with her. But soon she got over it, as she stood there looking at all the dresses. The objects that quickly caught Guille's eye were the mannequins of the little girls wearing dresses that stood by the entrance of the girls' department. She was amazed at that.

Confused, she asked Estella, "How do all of those little girls stand there without moving? That must be hard to do."

Estella smiled and explained. "They are not real, just statues called mannequins."

She tried to get Guille to touch one to prove to her that they were not real. Guille did not want to have anything to do with them. The entire time we were there, she kept one eye on the dresses and one eye on those "girls" standing there. Those she did not trust.

Once inside the girls' dress area, she told Estella that she had never seen so many dresses at one time in all her life. Then she wanted to know why they were there. Estella explained that they were there for people to buy, just as we did in the shoe store. Estella told her that she had to find her size and look at the dresses to find one she liked. Then she would try it on in a small room to see if it fit and if it looked good on her. That explanation did not suffice. It looked as if the only way she was going to understand it was to start doing it. So off we went to carry out the adventure of "Buying Dresses."

Estella said to her, "This one would look pretty on you. Would you like to try it on, Guille?" Estella told me Guille was worried that she would not be able to put it on without getting into trouble. Estella then told her, "Yes, you can do that without any trouble. We talked about this earlier when we got off the escalator. Don't you remember?"

"Oh, yes" was the reply. Estella repeated the question of whether or not she liked it and Guille answered, "Yes, I do."

The two of them went to find the dressing room. I followed and soon we were in front of the room. The two of them went inside and I waited. I could hear someone making sure the door was locked. I did not have to ask who that was. I was quite sure it was Guille.

Before long, they reappeared. Guille looked extremely pretty in the new dress. The greatest parts of it were not only the dress but also the sheer fact that the dress fit her so very well and the look on her face. She kept looking around as if someone was going to do something about her wearing a dress that was not hers.

"Do you like it?" Estella asked me.

"Very much so. I did not think a well fitting dress added that much to someone's beauty and charm."

Estella told Guille what I had just said. She looked at me and presented me with that smile of hers. She was still a little mad at me due to the escalator episode, but after that translation, I was really back in Guille's good graces again.

I looked at Guille and asked, "Do you like it now that you have it on?"

She swiftly replied, "Yes, I like it very much, Papa."

I asked the same question to Estella and got the same reply so I stated, "Good, let's buy it."

With that, Estella told Guille to go back inside and take it off so Papa could buy it for her. By this time, Guille was getting the idea of what buying was and did not ask many questions, she was almost as quiet as she was in the shoe store. The only question she asked was if she could wear it now like she did with the shoes. We both replied that we could see no reason why not.

The answer made her extremely happy and she proceeded to the closet mirror to look at herself again. She stood there looking first at one side of herself and then the other. She even tried to look in the mirror so she could see how she looked from the back. She walked further away from the mirror so she could see how the dress and shoes looked together. She twirled so the dress flung wide from her side. She did that two or three times. She was so very happy.

Estella and I glanced at each other and smiled. I had a feeling inside of me that I cannot seem to put on paper. The feeling was something like an inner glow and happiness for a child who wanted nothing but yet enjoyed everything, small or large, a child that loved for the sake of love and nothing more. God, what an excellent feeling it was to stand there and watch her twirl. It was as if you were watching Cinderella after the fairy godmother had placed the gown on her prior to the prince's ball.

We went to the counter and paid for the dress. After the new dress was bought, she placed her old dress in the bag. Once more, it was done only after she was sure that no one would see her putting this old dress in the bag. She was ashamed now of the fact that she had worn it.

Once that was done, we proceeded hand in hand to the "devil stairs." Upon arriving there, Guille, much to my surprise, held my hand very tightly and proceeded to gingerly step on the escalator with me. She kept one hand in mine and the other on the railing of the escalator, as she had seen the girl in front of us do. Guille had conquered her fear of the stairs that move. By the time we had gotten to the first floor, she wanted to go back up.

So up we went again to the third floor. Then we promptly departed for the first floor once more. She wanted to do it yet again. However, we said we were running out of time. She relented after the third time but only after we promised that the next time we came to the plaza, she could ride them again.

As we walked back to the car through the plaza, I noticed that the look of absolute amazement was not there. She still looked wildly at the shops but it was the same way other children do when they are at a new shopping plaza. Guille, after all, was an "experienced" shopper by now. Not only was she an accomplished shopper, but she held her head high and proud as she strutted down the plaza street dressed head to toe like a queen.

I thought, as I looked at her walking with her head held high, something was missing, something that the other girls had as I watched them pass us. "What was it?" I pondered. There's something missing in Guille. I looked at Guille, back at the other little girls, and then again to Guille. At last, it struck me. How dumb could I be? The problem was so obvious that I had completely overlooked it. It was something that all the other girls had and you just accepted it in your mind as being there without thinking.

The average Mexican child had her ears pierced at about five months of age, just as every little boy of the Jewish faith is circumcised at birth. It is a custom. Well, due to Guille's birth circumstances, she had never had her ears pierced. That was it. Hence, she had no earrings in her ears.

I suggested to Estella that we get Guille's ears pierced. She agreed. We then asked Guille if she wanted that. We first had to explain it to her and then showed her the other girls that were walking by that had their ears pierced. Guille agreed and we went to a jeweler to have them done.

Guille sat in the chair without any fear whereas I was petrified for her. The woman took a pistol-looking piece of equipment out and the ears were pierced in a matter of seconds. Guille did not let out a single sound as it was being done. I almost passed out. The woman in the store then put little gold earrings in Guille's ears and told us to leave them in her ears for about two weeks. After that, we could come back and pick other ones if we so desired.

These little gold earrings were the first pieces of gold that Guille had ever had. Soon, Guille was to have gold and diamonds around her neck and on her ears and fingers. I promised myself this, as I stood there watching this poor little waif. She would no longer do without anything for the rest of her life. This I swore to God in that very instant. Those earrings made her very proud. As she said, "I will be the only girl in the Casa that has such things."

At the exit to the plaza and by the street that separated the plaza from the parking lot, she stopped and looked both ways for cars. When she saw that there were no cars coming, she promptly let go of our hands. Guille looked at us for the okay signal, which we gave her, and then she ran across the street and waited for us on the other side.

Once in the car, Estella said, "We ought to get back to the Casa."

"What about lunch for Guille?" I answered.

Estella responded, "We can pick up a hamburger on the way back. Okay?"

"'Sounds good to me, let's go that way then, but first the ice cream sundae that I promised Guille. Then the hamburger next stop, okay?" Everyone agreed so we were on our way.

As we proceeded to a store that I knew specialized in ice cream and sundaes, Guille was asking what ice cream was. Estella tried to explain, but to no avail. Guille just did not understand, no matter how the both of us tried to describe what it was. Soon we were there. I parked the car, and we all got out and went into the ice cream store. Once inside, we could see a showcase full of 55 different kinds of ice cream. Guille ran up and down the showcase asking what this was and what that was. We told her that each was a different flavor. Then we had to define what a flavor was. How do you try to explain "flavor" to someone that has no idea of the word? Try it sometime; it is not easy.

We gave up and picked chocolate, vanilla, and strawberry for her in a banana split. These flavors every child likes. We did not feel Guille was ready for a cone of ice cream just quite yet. When presented with her treat, Guille took it and we went to an outside table to sit down. Guille grabbed the spoon with all four fingers wrapped around it. She then put it in the soft ice cream and gingerly placed the chocolate into her mouth.

She said, "It feels cold." For that reason, she did not like it. She then tried the other flavors but did not like them either for the same reason. "They are cold too," she announced. "The banana would have been good if that cold stuff was not on it." In summary, she did not like ice cream or ice cream sundaes. To this day, she will not eat ice cream.

With that failure in place, I said, "Well let's go for those hamburgers. There's a place I ate in nearby that serves hamburgers. It's similar to our fast food places, with a drive-thru window."

Once more, I just assumed that Guille knew what I meant. Well, I had forgotten that Guille not only did not know what a hamburger was, but also did not know what a drive-thru window was. I was quickly learning that when I said and did things, I had to be very careful, as Guille did not understand the simplest of things that every other child knows.

When we arrived at "Hamburger Heaven," as the sign said in Spanish, Estella once again had to clarify where we were going. Guille was trying very hard to understand what a hamburger was but was not really able to contemplate what Estella was explaining. Moreover, the ice cream episode had left her very suspicious and leery of the food outside the Casa.

I drove to the drive-thru window and ordered three burgers and some drinks, including milk for Guille. As we parked by the window, Guille peered out the car window, trying very hard to see what they were doing on the inside of Hamburger Heaven. After a while, the man returned with my order. I paid him and started back on my way to the Casa. I figured we could eat as we went, once more the wrong decision.

As I was driving, I handed the food and drinks to Estella to dispense. Estella unwrapped the tinfoil that surrounded the burger and showed it to Guille. Guille took it and just held it in her hand. She did not know what to do with it now that she had it, even though Estella had explained what to do earlier.

Due to the bumpy back roads, Guille started to drop the fixings inside the hamburger on her dress. When I saw that, I pulled over and actually had to show Guille how to eat one. After a couple of bites on mine, she did the same. The expression on her face showed that she liked it. In fact, she liked it so much that she had finished hers while I was still on my second bite.

The drink we ordered for her was milk. I figured she would know what that was and would have no problem at least with that. Once again...wrong. In the Casa, the milk they had came straight from the cow. It was not put through the pasteurizing process that our milk goes through and it was warm. Thus, the taste was not the same. She did not like the milk because she thought that it tasted funny. She would not drink it no matter what we said or did. After the completion of the burger, she asked for a second one. As time was short, we told her that when we took her out again next Saturday, we would have more time for that and other things. She said that she wanted to go again and could hardly wait.

For the rest of the trip back to the Casa, I thought of the day's events. In my mind, they went very well. I was expecting to teach Guille all sorts of things, which I did. Yet, I never expected to be taught myself. This day's events taught me more about the early life of a child than I had ever known or read. This day was, and still is, the greatest day of my life. Acquiring the understanding of how a mind of an infant, in relation to the world's environment, can exist within a physically normal eight-year-old child truly changed my life.

CHAPTER ELEVEN

MADRE STARTS TO TRUST AND I START TO COMPREHEND

As we entered the huge gates of the Casa from our plaza adventure, it was about 1:45. After I had parked the car and we all alighted, Guille asked me, through Estella, "May I throw my old shoes away?" She promptly added, "Would you go with me?"

I nodded, "Sure, you can throw them away, and I'd be happy to go with you to do it." I then asked Estella if she wanted to come with us. Her answer was a rapid, "No, thanks, I'll wait here for you two."

Guille then took the old shoes in one hand. She held them as far away from her as far as possible, as you or I would do if we had to carry something that was unpleasant. Taking my hand, she led me across the inner courtyard to a small door leading behind the Casa where the garbage was kept.

What was behind that door was a sight to behold. One small narrow corridor appeared. I could see why there was a door at the entrance to this abomination. At one end, I saw the garbage ditch. On our way to our destination, we passed where the children relieved themselves when they needed to go to the bathroom while eating or working in the courtyard or in the kitchen.

These facilities consisted of five stalls on one side of the corridor, all in a row. Each cubicle was about four-by-five. They were constructed of rough-cut wood and none of them had doors for privacy. As I passed, I could see there was a hole in the ground with no toilet seats, only holes. A basket was at the entrance of each stall. Flies were all over the place. The stench was absolutely unbearable.

The other side of the passage was strewn with garbage and some paper where the children had missed the baskets. We finally reached the garbage dump, which was about eight feet from the last toilet stall. I could hardly breathe as we made our way to the dump. Guille walked as though there was no stench at all. I guess that after six years of living with this, you could become accustomed to it.

When we got to the edge of the garbage ditch, Guille raised her hand and threw in the shoes with a great deal of flair and enthusiasm. The look on her face was that of sheer pleasure and delight. It made me realize that she had probably never thrown anything away before this. There was always some use in the Casa for an object or piece of clothing that the children had outgrown or broken.

After that majestic gesture, she whirled around and happily pronounced in very poor English, "Feel wonderful." She took my hand and led me past the toilets again to the inner courtyard where Estella was waiting for us. I quietly mentioned to Estella, "Now I know why you didn't want to go with us." She just smiled and gave a small nod with her head to indicate that my assumption had been correct.

Estella looked at Guille and said, "Get that new dress off and put it under your bed with the rest of your clothing. Then get dressed for dinner. You can wear the new tennis shoes if you want." Guille nodded and then ran swiftly to the dormitory to fulfill Estella's wishes, but only after the customary goodbye kiss on my cheek.

When Guille returned, eight of the other girls, from eight to twelve years old, were being loaded into the back of the Casa's pickup truck to go somewhere. The girls all wore their Sunday dresses and shoes. In addition, they all had their hair fixed into tidy ponytails. Some of the older ones were even wearing lipstick. Estella excused herself from me and went over to Felipe, who was going to drive the truck. I heard her say something about joining him after she got finished here. When Guille asked if she had to go with them, Estella replied, "No, the Madre said that you did not have to go now since you have a Papa." A huge smile came over Guille's face.

I asked Guille where the girls were going at this late hour. I knew she understood me, but she did not reply. All she did was to look at Estella with a funny face.

Estella then took up the question and answered, "Oh, they are just going for a ride to the park. They will be back in a couple of hours." I thought it strange that they should go to the park at this hour all dressed up and wearing lipstick. However, I let it drop. I just chalked it up to "Boy, these Mexicans have funny ways."

Guille came to me and gave me a big hug and a kiss on the cheek. As Estella translated, she quickly said, "Goodbye, Papa, eating time. See you tomorrow in school. Love ya." As Guille chattered away, she watched the girls in the truck to make sure they all saw and heard it. The girls in the truck were likewise trying to talk to her before they left. They wanted to hear what had happened on this glorious day when she had gone beyond the great walls of the Casa to the places beyond. Guille paid no attention to them. Instead, she turned to me and said, "Goodbye," again when Estella told her to go to the kitchen and prepare for supper. Guille then quickly disappeared.

As the truck was leaving, all the girls in the back waved to me and said, "Goodbye, Teacher." They also blew me a kiss with their hands. Their eyes had an expression of cloudiness and total disregard of their surroundings. They seemed strange. I tried to recall where I had previously seen this type of look. At the time, I was not able to recall it. However, I did later when I found out what was causing it and where the girls were really going. In addition to how the girls looked, Felipe had a camera in his hand. Upon seeing me, he tried to hide it. I also thought that was strange.

Estella and I now stood alone in the courtyard. We were engaged in small talk about the day's events and what was to happen next with Guille. As we were talking, the Madre started to come towards us. We both stopped talking and gave her a wave. She responded similarly, accompanied with a big smile. Upon arriving, she extended her hand for a handshake. While doing this, she said, through Estella's rendering of her words, "I'm sorry that I missed the class this morning. I enjoyed it yesterday. Tomorrow, I shall surely be there. Do the children still enjoy the 'toys' you use? You know the ones I mean. The little boxes that talk to you?"

"Yes, Madre, very much so. They also seem to take delight in being in the class," I responded.

"I have heard that too. The children look forward to your classes so very much. They talk a great deal about them and how much they are looking forward to learning more English."

After the completion of that discussion, the Madre told me she had contacted a man who would provide the Casa with the new reservoir for water, which I had volunteered to buy. She then told me how much it would cost and asked if that price was a worry to me.

"No, it is a very reasonable price. When will he be able to start?" I inquired.

"Right away, as soon as you bestow your contribution." With that, I reached for my checkbook and presented her with the proper amount.

I bring these contributions to the reader's attention when they take place in the course of Guillermina's story. It is not to portray me to the reader as a Good Samaritan or a great person. I was presenting them for the well-being of the children, along with hoping that they would likewise help to place computers in the Casa, but those were the only reasons. However, unbeknownst to me at the time, they would play one of the most important parts, if not the most important part, of this tangled web that was now being spun by Estella and the Madre to catch their precious fly: me. Therefore, bear with me while I disclose them as they occur. Their significance will become quite evident in the ensuing chapters.

After I handed Madre the check, she suggested I examine the progress of the boys' bathroom renovation again. Since I had contributed to it on the first day that I ever entered the Casa, I indicated that I would be happy to see it. Thus, we all then advanced towards the objective.

The last time I had visited this room, the men were still working on it. Now there were no tiles off the walls. The showers themselves were neatly in place and the floor was repaired. Although the toilets still did not have seats, they all operated now when flushed. Beside each bowl was a basket for the used toilet paper. But I observed that there were no toilet rolls or paper holders in the entire bathroom.

Later, I was to find out that when they had to attend the washroom, the children first had to obtain the Madre's permission. At that time, she would bestow upon the child either one or two sheets of toilet paper from a roll of paper that she kept locked in a closet. The bestowing of the number of sheets was dependent on for what purpose the children were to visit the washroom.

The only bathroom in the Casa that had a toilet roll holder supplied with paper was in a bathroom that was off the Madre's little living room where she entertained visitors such as myself. During my years there, this was the only washroom that I used. I also put the paper in the bowl prior to flushing it. I always felt a little guilty when I did it but, at the same time, it made me feel good to have my small rebellion.

After the tour of the boys' washroom, the Madre, Estella, and I moved to the nuns' dining room for a Coke and something to eat. I was not really hungry because we had just had those hamburgers. Nevertheless, I speculated that this would be a good time to develop a closer relationship with the Madre, since she did not seem too busy at this instant. One of the biggest obstacles to obtaining a closer relation with the Madre was the availability of Estella for interpretation. Thus, with both of them and the solitude of the dining room, it was an ideal situation.

On our way to the dining area, we had to pass straight through that stretch where the children eat. There were two or three girls washing down the area. Guille was not one of them. She was in the kitchen helping the women there to prepare food for the children. The children who were cleaning the eating area were all dressed in skirts and blouses. I tried not to look as we passed through on our way to the Madre's room. However, I was not successful because the Madre stopped and walked over to one of the girls. Apparently, the child was not doing her job well enough and the Madre seemed very upset as she spoke to the little girl. Estella saw I was becoming concerned over what I was witnessing so she took me by the arm and continued to the nuns' dining area, where I was not able to observe or hear what was going on with the child and the Madre.

Inside, I sat down and we awaited the Madre. Estella poured me a Coke and started to speak. Before her first word was completed, I heard a cry from the room that we had just left. The cry was that of a child in pain. I started to get up to see what it was but Estella stopped me with "Bob, you better stay out of it. Sit down, drink your Coke, and wait for the Madre to finish. She knows what she is doing." I took her advice and returned to my seat.

Soon the crying stopped and the Madre appeared. "There are times you have to point out to a child what they are doing wrong or else they will not learn. Is that not correct, Senor Nielsen?" she stated as she rejoined us.

"Absolutely, Madre," I answered. I left it at that, but I wanted to add, "It depends on how you 'point it out' that a child learns." Then I saw the little girl to whom the Madre had just "talked." She had walked by the open door to the Madre's dining room on her way for something. She had on a very short skirt so you could see much of her legs. Across the back of her legs were several red marks, as if they had been hit by a stick or a belt. She was also naked from the waist up and one of her nipples was very red. Since only one side of her was visible, I do not know if the other nipple was in the same condition. She had been wearing a blouse when we passed her just minutes ago. Yet, for some reason, now she did not have it on as she scampered by the door.

Madre saw me looking so she quickly got up and shut the door to block my view of the children's eating area. "Well, Senor Nielsen, how do you think the children are doing in the speech school? Is everyone paying attention and learning?"

After what I just heard and observed, there was no way I was going to answer that question in the negative. "Each one of the children is just wonderful, Madre. They all pay attention and are quick to learn, especially Guille," I countered, hoping not to get any of the girls into trouble inadvertently.

"Yes, she has told us that she wants to learn English very quickly so she can speak directly to you without having to have all her words explained. She also added, "Guille has a wild imagination and at times does not always tell the truth. She loves to make up stories so people feel sorry for her. So when you and she start to understand each other, remember that 'fact.'" I thought that was strange. Why would she make an issue of that particular trait? She had not made any other issues before of Guille's characteristics.

"Speaking about Guille, did you enjoy your day with her? What did you all do? I was watching from the upstairs window when you all returned. She seemed very happy. I have not had an opportunity to ask her how the day went. I will do that this evening when she gets ready for bed. Did she behave herself?" At this point, she looked more towards Estella for an answer to the question rather than me.

Estella took the indication and replied, "Yes, Madre, she was very good. She behaved in every way." I wondered what would have happened to Guille if Estella had said she did not behave. After witnessing the Madre chastising the little girl in the children's eating area, I was shaken.

Estella then moved on to explain in detail what went on this morning. Estella did not stop too often to tell me what she was saying to the Madre of the day's events with Guille. However, I thought by the smiles and laughter that the both of them were enjoying the account. I could see that whatever Estella was saying pleased the Madre. This made me feel a little better.

At one point in the conversation, they stopped talking and the Madre looked at me and laughed aloud. When I asked what was so funny, Margaret replied, "I was explaining how you picked Guille up to take her on the escalator and how the people were looking at the gringo." I then laughed with them. I wanted to show the Madre that I could see the humor in the event so as not to embarrass her for laughing at me. She nodded approval at my laughter and laughed a little harder herself.

Soon Madre got up and came over to where I was sitting. To my surprise, she put her arms around me. I wondered what this was about but, thankfully, Estella was quick to clarify her actions. "This is the way the Madre shows that she likes you very much and takes great happiness in you being here with her and the other Madres." She then proceeded to say, "You should now stand up an embrace her. This demonstrates that you have a mutual perspective."

Upon taking her advice, I stood up and embraced the Madre in my arms. She enjoyed it very much and patted me on the back. This is another method of showing great pleasure in the Mexican culture, especially with the men.

We all then sat down again and Estella finished explaining the day's events to the Madre. At that point, the Madre looked at me and asked, "Are you planning on taking Guille out tomorrow after speech school?"

"Yes, if it's okay with you and if Estella is available to accompany us," I answered.

The Madre did not wait for Estella to express her wishes before she replied. "Estella is available. Any time you want to take Guille out, you may just see me first so I know where she is. Guille is one of my favorite children here at the Casa. The child has never had anyone really pay attention to her, except every so often some friends of mine will take her to their house for the evening. Their house is only two blocks from the Casa so she does not get to see much. Also once in a while, Estella will take her and the other children to the park on the outskirts of town. However, with these two exceptions, you are the only contact she has had with anyone.

"The other children seem to go out more often with friends of the Casa. Guille has never been one of them. The people always overlook her when they come here to visit and assist the children. You are the first person who has really seemed to enjoy being with her and whom Guille enjoys being with."

After the explanation was finished, the Madre asked Estella to invite me for dinner. I really did not want to stay. However, when the Madre saw my expression, she quickly added, "If you do stay, Guille could join us in the nuns' dining room this evening."

Boy, she was a smart old bird. How could I turn that down? She knew I could not. I was sure she was also testing me to see how serious I was about Guille and her welfare. Turning the invitation down or accepting it would now provide the Madre with a great amount of insight into my intentions towards the Casa and Guille. On my side of the coin, I thought that my acceptance or refusal would help or hinder me in the trust that I needed to secure from the Madre if I was ever going to position my computers in the Casa.

I looked at the Madre and articulated with my most pleasing voice, "Thank you, it would be an honor to eat with you this evening. If you could also arrange to have Guille there, it would endow my heart with great pleasure and joy."

The Madre indicated her approval and announced, "I have to do some work in the office. Estella will see to your comfort until it is time to eat this evening." She then came to where I was sitting and bid me farewell until six, which was when they ate.

After the Madre left, Estella turned to me and exclaimed, "You really have made a 'hit' with the Madre. She is genuinely fond of you and trusts you. To allow you to remain without her being here, places you in great esteem. She only does that for a few people. The only reason she wants me with you is for interpretationif you so desire it." Estella then asked what I wanted to do since she also had things to finish before dinner.

I said, "I will just wander around if that is all right with you." The reply was in the affirmative.

She walked me to the outside door that exited onto the inner patio, just past the children's dining area. By this time, the area was spotless. The children who had accomplished the task were gone. I stood there and waved goodbye to Estella as she vanished across the yard and into a car to join Felipe and the children at the park. Now that I was alone for the first time, I was free to see what some of the places in the Casa were really like. With the privilege granted to me by Madre Esmeralda to enter into the girls' area, I now had an opportunity to exercise my curiosity. Thus, I set forth towards that area.

It was only a short distance from where I was standing to the entrance of the secluded area. I entered and was almost immediately confronted by Felipe. He must have returned while we were in the dining room speaking with Madre Esmeralda. However, when he saw me, he stepped aside and let me pass unmolested. I exited the passageway into the girls' play area.

There were four or five girls there about seven to nine years old and all the rest were about three to six. In that group, there must have been about fifteen or twenty young girls. Most of the older girls were out for that "ride."

I spied the children who had been cleaning the dining area earlier. They still had on the same clothes in which they worked. I also saw the one who had the marks on her after the Madre had "talked" to her. I went over to examine her closer. The marks on her legs were definitely from a stick or a belt. Since I could not speak Spanish, I was at a disadvantage as to ask how they got there.

I tried to say something in Spanish that I had learned since I had been at the Casa these past couple of days. However, it did not go over too well and all she did was to look at me with a puzzled look on her face. Her expression clearly asked, "What are you trying to say?" After a few minutes, I stopped trying to speak a language that I knew nothing about and just went about looking around the area.

The small children were quick to gather around but the older girls kept a safe distance from me. I could advance to them but they would never come to me on their own. At the time, I thought it was strange, but blamed it on life in an orphanage. Later, I was to discover why this lack of trust was present in the older girls and not so prevalent in the younger ones, although some of the little ones did show the same mistrust and wariness that the bigger and older girls had.

As I was gazing around, a Madre came out of the dormitory and blew a whistle. All the girls ran to the sleeping enclosure. The Madre came over to me and gestured with her hands that it was siesta time for all the girls. She invited me into the girls' area to see how this was done. I followed and soon I was within the sleeping quarters.

There I saw all the girls that had just been just outside. In the dormitory, the beds along the sides of the walls were neatly made with pillows and a small doll on each bed. Yet, the girls were not on top of the beds. They were all stretched out on the cold concrete floor in tight human balls trying to keep warm. Not one of them had a blanket. All their shoes, if you would call them that, were taken off and placed neatly beside them as they tried to take their siesta.

I stood there watching this horror until my meditation was broken by the Madre who was assigned to the girl's area. Not realizing we were there, she approached one of the girls who had her eyes opened and was not trying to sleep. The Madre made a motion to the child to get up. The child was not fast enough so the Madre grabbed the child by a handful of hair just above the ears and pulled her to her feet screaming. Once on her feet, the girl promptly placed both hands over her breasts. The Madre then started to pull her hands away so she could open the blouse. That is when the Madre noticed me.

Once she was aware that she had an audience, she suddenly turned to me, smiled, and let go of the girl. The child promptly resumed her position on the floor. This time her hands stayed on her breasts as she laid there.

The Madre who accompanied me then continued the tour of the rest of the dormitory. I saw the same washrooms I had seen earlier. Completing that, I was led to the passageway to the inner courtyard outside of the girls' quarters.

I then just wandered alone around the yard and spent some time in their beautiful church, which was part of the inner yard. The time passed slowly but soon Estella returned with the other girls. The girls went quickly to their dormitory without stopping, although I noticed they did seem to have a hard time walking. As they went to their area, they never once looked in my direction, completely different from when they left a couple of hours ago. Their dresses were wet and their hair was no longer in the cute ponytails that they had been in when they left. Now their hair was in disarray. I assumed that they must have had some time at the park to get that wet and messy.

After waiting a few minutes, I signaled for Estella to come over to me. When she did, I asked her to ask the Madre why I was led out of the girls' area after the tour. Estella asked the Madre and then smiled. Estella said, "She was not leading you out. You could have stayed if you wanted. She thought you were finished and she wanted to get back to work."

I wanted to ask Estella why the little girl inside held her breasts when the Madre put her on her feet and why the girl in the dining area had no blouse. I really wanted to ask, but I was afraid of the answer. I was also afraid that Estella would not really give me an answer. For the time being, I decided to let the questions die.

The hour was about four thirty now and soon I would be eating with the Madres. Feeling a bit tired, I told Estella that I would go back to the hotel to freshen up a bit and then return at six. She agreed to tell the Madre, so I got into my car, made my goodbyes to Estella, and then proceeded through the gates.

As I drove back to the hotel, I wondered why the Madre was allowing me to have free rein of the Casa. Why would she punish a girl with me present? Wouldn't she be afraid that I would say something to the authorities? But I then thought that if I did say something to someone, who would believe me? In addition, I would never see Guille again if I caused trouble. Ah, there was the reason. I would never see Guille again. That's why she was happy about the fondness that I was starting to feel for Guille. If I said something, she would cut me off instantly from ever seeing her again. She now "had me" via Guille, lock stock and barrel, along with my "contributions."

She had no need to hide anything now. As I said before, she was a wise old bird. Now that I was to be part of the Casa life, I wondered what I was still to witness and what I would have to take part in by my silence. Little did I realize what I was about to uncover.

CHAPTER TWELVE

GUILLE DINES AT THE CASA

When I arrived back at my hotel, I had a message to call Diane, my secretary. She knows never to bother me when I am on a trip or a job. The only reason she would do so was if it was significant, so when I received the message that she had called, it disturbed me.

Diane was my right arm. I almost never made a move without her knowledge. The only person who always knew where I was at all times was Diane. Even my director did not know where I was half the time. He always had to ask Diane, "Where is he now?"

She not only did my office work but also all my outside business, such as paying my electric, phone, and gas bills for my apartment in Texas. I would be lost without her. She was a once-in-a-lifetime secretary whom every man or woman dreams about having at the office. She was a virtual "Girl Friday." They actually exist, and I had one.

I called Diane at home since it was way past working hours for the office. "What's up? Is my ex-wife causing more trouble?" I asked.

She laughed and replied, "No, not this time. I had a phone call from Bob Hess in San Diego." Bob Hess was the man whom I was doing business with in San Diego, the man who was not able to keep that appointment a couple of weeks ago, which allowed me to have the free day that started my present adventure.

She continued, "Bob called and said he had a conversation with a good friend of his that lived in Mexicali, Mexico. He is a Dr. Jesus Galaz who had a prekindergarten school. This doctor is interested in starting a computer school in Mexicali. Since you are in Mexico, I thought you might want to give him a call. Bob spoke very highly of this man."

Diane usually had very good insight as to whom I should talk to and whom I shouldn't. Therefore, I responded, "Why do you think this is a good thing?

Diane answered, "Well, according to Hess, this man not only runs a school but also speaks perfect English. That should help you in the Casa. Also, you mentioned that you were interested in prekindergarten children."

As always, she had a good answer. One of these days, I will stop asking her, "Why." She always had it all well thought out.

I said to Diane, "Sounds good, as always. Let me have his phone number. I'll call him this evening before I return to the Casa for dinner." She gave me the number and said her goodbyes.

I took a fast shower and then called Dr. Jesus. To make this call, I wrote down the number on a piece of paper and presented it to the hotel operator. I had found that this was the only way to get through the language barrier. The phone soon rang and a man answered in Spanish. I introduced myself as Dr. Nielsen.

At that point, the man presented himself, in perfect English, as Dr. Jesus. His voice was that of a young man. He struck me as a person of much intelligence as he continued speaking. "Dr. Nielsen, Bob Hess asked me to give you a call. He told me what you were trying to accomplish in Tijuana. I thought that I could be of assistance to you there. I am there many times during the week to teach at the university. Also, I have a school in Mexicali in which I would very much like to place computers. If you and your company could assist me in doing so, I think the results and findings could benefit you in your overall research of education in Mexico. May I fly to Tijuana and speak with you?"

"Yes, I would like that very much. How about sometime this week?" I replied.

"I could be there this Friday at one in the afternoon. Would that fit into your schedule?"

"Yes, that would fit perfectly," I answered. I told him at what hotel I was staying and then I added that I would meet him in the lobby of the hotel. He informed me that it was the best hotel in all of Tijuana before I had to say, "I hate to cut you short but I have a dinner engagement this evening." We hung up the phone. It was now five thirty and I had to be at the Casa at six.

As I drove through the narrow streets, my mind was on the dinner that was about to take place. Intertwined with those thoughts were others of Dr. Jesus. What was he like? Why did he suddenly pop up right when I needed someone like him? What was his real reason for wanting to put computers in his school? What did this man actually want? Would I truly like him when I met him in person?

My thoughts finally ended. I was once again entering the Casa and heading for my now-usual parking space within the Casa's colossal walls. Estella and Guille were standing by my parking space. The child was waving at me fanatically as I approached. When I parked the car, she quickly ran up and spoke through the open car window. "Hi, Papa, I was waiting for you ever since Madre told me you were coming and that I could eat with you!"

Estella interrupted and added to Guille's words. "She has driven all of us mad with questions. When would you be here? What time was it? How should she fix her hair? All sorts of things a little girl would ask." I stepped out of the car and Guille immediately jumped into my arms with such speed and tenacity that it almost knocked me over. She gave me a big hug and a kiss on the cheek. "Hi, Papa," she kept repeating as I held her in my arms trying to regain my equilibrium.

Her weight was hardly anything at all. I would say she weighed about forty-five pounds, not much for a girl of this age. Her hair was done up in two very neat ponytails, one on each side of her head. Her dress was the one that we had purchased earlier in the day. She was also wearing her new shoes. She looked beautiful. On her face was a smile from ear to ear.

Estella said, "I have not seen this child so happy since I don't know when. You have changed her life. She is now popular with the other girls. She is also starting to laugh and smile a little now. They no longer call her flaco [skinny.] These things never happened before you came. I had often worried about her. Well, I guess she has adopted you as her new father and it looks like now these worries of mine will become yours."

I smiled and agreed. "It is starting to look that way but don't leave me alone with her yet. I will need lots and lots of help with this newfound parenthood."

Estella looked at me and sort of gave me a half grin and nodded her head as if to say, "Don't worry I'll help." With that, Estella stated, "The Madres are waiting for us in the dining room."

"Let's go," I answered and put Guille down. She promptly took my hand and we started for the dining room. As we walked to the area, Guille kept looking up at me, smiling, and squeezing my hand.

During the passage to the nuns' dining room, we had to pass through the dreaded children's dining room, and this time they were all eating in there. As we walked past them, I could see Guille out of the corner of my eye. She was looking at the other girls who were eating there. She would look at them and then look at me, as if to say, "See this is my Papa and we are going into the forbidden area to eat, the Madre's dining room. See, I, Guille, am something special." Her chest, what there was of it, was sticking out a mile in front of her. She walked with her head almost up. She was so very proud as she strutted past them all.

The first children to notice us looked at her with an expression of envy. Then they quickly turned to the girl sitting next to them and said something. Then those children would look up too. The whole area that was always very quiet was now alive with whispers. I assumed this was all because of Guille and me.

Noticing my concern, Estella said, "The children have never seen one of their own enter into the nuns' dining area other than to work there. None of them has ever eaten there so they are now talking about it and why Guille is doing so. Guille told them earlier that she was to do so, right after the Madre had told her that she was being so honored. But they did not believe her. So now, they all want to make sure that everyone knows why Guille is doing such an unheard of thing."

"Bob, you have to realize that since you've come here, you have stirred up quite a fuss. In all honesty, things like computers, education, and English-speaking classes were unheard of. So, please, bear with it. Soon they will be accustomed to you coming and going. Then they will take no notice of you, your association with Guille, or your strange machines that talk and think. You will become part of the Casa and be accepted."

"Also, before you, the only American or white person they have ever seen here more than once or twice was myself. The other white people whom they saw were only here on Saturdays and Sundays and then for only a short time. The only other people were the social workers who came here, and they were always of Mexican/American descent, one of the Madre's requirements. You, again, are most unusual. You are here during the weekdays and are totally white. They really do not know how to act or behave while you are here. Most of them only know about you from the stories that are being told by the children who attend your English classes."

We arrived at the sanctimony of the nuns' eating space and Estella opened the door. At this point, I could feel Guille clutch my hand even tighter. It was wet from nervousness. All the nuns were already seated and waiting for us to arrive.

Guille's eyes lit up like candles and her mouth dropped almost to her chin. Her eyes were telling me that she had never seen anything like this. There in front of us was a finely set table. An Irish linen tablecloth was neatly covering the table, accompanied by matching napkins at each place setting. The silverware and dishes were among the finest that I have ever seen. These were placed neatly on the table in front of each chair that surrounded the table. All the chairs, except three, were occupied by the nuns. In the center of this elegant table setting, there was a gorgeous arrangement of flowers. Rolls, bread, and Mexican salsa were in abundance. Two lit candelabras glowed with a tastefulness fit for royalty. The room was pleasantly heated by four electric heaters, one in each corner of the room. The fragrance of the flowers filled the room with a pleasing aroma.

I wondered how Madre Esmeralda explained this to her superiors. After all, this order of nuns was supposed to be dedicated to poverty. I felt very ashamed to be sitting down to a feast like this when the children just outside this room were eating in a cold, sordid atmosphere. The bread on this table was the only thing that the children were eating in their dining area outside, along with a glass of warm milk straight from the cow.

Upon us entering, Madre Esmeralda stood up and walked over to me. She gave me my newly acquired customary Mexican welcoming embrace and then bent down so Guille might give her the expected kiss on the cheek. With that, Madre patted Guille on the head and gave her a big smile. Guille looked down at the floor again in humbleness.

Madre greeted me by saying, "Welcome, Senor Roberto. We have been waiting for you." She showed Guille and me to our places at the table. I was to sit next to the Madre, who sat at the head of the table, and Guille would sit next to me. Estella was on the other side of the table next to the Madre. This I assumed was to make translating the conversation easier during the dinner.

Guille took her seat at the table and looked at the strange things that were placed by her plate, the silverware. Once seated, she quickly placed her hands in her lap. Her feet did not touch the ground; they just hung there. Guille constantly looked first at me and then the Madre. I could see that she was very nervous. When she was not looking at either of us, she was quick to return to gazing at her hands in her lap. She never looked anywhere else but one of those places.

As we sat there, the phone rang and Guille jumped about ten feet off her chair and grabbed me tightly with both arms. Her face had an expression of immense fear. Estella said something to her in Spanish and Guille then gave me a little room to breathe, as her arms loosened slightly. Estella continued talking to her in Spanish and after a while, Guille let go of me and sat back down on her chair, but she kept a steady eye on the black devil thing on the table that had made such a terrible noise from nowhere. After calming down Guille, Estella told me that this was the first time Guille had heard or even seen a phone and that is why it scared her.

Estella explained to Guille that it was something people used to talk to each other and Papa would teach her about it later. With that explanation, all was well and the room returned to normal. After everything settled down, Guille remained seated and now held my hand very tightly under the table so no one could see it. However, she still kept one eye on the phone throughout dinner.

The Madre spoke to Estella, who then translated for me. "Roberto, the girls are very excited about your English classes. They are practicing on each other the words that you teach them each day. I hope you will be able to continue this class. If you want anything, the Casa is at your disposal."

I thought to myself that it was wonderful to work with someone who cared so much about the children. I thanked the Madre and then asked, "Have you ever heard of a Dr. Jesus Galaz from Mexicali?"

"Yes, I have heard of him during my visits to Mexicali when I went to see our other Casas that are located there. He is very famous in Mexico, but I have never met him."

A point of interest, in this order of nuns, was that there were 59 similar Casas spread throughout all of Mexico. Of these, there were three in Tijuana and two in Mexicali.

I told the Madre that Dr. Jesus had called me and expressed his desire to help on the project. Then I asked if she would mind if he did so. The Madre indicated that she would enjoy having such an upstanding, famous man come to her Casa and work with the children.

Guille was still just sitting there looking down while Madre and I spoke. She was also still holding my hand under the table. I could feel her hand becoming increasingly wetter with nervous perspiration. Soon one of the workers came from the kitchen with soup that contained spaghetti and a broth-like substance. Upon spying Guille at the table, she stopped and stared, as if she had seen an unbelievable sight. Madre Esmeralda quickly motioned her to continue her work. The woman then placed the first bowl in front of the Madre. Then the second was placed in front of me. Two more people came from the kitchen with more soup, which was dispensed to the other Madres and Estella.

Guille was the last to be served. They served it in such a fashion that it looked like they were throwing it at her. That rather got to me, but I did not say anything. However, due to this incident, I always made a big fuss later in Guille's life, regardless if we were eating at home or in a restaurant, if she was not served first. Not only was she to be served first, but she was to be served in a very gracious manner suitable for a lady.

Madre then indicated permission for us to eat. Guille let go of my hand and lifted the plate to her mouth. She started to slurp the soup with an abundance of noise. I looked at her in astonishment. I wondered why the Madre did not say anything about her method of eating soup. Nevertheless, she did not, so I didn't said anything either. Yet I thought to myself that I would teach her to eat properly while on our visits outside the Casa.

Her lack of table manners did not stop there. When her face became wet with the soup, she would then use the back of her hand to wipe her face dry. She had a napkin at her place setting, but she had never before seen one. Therefore, she did not know what it was or how to use it. She would wipe her hand on her slip beneath her new dress. She was very solicitous about not getting anything on the new dress. While doing this, she would quickly glance at me to make sure that I could not see her slip, as to do so would be a sin in her mind. The Madres had told her so.

When we had all finished the soup, the main course was served. This consisted of ham, potatoes, corn, beans, and rice. As I had mentioned earlier, the Casa children had never handled a knife and fork so when this main course was served, Guille was lost. She looked at me with great concern as to which utensil to use and how.

Estella, spying Guille's concern, said, "Bob, why don't you cut the meat for her? Guille has never seen a knife before."

I promptly picked up her knife and fork and proceeded to do as Estella had suggested. Guille let out a sigh of relief. As I was doing this, Guille carefully watched my actions. She was very intent on how I was holding the knife and fork while I was doing the cutting. It seemed to fascinate her, this action of cutting this unknown entity called meat.

Once that was done, the problem now arose for Guille of which utensil to use to eat the meal. She picked up the spoon and started to eat. After all, this how she ate when she was outside with the other girls. We at the table did not say anything to avoid embarrassing her, but the Madre picked up her fork. Upon seeing this, Guille promptly put down the spoon and picked up the fork. Picking up the fork was easy. However, now that she had it, she had no idea how to hold or use it. I picked up mine very slowly so she could see how I held it. She then did likewise. Gradually, I started to eat, first the meat and then the other items on my plate. Guille closely watched every action that I did with the food. She then mimicked me. What I ate, she ate. This went on for the entire meal.

It was comical to watch her try to eat with a fork. She used it as you would use your spoon. She tried so hard to look natural with the fork and had so much trouble with it. She sometimes would try to pick up something from her plate and it would shoot off the plate and onto the table. She would swiftly pick it up with her hand, place it back on her plate, and then try again. No one said anything, nor did we look at her directly, only out of the corners of our eyes. Have you ever tried to eat corn with a fork when you did not know how to use one? Someday, try it as if it was your first time; it is not easy.

During the meal, I made more inquiries about Dr. Jesus. Coupled with this, I started to feel out the Madre's opinion again on computers in the Casa. She was still as adamant as she was when Dr. Adolph queried her on this subject. So once more, I let subject drop and quickly changed it to something else.

After dinner, we all retired to the Madre's little living room at the end of the inner patio. Upon entering, Guille once more just stood there and stared. She had never before been in there. Nor had she ever sat on a soft chair. She sat next to me and kept feeling the cushion to figure out why it was so soft. We just sat making small talk.

Before long, the Madre said, "It is way past Guille's bedtime."

I looked at Guille and agreed with the Madre. Guille was sitting next to me, holding my hand as usual, with a very tired look on her face. I told her, "I will see you tomorrow; it is bedtime."

Guille replied, "Okay, see you tomorrow, Papa." With that, she gave me a kiss and a hug and then went to the Madre. After the customary kiss to the Madre, she exited the little room with a smile and a wave, saying once more, "I love you, Papa. See you tomorrow," before heading towards the girls' dormitory.

After that, the adults soon stood and said our own goodbyes. I then got into my car and was on my way back to the hotel. It was now nine thirty and I too was tired. Psychologically and physically, I'd had a very long and busy day.

CHAPTER THIRTEEN

THE COMING OF JESUS

The next morning, I was up at about five thirty. I think that it was in anticipation of Dr. Jesus' visit, which was to take place today at one. I was trying to picture in my mind what he would look like; short or tall, fat or thin? I was also wondering why he was so interested in the project here at the Casa in Tijuana. During my phone conversation with him last night, the man seemed very knowledgeable in early education. On the other hand, he seemed to know very little about computers.

I shaved and took a shower. Then I proceeded downstairs for breakfast. It was now about eight in the morning. In the restaurant, I ordered the same thing as yesterday, hotcakes. It was still the only item on the menu that I was confident enough to order. After completing the meal, I now had some time on my hands before school would start at the Casa. I walked out to the terrace and looked towards the pool. There was no one swimming at this early hour. As mentioned earlier, the Mexican nights and especially the mornings are extremely cold. The temperature sometimes goes from 95 in the afternoon and early evenings to 45 or 55 in the very late evenings and early mornings.

From the terrace, I continued to the lobby. There were quite a few people leaving or checking into the hotel. The lobby was alive with Mexican families. I sat in one of the chairs and just watched. I enjoyed doing this very much when I was at the hotel because the Mexicans have such a great love for their families. It shows in their mannerisms when they interact among themselves. The attention that a mother shows to her children and a husband's devotion is unbelievable. The husband carries a bearing of being the all-knowing man. Yet, when his child needs fatherly attention, he somehow is always there to perform the role of the all-loving Papi.

Before long, I got up and went to my car in the hotel's parking lot. As usual, I counted the tires before getting into it to make sure that none of them had gone for a "walk" during the evening and failed to return. As I drove, I noticed all the street children of Tijuana. They are always out bright and early to pounce upon your car when you stopped for a red light or a full stop sign. These children are anywhere from four years old to about eleven. They have no home, no family. They live together in a sort of commune, finding shelter in an abandoned car or under cars that park in the street for the night. When you do park your car in the street for the evening, you must always look under it before you start it again to make sure that some of them are not still there.

When morning comes, they all go scrounge for food in garbage cans. Then they head for their respective locations where cars are forced to stop. There they wash your car windows as you wait. In return, they expect a small reward. This is what keeps them alive and somewhat fed. I was always a sucker for them and I guess I always will be.

Upon arriving at the Casa, the gates swung open to allow me admittance. Felipe seemed to be expecting me at this hour. He waved a good morning and said some form of greeting to me in Spanish. I waved back pleasantly and gave him a smile. I never ceased to marvel at the size and strength of that man every time I saw him.

Standing there at my usual parking space was Estella and Guille. Guille was jumping up and down in expectation. I parked and got out of the car. Once more, the wild dash to me while I was getting out nearly knocked me off balance. My biggest job at these times was trying to stop from falling when she sprang forward into my arms. "Hi, Papa, did you sleep well?" Estella translated the words Guille spoke as she clutched me around my neck so hard that I could hardly breathe.

"Yes, I slept very well. Did you?" I countered.

"Yes," she said and then continued chattering without taking a breath. "Do you know what?"

"No," I responded in amusement.

"The girls kept me up most of the night asking me what I did when we ate with the Madres. I told them everything. About what meat is and how good it tasted, the silverware, especially the knife, and the cover that was over the table. Everything, Papa, I told them about everything," Estella interpreted as Guille rapidly spoke in Spanish.

"Really, did you like that?" I replied.

"Yes, very much. They hardly ever talked to me before. Now they all want to talk to me and be my friends. Isn't that wonderful, Papa?"

"Yes, it is. You are a good girl. Why shouldn't they want to be your friend?" That was all I could think to say at the moment. I was quite choked up with emotion over the happiness of this little girl. She never before had friends, and now she was so excited because she had some. "Well, it's time for class; let's go," I finally uttered as I put her down and took her hand. We then headed towards class.

As we walked across the courtyard to the classroom, I observed a man coming from the servants' sleeping quarters. I had not seen him at the Casa during my previous visits. He was definitely not of Mexican origin. He was white, blue-eyed, and had blond hair. The man was in his early thirties and he looked and dressed like a European. His pants were baggy and his shirt had the first three buttons unbuttoned to expose his upper chest. In his hands were two small plastic bags. They looked like they were bags of sugar. Upon seeing me, he quickly retired back into the sanctuary of the servants' sleeping quarters.

I asked Estella, "Who was that?"

She replied, "I did not see him."

I knew damn well that she saw him. The man had looked directly at Estella after he saw me. I figured that it was none of my business so I did not push the issue with Estella. Still, I thought it strange and sort of puzzling why she would lie like that. Guille also saw him but since she could speak hardly any English, it would be pointless to ask her. However, I doubted that, even if she could speak English, she would tell me who he was after Estella said she did not see him.

We continued our walk to the classroom without further interruptions. Upon arriving at our destination, the rest of the girls were there waiting. When we entered the room, they all stood up and greeted me with the now familiar, "Good morning, Teacher." They then waited for permission to be seated.

After I gestured for them to sit, Guille let go of my hand and took her assigned seat. The girls had all waved and smiled at Guille when she walked in with me.

We commenced with the lesson. The girls were learning English much faster than the children whom I had taught in the past had. Their desire to learn was very strong, coupled with the fact that they had no outside distractions except their work at the Casa. Guille was learning the fastest of them all. I was to find out later that this was due to her great eagerness to speak to me in my own tongue without a third party to translate her words. This observation was eventually to lead me to an important conclusion that was contrary to the very basic philosophy of the great child psychologist, Piaget.

The class time went rapidly. When it was time to wrap up the session, they all pleaded to continue. I reminded them that if I did not stop on time, you-know-who would be standing at the door of the classroom. This statement of mine quickly stopped any more aspirations of extending the class. The girls got up and left to do their many chores before lunch and regular school.

Guille stayed behind with me after I checked with Estella for permission. Estella glanced at me and said, "It's okay if she stays with you. Madre told her last evening that if she wanted to stay after class and it was all right with you, she could. Is that all right with you?"

"Yes, by all means," I responded.

Estella then explained that she had other tasks to do in the Casa so she had to leave. She told me to bring Guille back to the dormitory by 12:00 because she had to get dressed to go to regular school at one.

The time remaining was spent in private lessons for Guille in English. By noon, Guille's quitting time to get ready for regular school, she was speaking many words and phrases in English, and using them correctly in sentences. We were really starting to communicate. I started to see something unusual with how Guille was learning. Not only was she speaking the English words and sentences, but she was also apparently thinking in English. None of the other girls seemed to do this. By thinking in English, she did not have to digest the English word in her mind, transfer it mentally to Spanish, and then back again into English for the response.

This action can be detected by observing the speed one takes when responding to a question in a foreign tongue. With Guille, her response time to my questions was beyond my understanding and experience, especially with someone who had just started to undertake the learning of a second language. I believe that it came from the "want" to understand that was so much more prevalent in Guille.

The only person whom I knew who could really explain her response time was Dr. Adolph. I planned to call him at his home that evening to ask him about it. I also wanted to inquire if maybe he could find time to come to the Casa and personally witness the phenomenon that was taking place within Guille.

After checking the clock, I said, "Guille, time for regular school now. I'll walk you to your dormitory and say goodbye there."

She responded, "Okay, Papa," in English and off we went, hand in hand, to the dormitory. Upon arriving there, it was obvious that the Madre was not expecting me. Nor did she see me at first. As I entered the door of the actual sleeping quarters with Guille, I fully witnessed my first actual view of the many abuses to the children that I was to see during my stay at the Casa. While I had previously caught glimpses, attempts had been made to keep it hidden.

It seemed that one of the children had done something wrong. It was a girl of about nine years of age. The girl had opened her blouse and was kneeling. Then the Madre would squeeze and twist her little nipples. This caused the child to scream quite loudly. The more she screamed, the more the Madre seemed to apply pressure to the nipples.

Out of the corner of my eye, I could see Guille looking at me with an expression of embarrassment as I watched what was taking place. Guille did not say anything. She just dropped her head and looked at the ground while tightly gripping my hand.

What I was observing was of course the answer to what I had seen and described earlier. This was why the children would hold their breasts when the Madres became mad at them. This was why that little girl in the dining room had yelled in pain and was briefly seen with a painfully red nipple after the Madre had "talked" to her about being bad.

Upon seeing me, the Madre quickly told the child to go to the washroom. Then she came over and greeted me. She did not say anything about what I had just seen. She behaved as if it never happened. I presented the same attitude and greeted her with a smile and an "hola." She told Guille to say goodbye to me and get dressed for school. The Madre then patted her on the head and asked if she had learned anything today at the English school.

Guille nodded, "Yes." Then she quickly gave me a kiss on the cheek, said, "Goodbye," and vanished into the washroom after grabbing a handful of her school clothes from the top of her bed. After Guille left the room, the Madre escorted me to my car. Then she told Felipe to open the huge gates, which hid the abuse and neglect from the outside world.

I left rather quickly. I was so mad at myself for not saying anything about what I had just witnessed with that little girl. I also wanted to ask Guille if they have ever done that to her. If they had, I was going to ask that it never happen with her again. How could I do that? It was going to be a great act of diplomacy on my part. Unfortunately, diplomacy was one of the many virtues that was lacking in my makeup. I didn't know how I was going to protect Guille from this punishment without getting both Guille and myself in trouble with the Madres.

The time was about 12:45 and I had to meet with Dr. Jesus at one in the hotel lobby. While I was interested in meeting him, in all truth, I was distracted. My mind kept returning to wanting to call Doc Adolph about why Guille was learning so fast. I thought about the incident in the dormitory, if Doc thought this has happened to Guille, and if so, how to stop it from happening to her again. I also worried about that strange man whom I saw at the Casa this morning.

I wondered if Doc had suspicions of things like this when he was last here. I now pondered if that was he was trying to tell me that evening in the lobby of the hotel. He had said, "I believe a lot more is happening at the Casa than meets the eye," and, "Do not be surprised at what you find."

By this time of the day, the street children were very active, and blocking traffic. Thus I arrived at the hotel lobby fifteen minutes late for my appointment with Dr. Jesus. As I entered the lobby, I spied a young man sitting in a chair by the entrance. One of the bellboys whispered something to him and pointed at me. The man then rose from the chair and started moving towards me. He appeared to be about 29 or 30 and was dressed in a shirt and tie. His pants were worn blue jeans and his shoes were white sneakers, typical of our younger intellectual generation. His raven black hair was long but kept neatly combed. He was of average build and had a light complexion. His lips were that of an English man, not the thick, heavy lips that always accompanies a man of pure Mexican descent, and his face was clean-shaven. Overall, he looked like a handsome, young, intellectual gentleman.

We introduced ourselves, then I asked if he wanted to go to the bar to talk. I really wanted to hear what he had to say but I was extremely thirsty. Once in the bar, we proceeded to find a quiet table in the corner of the room. We then found a waiter and ordered our drinks. I assumed that we would wait for the drinks and then have some small talk before discussing business, but I was wrong. Without delay, Dr. Jesus started the conversation by remarking, "I think what you are trying to do with these children is a wonderful thing. More people in this world should think of the foundlings that are so prevalent throughout the world."

He looked at me with an expectation of response but I was so taken back by his rapid method of getting right to the point that I was speechless. This was not what I had come to expect from a Mexican's approach to conversation. Very seldom would a Mexican get right to the point. Only after a discussion of your family or other things was the point ever reached.

When I kept silent, he continued, "As I explained to you before, I run a prekindergarten school for middle class Mexican children. I feel that computer-assisted education is here to stay. The aim in the past has always been to start the children with computers in the higher classes, such as the eighth or ninth grade. This I believe is erroneous. We should start children at a very young age. In fact, I would like to start such an analysis in my school. However, I do not have the funds to procure the computers. This effort would not be to study how a computer operates, but to discover the advancements that a very young child can make when teachers use computers as a tool."

In the process of listening to this discourse, I thought of how Doc Adolph, myself, and Dr. Papet of MIT, the famous educator and a student of Piaget, had discussed the very same principle many times previously. Our approach was to start teaching children at the youngest age possible, such as the age of two or three. This young man was sitting here explaining the same reasoned doctrine that my colleagues and I had discussed so often in the past. It thoroughly astounded me; not only were his thoughts similar, but he was so young. Most young people in the field whom I have had the pleasure to meet would not even listen to our theories of early child education via computers with any sense of credence, even those who were supposed to be bright and open minded.

My colleagues and I had often discussed staring such a prekindergarten school but could never find anyone interested enough in the study to participate. Now all of a sudden, this man shows up in Tijuana of all places. I started to think that if we were to start the effort here, we could not only get the benefits of his preschool but also receive important data on how culture affects preschool and early education also. This man, Dr. Jesus, was an answer to our prayers.

The waiter finally put in an appearance with our drinks. At this time, Dr. Jesus was gazing at me in silence, awaiting my reply. I raised my drink and took a couple of sips before reacting to his dialogue. This was my way of not displaying my excitement over his parallel thoughts. I needed time to collect my wits enough to respond.

"Well," I started, "you are a man who gets right to the point. I like that in an individual. Your thoughts are quite correct. May I ask how you came to such a wild conclusion? You must know that you are one of very few people who believe in that postulate."

His reply was even faster than the last. "It's only common sense if you understand the workings of a young child's mind. My only problem is that I don't really understand the operations of a computer and its associated equipment."

"That's the easy part of it all," I interjected.

He then carried the conversation forward by adding, "I have followed your work through Dr. Bob Hess, one of your consultants. He speaks quite often of the commitment that you and the rest of your colleagues have to early education. I have wanted to become part of your effort for a long time; however, you were never here in Mexico to speak with about it. When Bob told me that you were here to start working with the children in the Casa, I decided that this was the time to contact you."

I leaned back in my chair and stared at this man for whom I felt an instant liking and respect. He and I were on the threshold of one of the most unbelievable and phenomenal journeys that any two people of this day and age could take in the subject of human behavior, both for the child and the adult. He was a man that was to become one of my greatest and closest friends and would help me through some of the most, if not the most, trying times of my entire 57 years of life. If it was not for this man, I do not think I could have reached this point to write about the events that took place over the years. In addition, he eventually became an adopted uncle to Guille.

Before long, I answered him. "I have often thought of your statements in my own mind. My problem was that I have never found anyone who was bright enough to undertake such a project, until this moment. Yes, by all means, we will be thrilled to include you and your school in our project. In fact, let's start tomorrow at the Casa. I want to show you some unbelievable results that I have obtained from these children so far, especially one named Guille. Maybe you could assist me in unraveling some of the remarkable results that I have obtained with her.

"This evening I have to call a friend of mine, Doc Adolph in New York, to help me in understanding why some of these events are just now starting to show up after three years of experimenting and not earlier. I must inquire from Doc if we went wrong somewhere in our approach in the past. Or is there something now that we are doing that we had not done in the former trials?"

Jesus looked at me with an expression of total bafflement over what I was saying. I saw this in his face and added, "I know I am rambling and remarking on things that I have not told you about yet. Please, bear with me and tomorrow, I will show you these results in the flesh. Then we can talk about it at great lengths tomorrow evening. However, in closing, let me just say that tomorrow you will see a child who not only absorbs a language immediately but also thinks in the foreign tongue."

Jesus exclaimed, "This I will have to see to believe. I'll be happy to go with you tomorrow to the Casa. You and I both know that for the short period of time that you have been with these children, it is impossible to accomplish such a feat of understanding foreign linguistics to do what you just claimed."

I replied, "I know it is. But, damn it, it is happening right before my eyes. I really can't explain why it is taking place, but it is. Tomorrow you will see it. Then you can form your own judgment on whether I'm crazy or not."

Jesus wanted to confer more on the subject. I told him that I was tired and still needed to call Doc before I retired. After a moment, I added that I would see him tomorrow at seven in the morning for breakfast. That would give him some time to think about what I had just said and maybe come up with some hypotheses. It would also give me time to confer with Doc about the possibilities of why such an event was taking place within Guillermina. In addition, he could interpret the menu for me at breakfast. Hotcakes every morning was starting to get to me by this time.

Thus, I bid Jesus good evening, and he did the same to me. We both then proceeded to our rooms.

CHAPTER FOURTEEN

JESUS MEETS ESTELLA AND GUILLE

Upon arriving in my room, I promptly placed a phone call to Doc. In Mexico, when you say, "promptly place a phone call," it could be anywhere from a minute to all day and then some. That would still be considered promptly in their minds. Mexican phone systems are not the greatest in the world.

But, as luck would have it, I unearthed an operator within three minutes. Not only was it done in record time but the operator also spoke fairly good English. She found a phone line within a couple of minutes and soon Doc's phone, I hoped, would be ringing. In record time, then, a pleasant voice answered the phone. It was Grace, his wife. "Hello?"

I said, "Hi, Grace, this is Bob. Is Doc there?

Grace responded, "He is in the computer room. I'll get him." She jokingly added, "Since you came into our lives, he has done nothing with his violin. All he does now is work in that room with his second wife, the computer."

Before I met Doc and convinced him to work with computers in early education, Doc had been a very great violinist and played at Carnegie Hall, along with other many concert houses throughout the world. In the past three years, he had hardly touched his violin, even to practice. In addition, he had not given a single concert during that time. I always said to Grace, "It is the fine arts' loss and the world of computing's gain."

Doc, after a minute or two, was on the phone. He said, "Sorry I took so long getting to the phone but I was right in the midst of a paper I'm writing for the *Psychiatrist Journal*. It's on the use of computers to diagnose mental illness. What's up, Bob? Grace said that you sounded excited over something."

I forgot to mention that Grace was also a psychiatrist of some renown. Every time that I have been in their house or out to supper with them, I always had the strange feeling that I was under total scrutiny by the both of them.

"Doc, I have had the strangest thing happen to me these past couple of days. I need your advice and your help in interpreting what seems to be impossible," I announced.

"Calm down." That was his answer to my deep concern.

"Calm down? How can I calm down when I think I have uncovered something great and most wonderful? It may be the greatest feat of my life!"

In his usual calm approach to situations, Doc replied, "Bob, I'm sure it is if you say so. However, getting this excited about it does not do anyone any good."

Here I was with something on my mind that is beyond expression and he's psychoanalyzing me on the phone. "Doc, do you remember that little girl, Guillermina, whom you met at the Casa?"

"Yes," he answered cautiously.

"Well," I continued, "during the past couple of weeks, as you know, I have been teaching her and the other girls at the Casa our method of language instruction. They have all done exceptionally well and learned quite fast, but that's not the amazing thing. This little girl, Guillermina, not only learns swiftly but she thinks in English after only a few lessons. How do you explain that?"

"What do you mean she 'thinks' in English?" Doc exclaimed.

"Her replies to my questions are extremely fast. She does not seem to have the usual hesitation in mental translation from native tongue to English that all people learning English have, especially children. It is as if she has been speaking English all her life. She learns very quickly but the response time in English to my questions is unbelievable."

"As we both know, the response time to a different tongue is usually quite long when you are first acquiring a new language. This time reduces as your understanding and vocabulary increases. In a child, it is usually faster than in an adult, but this phenomenon still takes place over a period of years not days. If what you say is true, then you really have found something new," admitted Doc.

He continued. "If it's all right with you, I will be there this weekend to examine her. The only thing I can contemplate at this moment for an answer is what Piaget found many times in his experiments and could never really elucidate. That is, if a child genuinely wants to learn something, there is no stopping the child. For some reason, the child's mind will seem to absorb the instruction at an accelerated pace. While I was at the Casa last time, I could see something in Guillermina that was strongly attracting her to you. Therefore, that want must be deeply rooted in her mind. This is the only conjecture in my mind until I see and talk to her. So, is it all right if I come down this weekend?"

I hastily replied, "You and I are on the same wavelength. I was going to ask you to come down this weekend. Yes, by all means, come down.

I will pick you up at the airport. We can talk about it on our way to the Casa. I'll make reservations for you here at the hotel where I'm staying so you do not have to face those border crossing guards each evening on your way back to an American hotel."

"Good, I will be there on the four o'clock plane to San Diego. I'll book the seats right after I hang up," Doc answered.

"By the way, there is a man by the name of Jesus from Mexicali that I want you to meet. He will be here also. He a very bright guy. I think you'll like him. Nevertheless, I would like to have your opinion of him to see if you think we should or shouldn't add him to our team here in the Casa. We can talk more about it when you are here," I informed Doc.

Doc replied in a positive fashion and then hung up after his usual pleasant goodbyes.

I did not mention any of the other odd events with the children and that strange man that I had witnessed. Although I had planned to mention them, I had second thoughts when I finally had him on the phone. I figured that I could tell him when he was here.

After finishing the call, I undressed, left a wakeup call for seven the next morning, and went straight to bed. It seemed that each evening, it took me longer to go to sleep as my questions about the Casa were piling up so very rapidly. Before I could explain one idea, a new one would pop up. Who was the European man that I saw that Estella would not discuss? Why does Guille think in English? Do all the Madres punish the girls the same way? Is Jesus for real? These and many more thoughts were racing through my mind as I lay in bed.

One thought that always dominated the others since I met Guillermina was the belief that this was meant to be. All of this was preordained. My reasoning for that thought was based on the sudden changes in my life around the time that I had met her. Last year, I did not care about much of anything, as I had just gone through a rather bitter divorce. Yet now I had so much for which to live and be happy. My life had completely changed.

Just before coming to Tijuana in February, I was in Boston and was drawn to a church by my hotel one Sunday. Don't ask me why. I hadn't been in church since my last daughter turned out to be what she was. However, for some reason, I decided to go to church that day. After the church service, the little children from the church's school were outside selling peanuts to finance a trip to a summer camp. I donated. In fact, I purchased all the children's peanuts and also gave them a check for $500.

After that encounter, I made inquiries to an adult who was supervising the children. She pointed to a very beautiful school across the church parking lot. I then proceeded to the school and met the person who was to start the changes in my life. Sister Mary Peters, the director of the school, promptly invited me into the convent and we discussed the plight of some of the parish children who could not afford an education.

Being moved by our discussion, I asked if I might finance some of them to attend her school. This offer she accepted and the only stipulation that I set forth was that they were never to know who was sponsoring them. To this, she agreed and said that tomorrow she would contact the parents of the children. She knew that they would be excited to attend the school next semester.

About a month after that encounter, I took an unexpected spur-of-the-moment trip to Jerusalem and Bethlehem during the Christmas season. Dr. Papert of MIT talked me into going with him. There I did not do much touring, except for in the old walled city of Jerusalem. I spent all my time there wandering through its narrow and well-worn streets. I walked the path of Christ to Calgary many times. Each time that I did, I felt more alive. I had tickets to go to the church in Bethlehem where Christ was born to celebrate midnight Mass but some friend asked me for those tickets as a favor.

Christmas Eve, I stood alone by my bedroom window in the hotel that overlooked the old city. My thoughts that evening were on the beauty of the world and not my usual ones about what did I have to live for. For some reason or another, the old city of Jerusalem gave me a feeling of a great inner glow and happiness that evening. Those days that I spent in Jerusalem were the most wonderful days of my life until I met this little child, Guillermina.

Was this encounter in the Boston school and my trip to Jerusalem preordained? Was I destined to meet Guillermina? Was this the Lord's way of telling me to love again and not hate all that I see and know? Was this now to be my final chore on earth? Had this little child, for whom I had grown so hopelessly fond, been born and allowed to suffer as I had these past years, just so the rest of my life would be dedicated to her and her care? Have both of us suffered the unrestricted horrors of life these many years as a test? Was it significant that Dr. Galaz's first name was Jesus and Doc's last name was Christ?

Whatever the reason, I truly felt that I was supposed to come to Tijuana and meet this child. Many future events merely strengthened my belief in this. Soon I was fast asleep with these thoughts racing through my mind. Knowing that Doc was on his way to help relieved some of the anxiety. It was the first good night's sleep that I had had in many a day.

The next morning, I was awakened by the hotel operator with the prearranged wakeup call. I quickly arose, showered, and shaved. Shortly after waking, I was on my way to the hotel restaurant for my breakfast appointment with Jesus. It was 6:59 when I entered the dining room. A wide-awake Jesus was already sitting at a table by the window. He looked up and said in pleasant voice, "Good morning;

you are right on time. You should consider changing that if you expect to be in Mexico for very long. Very few, if any at all, Mexicans are ever on time for anything."

I smiled and replied, "I have found that out already. This will be the first time here that I will not have the hotcakes because now I have someone that can read this damned menu."

We finished our meal and were soon on our way to the Casa. I could see in Jesus' eyes that he was excited as we wound our way through the back streets of Tijuana. When we arrived at the huge gates of the Casa. I sounded my car's horn and the enormous giant Felipe immediately appeared. He opened the gates wide to allow us to pass and then, just as quickly, he had them closed again behind us. Out of the corner of my eye, I could see Jesus looking at Felipe and Felipe at him. I think Jesus was astonished by the man's size, much like I was the first time that I saw him.

I looked towards my parking space that Madre Esmeralda had generously assigned to me. Standing there with her ever-faithful shadow, Estella, was my precious Guille. I looked forward to her being there so very much when I arrived. It was as if my heart jumped for joy. Corny as it might sound, that is the only way I can describe the feeling within me.

She was waving frantically as we approached. She was saying something that I could not hear until I was almost there. Then I heard it. "Good morning, Daddy. I missed you very much last night," she spoke in perfect English. It was no longer "papa" but "daddy" now. She had learned that word in our English class.

She opened the car door and gave me a big hug and kiss on the cheek. Then she just about dragged me out of the car so she could embrace me more. As I smiled at her antics with fond amusement, it made me think of Doc's response to my questions last evening on the phone. Yes, the want of this child is there, and thus the drive to learn to speak English so rapidly. Yet, it still did not explain her ability to think in English.

I held her a while and then said, "Good morning, Guille, did you sleep well last night?"

"Yes, very well, thank you," she declared instantly in her newly improved English.

As all of this was taking place, Jesus alighted from the other side of the car. Upon seeing him, Guille suddenly became withdrawn and stood very close by me with a tight grip on my hand.

"This must be the Dr. Jesus whom Madre Esmeralda said was coming today. Good morning, Doctor. Say good morning to the doctor, Guille," Estella said when she saw Jesus. Guille's only response was a look of fear and a death grip on my hand.

I tried to comfort her. "Guille, there is nothing to be afraid of. He's a friend of mine. He has come to see what I have been talking about. I have told you that I speak about you all the time. He just wanted to come and see for himself what wonderful children you and the other girls are."

She looked at me and smiled. Then she let go of the tight grip she had on my hand, not all the way, just enough to let the blood start flowing again. She understood about every other word that I had said. I wondered why men frightened her so much. Every time that we went out and there were only women around us, she was all right. However, once a strange man entered the scene, she always grabbed for my hand or sat closer to me if we were sitting down.

Finally, Guille peered out from behind me and said, "Good morning, Dr. Jesus." Then she immediately disappeared behind me again. Jesus stepped forward to shake her hand and Guille moved away. In a rather sharp tone, Estella said, "Guillermina, shake the doctor's hand and come out from behind Dr. Nielsen."

Guille, upon hearing this command from Estella, was quick to obey. Both Jesus and I looked at each other in response to the way that Guille obeyed Estella so automatically. Children do not normally respond so promptly, even well behaved ones. Something in her past or present had prompted that rapid action. As I stood there watching, Guille swiftly moved from behind me to my side, even though she was obviously terrified.

Jesus came over to Guille and knelt down beside her. He started to speak to her gently in Spanish. I did not know what he was saying; whatever it was, it was working. Soon a smile came over Guille's face and she was now standing in front of Jesus without that look of absolute fear, though she still held my hand tightly.

I asked Jesus, "What did you say? Whatever it was, it did wonders in how fast she accepted you. I have never seen her this way. I do not know what got into her. She's usually a happy, outgoing child."

Estella was quick to accept my quip and said, "Last night, the girls had a scare. They thought someone was breaking into their dormitory."

Jesus looked at me with a look of disbelief after he made sure that Estella was not looking. He had only been here a few minutes and already knew something was wrong. Estella also forgot that Guille now understood English quite well. Therefore, when Estella made her excuse, Guille looked at her with a strange expression, giving away the lie.

After this, as we walked towards the classroom and Estella was out of earshot, Jesus told me, "No, that was not the reason she was apprehensive. She is afraid of most men."

"Why do you say that?" I asked.

"Well, it's something that she said to me when I was talking to her in Spanish. I asked why she was afraid of me and she said, 'no reason.' She added that she was not scared of me. It was just that she did not know what I wanted her for. That was the tip off," Jesus explained. "When she said, 'what I wanted her for,' she was afraid that I was going to take her some place without you. I assured her that she would not go anywhere with me if you were not there. That was when she loosened up a bit. Have you any idea of what she was talking about?"

"None," I answered in frustration. "I have been wondering myself what is going on around here."

"Well, never mind, I just thought I would mention it to you so you can be on the lookout for any other strange behavior that she might exhibit. I would also be interested in any other strange things that she might say if you spot them when I am not here. There is more going on here than you think, Bob, so keep a sharp eye on Guille's behavior, along with the other children."

I was amazed. My God, I thought, he has been here only 15 minutes and he is already expressing the same observations as Doc. Both were child psychiatrists; what were they seeing that I was not?

CHAPTER FIFTEEN

JESUS CONVINCES MADRE ESMERALDA

Jesus and I walked with Guille at my side holding my hand. The faithful Estella followed behind us, within earshot. We proceeded towards the classroom, where the rest of the girls were waiting for their English lessons.

Upon entering the room, I was greeted by the girls in the class. All the girls politely said, "Good Morning, Teacher," in impeccable English. Jesus looked at me and asked, "How long did you say they have been speaking English?" He was obviously astonished by the perfection of their response in English.

I rejoined, "About two months now." Then I returned the children's greeting. "Today we have a visitor, Dr. Jesus from Mexicali."

Once I spoke those words, all the girls seemed different. They were looking at Jesus with suspicion. They seemed to be afraid of him, much as Guille had acted when she first saw Jesus getting out of the car in the courtyard.

Upon sensing this, I said, "Senor Jesus is a friend of mine and I trust him very much. He will do you no harm." Estella was quick to translate my words to the girls and that seemed to comfort them. Why were the girls so afraid of men? I pondered this while Estella was translating my words.

Jesus also noticed their behavior and spoke to them in Spanish after Estella was finished. Whatever he said, it worked because their faces turned from scared expressions to smiles. When I asked Jesus what he said, he replied, "All I said was that I too was an orphan and spent time in a home like this when I was young."

I said, "You never mentioned that to me."

Jesus said, "It's a lie, but it worked, didn't it?" It did work. They were happy that he could speak Spanish and he was one of them.

Guille took her usual front row seat. She turned to look at the other girls with that look of "See, I still have a daddy and he still comes each day. He is not like the others." The girls looked at her briefly and then turned to their handheld computers. They were eager to show me the homework that was assigned to them yesterday.

With the exception of Guille, they all looked tired and sleepy. When I commented on it to Estella, she replied, "They were up late last night with that scare."

I glanced down at Guille to get confirmation of what Estella just said.

Guille looked down at her machine and would not look at me. I could see that Guille understood what Estella had said in English. Although, she would not look at me, she did look at Estella with a sideways glance when she thought I was not looking. Her expression clearly said, "See, I did not answer his look." Even though she did not say anything, the look on her face was worth a thousand words. Once again, I found myself wondering what the hell was going on in this place.

I pushed the thoughts aside and channeled my energy into instructing the girls in their lesson for the day with Jesus' assistance. When the time was up, they were once more reluctant to leave. They had to be told in a strict voice to leave by Estella. Now that the girls' English was sufficient for simple conversation, Estella stayed with the class during the sessions and no longer left as she did in the past. That seemed strange to me also. I would have expected just the opposite, for her to leave now that translations were not needed.

The girls all left but Guille. She got up, stood by me, and grasped my hand after receiving approval from Estella. She had been told by the Madre that she could stay with her newfound daddy as long as he was at the Casa. Likewise, she would be excused from any duties, except for regular school.

Jesus came over to me and said, "The children have excelled in such a short time. You ought to feel proud of what you have accomplished here in the Casa. The greatest peculiarity that I saw was as you predicted back in the hotel. Guille's progress in English is amazing. She is far more advanced in speaking and understanding it than are the other girls. In addition, what you said about her thinking in English, I agree. She really does. I think as you do; it is because of your relationship and her great desire to communicate with you. That is obvious when you see the two of you together."

We all left and headed to the courtyard. Upon arriving there, we were greeted by Madre Esmeralda. "How did the lessons go today?" Estella translated the Madre's words.

"Fine, Madre. The girls are doing great. I would like you to meet Dr. Jesus, whom you graciously gave permission to visit."

Without waiting for Estella's translation, Jesus interpreted my words to the Madre. Madre extended her hand to Jesus. He did likewise. Then they spoke in Spanish for a short time. I could see by their expressions that they were getting along well.

After the conversation, Jesus uttered, "The Madre has invited us all to eat with her and the other Madres. Guille can also come. Madre seems to like seeing you two together. She said she is greatly pleased with the relationship that you two have developed in such a short time."

With that, we all commenced towards the dining room. The other girls had not come into the dining area yet. I was thankful for that. Upon arriving in the dining room, the Madre introduced Jesus to all the other Madres. Fulfilling that task, we all sat down and started to eat. I was on one side of the Madre and Jesus was on the other. Next to me sat Guille. She was a pro now at using the silverware and was eager to show off her newfound talent to Jesus. Under the table, unseen by the Madre, Guille kept a tight grip on my hand. Madre and Jesus carried on a conversation during the meal in Spanish. I asked Guille what they were discussing and she explained it well in her newly acquired English.

After dinner, Jesus suggested that I should discuss the placement of computers in the Casa, as he thought the Madre was almost sold on the concept. I had mentioned to Jesus on the drive to the Casa this morning that the Madre did not like the idea of real computers in her Casa and the reasons why. Jesus offered to translate now on that subject if I so desired.

I replied, "Well, if you think so, here goes." I then spoke again via Jesus about the placement. Low and behold, she did not stop me halfway through my dissertation, as she had done in the past. She allowed me to continue to list the reasons why I thought that it would be a good idea.

When I finished my spiel, the Madre uttered, "Roberto, I have seen what you have done in the past months not only with Guillermina but with the other girls and I now believe that there is a possibility of such a placement of computers."

With that, I quickly replied, "Madre, there is a school in Boston run by nuns who had the same reservation that you had at first. Now they would almost quit the order if I were to take the computers out of their school," I said jokingly. "May I invite you to Boston to speak with them as our guest?"

The Madre thought that was a splendid idea but first she had to receive permission from the Madre General, Madre Maria. The Madre declared that she would call her superior, who resided in Mexico City, this evening. She hoped that she would have an answer for me by tomorrow.

I said, "I will look forward to her reply." I then asked if Guille might accompany Jesus and me to town for some hamburgers. Madre approved, as long as her shadow, Estella, was available to accompany us. Estella said she was so we left the dining room and headed for the car and town. There we would purchase and eat Guille's now favorite food, hamburgers.

While eating the burger, Guille, as always, got more on her dress than in her mouth. She had learned to handle the fork and knife but not to eat a hamburger. Even though she was having a hard time with the burger, her desire to learn and, of course, eat the burger helped her to improve her burger-eating skills with each outing. To this day, when she eats one, she looks at me and smiles. I think she does it just to get that look from me that I gave her so long ago when she was mastering her eating skills in Tijuana.

Soon the burger was finished and we had to return Guille reluctantly to the Casa. When I exited the great gates that surrounded their prison and started back to my hotel with Jesus, Guille cried as she waved goodbye to me.

The ride to the hotel was quiet since we were both deep in thought. Jesus was reviewing his experience and I was concerned with leaving

Guille, coupled with worrying about what Madre Maria would say to Madre Esmeralda's suggestion. In truth, the former thought took most of my concentration, not the latter. My original purpose of being in the Casa had now become a lesser thought in my mind. All I could think about was Guille.

Jesus and I swiftly retreated to the bar upon arriving at the hotel. There we discussed the day's events. He was very interested in joining our project. He also asked if he might accompany me again tomorrow when I went to the Casa. He wanted to see the class again and to hear Madre Maria's decision about Boston and the computers. I was happy to invite him back with me.

It was late by the time we were finished discussing the day's events and we had to get up early. We soon said good night and each retired to our own rooms for a good night's sleep. At last, I had made some progress with the Madre, even if it was mainly due to Jesus doing the translation rather than Margaret. Madre seemed to take a likening to Jesus. When they first meet, Mexicans will usually trust another Mexican before they will trust a gringo.

The next morning, I was up bright and early to meet Jesus for a quick breakfast. Then we were on our way to the Casa to see if the Madre had gotten approval for the trip to Boston. I was hoping she would, as it would be a great experience for her to see children learning with real computers. Likewise, I was twice as happy on my way to the Casa because I would get to see Guille again.

As soon as I entered the Casa and reached my designated parking space, I could see Guille standing there with Estella. They had come to realize that I always arrived at 8:00 a.m. and was seldom late. As I pulled into the space, Guille was excitedly waving and saying, "Daddy, Daddy, Daddy!" She opened my car door, threw her arms around me, and kissed me on the cheek. When I managed to get out of the car, Guille took my hand and stood by me. Jesus came over and bent down. Guille bestowed a kiss to his cheek as well.

Estella asked if we would talk with the Madre prior to the start of class. The Madre had spoken to Madre Maria and now wished to speak to me. Estella added, "She did not tell me or discuss it with me. However, she did look as if it was positive. But, let's go and see as I am just as interested as you to find out what was Madre Maria's response."

All of us walked to a little office that the Madre had in the front part of the courtyard of the Casa. She had just finished speaking to some Americans in the office and they were leaving in the company of some other Madre. They were heading towards the children's area.

I asked Estella, "Who are they?"

Estella replied, "People here to adopt children."

They did not strike me as the average American couple. They just did not look like people who would adopt children. I could not put my finger on why I thought that, but I did. As they approached, Guille moved to the other side of me, opposite of their approaching path.

There sitting in that cold room was Madre Esmeralda with a serious expression on her face. We greeted her and sat down. Guille, chose to sit on my lap, something she still continues to do to this day. It was nothing to have her do it back in those days when she hardly weighed more than a fly. Nowadays, she seems to weigh closer to an elephant.

The Madre promptly began by asking how we were, how we slept, if we ate, and how we felt. This went on for about twenty minutes. You have to understand that even before a policeman in Mexico gives you a ticket, there is a conversation on the well-being of each person. They never just get right to the point about anything until they get those amenities out of the way. I will never get used to this custom. Jesus has been the only exception to this; after a relatively short time, he gets right to the subject.

"Roberto, last evening I called Madre Maria, as I said I would. She listened a long time and she is interested. She would like to come and speak with you in person about the placement of computers here in the Casa if that is all right with you."

I quickly answered, "I would be honored to meet with the Madre General and discuss the installation. Just name the time and place and I will be there." All this conversation was being carried on with the help of Jesus' interpretation.

"Good, I anticipated that you would say that and asked the Madre if she could be here tomorrow. She said that would be convenient for her as she was planning on being in one of the other Casas in a nearby town anyway tomorrow. Let's say about nine in the morning?"

"I'll be here," I eagerly replied.

With that, our conversation was over for now. The Madre nodded her head and presented me with a big smile as she patted Guille on the head. Then she proceeded to leave the undersized office. Guille got up and grasped my hand. She sort of pulled me to my feet and pronounced in her best English, "Daddy, let's go. The girls are waiting for us."

After receiving that order, we strolled out the office door, across the courtyard, and up the stairs to the classroom. As we walked, Jesus looked at me and gave me a big smile. We were on our way with the placement of computers in the Casa.

The girls all greeted us and I could clearly see their anxiety due to me not being there on time. I explained that we were talking to the Madre about placing real computers here in the Casa. This swiftly did away with the anxious looks and produced looks of pleasure on their faces instead.

With our explanations out of the way, Guille took her appointed seat in the front row. She turned and gave her now usual look to tell the other girls, "He's my Daddy." Then we proceeded to the instruction of the day.

After the completion of the class, we secured permission for Guille to accompany us to lunch. The permission was granted, assuming that Estella was not busy. At the time, I thought this to be a little strange, just like Estella's presence in the English class. I could understand why Estella was previously needed, since Guille was not able to speak any English until recently. However, she now spoke fairly well. Even if there were any problems in communication, Jesus was there to interpret for her. Why did we need Estella to be with us all the time? Even though it did not make sense, I had come to know by this time that the Madre did not appreciate anyone questioning her wishes so I never said anything to her about it.

Jesus and Estella got into the back seat of the car. To watch Guille jockey for the front seat was always a pleasure. She would open the back door and stand there to usher in the other people. These actions were to inform all that rode with us that the front seat next to me was her place. The only people whom she would give way to was the Madres.

During the ride, we all discussed the meeting tomorrow with Madre Rachel. Estella had met her several times and imparted many of the Madre General's idiosyncrasies to us. We listened with great attentiveness to her suggestions on how to entreat with Madre Maria. Jesus said he would remain here, if I so desired, to translate and discuss computers with the Madre. I happily accepted that offer.

While at the hotel a couple of days ago, I inquired about a good Italian restaurant. They had suggested Giuseppe's, which was just down the street. They explained that he had three restaurants in Tijuana, all of which were good. He also owned the most popular cantina in town.

Therefore, today my target was Giuseppe's. Soon we were there, and I silently hoped the food was better than what Giuseppe's looked like on the outside. We entered and found a table. Estella and I were the only Americans there. It soon became obvious that this was a Mexican restaurant and gringos were not appreciated. I could tell this by the way that they ignored us sitting there and from the looks from the other customers.

Soon Estella got up and said something to a man who appeared to be the boss. After that, service immediately was granted. Jesus said, "What did you say? Whatever it was, it worked miracles."

Estella's response was forthwith, "All I said was that these people are friends of Madre Esmeralda and that she had suggested that we try here. Bob," she continued, "Half the people of Tijuana have adopted children from Madre Esmeralda. She is an extremely important person to these people and they will do almost anything to please her. Giuseppe is no exception. Only last week, he adopted two more girls from the Madre."

"How many did he have before?" I inquired.

"Four," she answered.

With astonishment, I replied, "That makes six!" Jesus looked at me with an expression showing that he had similar thoughts. During my stay in Tijuana, I eventually found the ages of the adopted girls were from seven to eleven. Also, I discovered, they did not live at home with Giuseppe.

The waiter was soon standing beside the table waiting for our order. Everyone went for spaghetti since Estella suggested it was very good here. Guille was too busy looking all around to pay attention. When I asked her what she wanted, she was not sure. "What is spaghetti? Do you think I would like it?"

I informed her, "I do not know if you will like it, but try it and see if you do." Thus, all four of us ordered spaghetti.

The arrival of the food was prompt and we all proceeded to devour the best plates of spaghetti that I have ever tasted. "All" is actually the wrong word. It would be more correct to say that three of us were devouring it. Guille was still trying to pick it up. She had mastered most food but this was a new item and she was having a hard time getting it on her fork.

I asked if she wanted me to make it easier to eat. After she answered affirmatively, I took her plate and cut the spaghetti into smaller, more manageable pieces. Then Guille was able to join the rest of us in enjoying our lunch. From the way she was putting the spaghetti away, I did not have to ask if she liked it. It made me wonder what she would think of pizza.

Upon completion of the meal, we left and drove Estella and Guille back to the Casa, since still Guille had to attend regular school that afternoon. I left Jesus in the car and went to find the Madre to make our goodbyes. I inquired as to her whereabouts from one of the other Madres. She told me that the Madre was in her office with some Americans. I assumed they were the same people whom I had seen leaving her office earlier to inspect the girls for adoption.

As I headed to the office, I saw the shades were drawn and the door was shut. I did not want to interrupt so I looked through one of the windows that had a crack in the shade. The Madre was sitting behind her desk and the Americans were on the other side. Between them was one of the girls. I saw that it was nine-year-old Blanca from my English class. She was standing there completely naked. Her clothes were by the desk and the Americans were inspecting her from their chairs. Blanca stood there with her hands held tightly at her sides and was turning around very slowly as the Americans inspected her. Shocked, I decided not to bother Madre at this time and returned to the car.

Jesus said, "Did you say goodbye?"

I replied, "No, she was busy." I asked Estella to say my goodbyes for me when the Madre was free. Estella had a funny look on her face. She had watched me from across the yard by the car when I looked through the shades.

I did not to say anything to Jesus about what I had just seen, as I still could not believe it myself. Maybe I was jumping to the wrong conclusions. I could only hope so. Guille also had a funny look on her face and seemed a little stiff when I kissed her goodbye but, then again, she too had seen me peer through the shade into the office. I climbed into the car and waved goodbye to Guille. Then I was soon on my way back to the hotel with Jesus at my side.

It could have been part of the adoption procedures. I tried to convince myself of that as we drove back to the hotel. If so, it was a hellish procedure. That poor child in the office had been terrified. "*Bob,*" I thought to myself, "*stay out of it. You are here to educate the children and get results. In addition, you have a little girl to think of now. Don't cause any trouble. In the long run, getting involved with something that is not your business will do you and Guille no good.*"

I tried to concentrate on other things, such as the meeting tomorrow with Madre Maria. However, I couldn't stop wondering about what I had seen today and the light that it threw on previous events. I was also starting to get a strange feeling that Estella was not number one on Guille and the other girls' hit parade. These and other thoughts were constantly pushing to the surface as Jesus and I drove back to the hotel. Jesus was talking yet I don't think I heard a word he was saying. I just kept nodding my head absentmindedly.

Once back at the hotel, I agreed to meet Jesus tomorrow for breakfast and then headed to my room. As I lay on my bed, I tried to make sense of my thoughts. Before I got very far, I had drifted off to sleep. That evening I did not sleep well, waking often in a cold sweat from bad dreams.

CHAPTER SIXTEEN

THE COMING OF MADRE MARIA AND A TRIP TO BOSTON IS PLANNED

The next morning appeared quite swiftly. After a shower to wake up and prepare me for meeting the fabulous Madre Maria, I went down for breakfast. My excitement of the forthcoming day's events had finally driven back my concerns. I met Jesus in the lobby and we had a quick breakfast before leaving for the Casa.

As usual, Guille and Estella were there at my appointed parking space. Guille, after waving and running towards my car, threw her arms around me and knocked me back into the seat of the car.

Jesus laughed and said, "She really does love you."

Seeing that I was looking at Jesus instead of her, Guille pulled my head back to hers and planted a big kiss on my cheek. I finally extracted myself from the car while Jesus waited with amusement. Guille politely kissed Jesus on the cheek when she was done greeting me.

Estella came over and said her welcomes with a kiss to my cheek, along with one for Jesus, as the custom required. Then she said, "Madre Maria is here and is waiting for you in the reception room. She is quite interested in talking to you. I spent most of the early hours this morning explaining your proposal to her in person. She seems delighted with it. However, it all depends on how she takes to you personally." She meant those words to be kind but, instead, it made me very nervous. I hoped that nothing would go wrong during the meeting.

I turned to Jesus and said, "Jesus, if I do or say anything wrong, please stop me." He looked at me and laughed.

Guille was now holding my hand very tightly, the hand farthest from Estella. It suddenly occurred to me that Guille often held the hand farthest away from Estella. I suppose I was more aware of such things due to yesterday's shock. Hand in hand, Guille and I joined Jesus and Estella and the four of us proceeded to the small guest room to meet Madre Maria.

Estella and Jesus entered first and then Guille and I. Guille let go of my hand, ran to Madre Rachel, and gave her a big hug and kiss, completely bypassing Madre Esmeralda. This was the first time I had seen her act so affectionate with any of the Madres. After the hug and kiss, she curled up in the Madre General's lap and started to speak to her.

Jesus quietly translated. "She is telling Madre Maria how happy she is to see her and how happy she has been since you had come and how you are going to be her daddy."

When Guille finished talking, Madre Maria gently placed Guille back on the floor and then stood to introduce herself. Guille was now holding two hands, one of Madre Maria and one of mine. Guille seemed to cherish and love Madre Maria, unlike her attitude towards the Madres at the Casa. To me, this was sufficient to know that I was going to love this woman as well.

She was rather short and a little on the stout side. She wore the habit of her order. It was neatly pressed and clean. Her hair was snow white and, unlike all the other Madres I had seen, not pulled back into a tight knot on the back of her head. Her hair was neatly combed and kept rather short and fluffed. Her face was also very much unlike Madre's Esmeralda's. Her eyes did not flash. Instead, they had a kind, understanding, and loving look to them. Her face was rather round and seemed to glow. I could easily imagine an angel's halo hovering over her. I took an instant liking to her. I did not care if she was going to like me; I knew no matter what, I was going to like her. I would come to cherish our relationship as the years passed.

Madre Maria would play an important part of my life in the years to come. She definitely deserved that halo that always seemed to appear around her head. If God were to choose any woman for sainthood in this modern day and age, without a doubt, Madre Maria would be at the top of his list.

When we shook hands, I felt a unique sensation. A perception of warmth, kindness, and understanding fell over me. I started to see why Guille held her other hand so tightly. Her hand was not like Madre's Esmeralda's, unconcerned and frigid. After our introduction, I presented Jesus to her.

She spoke in Spanish and could not speak a word of English. Estella started to translate and I suggested it would be better if Jesus did the translation. Jesus then promptly picked it up. Estella retired to the corner with an expression that could drop a cow to the floor. She was quite insulted, but at this point, I did not care. I wanted to make sure that what was being interpreted was correct and did not have Estella's twist to it.

Madre Maria said, via Jesus, "It seems that you have made quite a hit with Guille. I had a long talk with her this morning about you and her. She is deeply and honestly in love with you. I have known Guille for years and she is one of my favorite children. Never before have I seen her so happy." After pausing a moment, she added, "This morning I spoke with the other girls and they are also very excited over what you are doing here. Therefore, I have been quite anxious to meet this wonderful man who has turned this Casa into one of the happiest ones."

We soon got the usual Mexican niceties out of the way as we stood there talking. Before long, Madre Maria and I sat down on the loveseat. Guille was not about to move a single inch away from us so she squeezed in between us on the couch. Madre Esmeralda and Jesus were on the other couch that faced us across a coffee table.

Coffee was brought to us by one of the young girls. In Mexico, coffee consists of a cup of hot water, a jar of instant coffee, sugar, and upon request, cream. At this point, you make your own coffee. As I was making my coffee, Madre Maria started asking questions about the computers and what advantages the children might receive from them.

The Madre said she had seen the ones that we now had in the Casa. However, she was aware that these were not the ones that I really wanted to place in her Casa. I opened up my attaché case and showed her a picture of a PC. Madre studied it quite hard and then passed it over to Madre Esmeralda for her scrutiny. After further discussion of the advantages, she said, "I have seen how well Guille and the other girls have progressed with speaking and understanding the English language. Do you think you can do the same with their school marks in the subjects taught in the Mexican schools?"

I explained that I was very positive that I could, since it has been done before in America. I figured this would give me a lead into the topic of her visiting the nuns in Boston who were having great results with computers in their school.

Being as astute as the Madre was, she quickly answered, "Yes, in America, but can you do it with children from a different culture and background?"

"I believe it can be done. However, that is what I would like to prove. This is why I would like to use your Casa to find out."

The conversation went on like this for about three more hours, with Madre Maria asking many pertinent questions. She soon earned my respect. It became obvious that she was a very intelligent and well-schooled woman, unlike Madre Esmeralda who had hardly any education at all.

After a while, Guille got bored with the discussion started to wander around the room to look at the flowers and pictures. Each time she got up or sat down, she would always kiss the both of us on the cheek. It seemed that every time she did this, it was always when I was about to say something. Thus, I would have to stop my conversation and bend my face towards hers for the appointed kiss. Madre Maria took notice of this fact and smiled.

Many more questions later, Madre Maria agreed to accompany me, along with Madre Esmeralda, to America to see this wonderful computer and what it might do for her children here and at her other Casas. I asked Jesus if he could come as an interpreter but he was unable to do so. Estella was fast to accept the post when Jesus turned it down. The plans were now made. Madre Maria, Madre Esmeralda, Estella, and I would be off to Boston in five days. I figured I would need the extra time to set things up with the nuns in Boston.

Since we had been talking for hours, I invited them all to the hotel for a meal. After Guille left to get dressed for lunch, Madre Maria said, via Jesus, "I wanted to talk to you without Guille here. She would listen and understand if I talked about her. Guille, as you know, is a lonely child and has never had anyone to love her. This is the first time anyone has ever paid her any attention. It is quite obvious from what I have seen today that everything Madre Esmeralda has told me about you two is true. Guille loves you very much. And you her. I now want to be very forward. What are your intentions towards the child?"

"Madre," I answered, "I have had two other children who are now grown up. These children are of my own flesh and blood. In all honesty, I would not give you a plug nickel for the two of them. I have never known a child like Guille. She wants nothing and asks for nothing. She is a beautiful child within her heart, a child any father could be proud of. I have come to love her very much. My intention, with your approval, is to adopt her. I believe she would give my life meaning. She makes my heart dance and sing every time I see her. I am happy when she is with me."

Madre replied, "Good, and I know she feels the same. Therefore, the two of you should be joined, as she needs you as much as you need her. I shall do all in my power to see that the two of you become one family." With that, she approached me and gave me a small kiss on the cheek and an embrace, along with the blessing of the cross with her hand.

In such a short time, Madre Maria had been able to see that Guille meant the entire world to me. Yet, more important, she could see the love that the two of us had for each other. This love that Guille and I possessed back in those days is still with us today. In truth, it has grown even more majestic since Madre issued those words many years ago. At this moment, Guille is looking over my shoulder and hugging me as I write. She is almost thirteen and still persists in sitting on my lap. If every father could have a child like Guille, then the families of the world would rejoice in happiness.

Guille returned in the dress that we bought in the shop a couple of days ago. She looked very pretty. This dress meant the world to Guille. These children never had anything but hand-me-downs, so a store where you could buy clothes that fit you was pure fantasy. There was a small spot on the dress, but Madre Maria took care of that. She led Guille into the bathroom that adjoined the living room. Then she produced a hanky from her pocket, moistened it, and removed the spot.

Guille thanked her, looked at me, and said, "Do I look okay, Daddy?"

"You could not look more beautiful," I responded.

With that, she gave both Madre Maria and me a big hug. Madre Esmeralda was left out once more. I could see from her face that all this attention for Madre Maria and none for her was starting to disturb her. Yet, what could she say? Madre Maria was her superior. I could not help but wonder what would happen to Guille when Madre Maria left.

To drive to the hotel, we all climbed into my car. Madre Maria sat beside me with Guille on her lap. Madre Esmeralda, the ever-present Estella, and Jesus sat in the back. We proceeded down the dirt roads that led to and from the Casa. These roads eventually turned into the main paved roads of Tijuana as we got closer to the hotel. As we drove, Guille was showing Madre Maria all the sights of her newfound city, as though the Madre had never before seen them. These sights, even though familiar to her by now, were still a wonder for Guille to behold. She was showing the Madre the traffic lights, car washes where machines wash your car, stores where you could actually buy clothes that fit you, and shoe stores where you buy shoes with a thing called money. These and many more Guille was quick to point out in excitement. The Madre graciously showed great astonishment and interest in every "discovery" that Guille showed her. I thought that it was very considerate of the Madre to care about Guille's feelings. At one point, Madre Esmeralda tried to quiet Guille. However, Madre Maria firmly said, "Madre, let her talk. I enjoy it very much." That ended any complaints about Guille prattling too much.

We finally reached the hotel. When we entered, all the bellboys and the front desk clerk nodded a hello to Guille. She had become quite a favorite with them all. As she walked though the hotel, she did her little skip hop. This was where she would lift up one leg, touch her shoe with the hand on the same side, place that leg down, and then repeat the action on the other side. Today her face was radiant and she smiled from ear to ear at everything she saw. She was looking forward to showing Madre Maria how well she had learned to eat.

We were shown to a table by the captain, who referred to Guille by name. He also bent over to be kissed by her. This made Guille even prouder. Once seated, Guille proceeded to show Madre Maria a menu and explained how to order from it. Her legs were under her on the chair as she sat at the table. She was not quite big enough to reach the table while sitting normally.

Madre listened to her with noble attention and then asked what she recommended. Guille was quick to recommend the hotcakes. Madre suggested it would be better to order from the luncheon menu rather from the breakfast menu. The suggestion was accomplished without embarrassing Guille. Jesus and I just looked at each other and smiled, making sure at first that Guille was not looking. Soon we all agreed on what we wanted and lunch was under way.

Throughout the lunch, Guille showed Madre Maria how to hold a knife and fork, how to cut meat, and other things in that vein. Once more, Madre Maria listened and made believe that this was all new. She took Guille's advice on all subjects of how to eat, what to order, how to order when the man came to you, and what pieces of silverware to use. Madre Maria handled the touchy situation extremely well.

During lunch, Guille and I carried on a conversation in English. I think she was trying to show off her language skills to Madre Maria.

The adults also continued their discussion of the Boston trip and I told Madre Maria about Doc Adolph and his upcoming visit.

After she had finished easting, Guille asked if she could ride up and down on the elevator while we adults talked. Permission was granted and off she went to ride the elevator, pushing all of its buttons to make the ride last longer. This was one of her greatest pleasures, along with patting every stray dog that she saw.

After we had finished discussing the trip, we rounded up Guille and headed back to the Casa. When we arrived there, I said my goodbyes. After giving Guille her kiss, Jesus and I returned to the hotel to make calls and set up the trip.

The first thing I wanted to do was to call Doc to see if he could postpone his weekend trip to the Casa, which we discussed a couple of nights ago. Due to this new twist of going to Boston, I thought maybe he could meet us there. That would give him the opportunity to meet Madre Maria. After the visit to Boston, we could reschedule his trip to see Guille at the Casa. I really wanted him to see Guille first; however, I still had a job to do. This job allowed me to stay with Guille; thus it was important to cover my responsibilities.

CHAPTER SEVENTEEN

BOSTON AND THE SCHOOL STARTED AT THE CASA

During the drive back, Jesus told me that he had to return home and attend to his school. He asked me to keep him advised of the progress in Boston and if permission were granted, he would like to be heavily involved with the research at the Casa. He hoped that our findings would be useful for the prekindergarten that he ran in Mexicali. He was also eager to meet Doc.

Jesus and I said our goodbyes at the hotel. I went to my room to start arranging the trip and to let Doc know about the change in plans. First, I placed a call to Sister at the Boston school concerning the visit. She replied that she would be pleased to entertain such a visit and would make preparations. I thanked her and then placed a call to Dr. Adolph to see if he could accompany us as well and reschedule his visit to see Guille at the Casa. He, I thought, would add a flare of dignity to the visit. Being of Mexican origin and fluent in Spanish, he would also be a great help with Madre Maria. Likewise, he knew of the Casa and Madre Esmeralda from his previous visit to the Casa.

The call went through rather easily and soon I was speaking to Doc. Dr. Adolph's reply to my request was positive. All people involved were agreeable and the times and dates were set. I then called my secretary and had her arrange the air travel and hotels. In addition, I spoke to our hardware people and got the shipment of computers on their way to the Casa in anticipation of a successful trip.

After finishing the calls, I leaned back on the bed and sort of smiled with pleasure at myself for pulling off this whole thing. Now if only it went as well as I hoped, I would be thrilled. I would be able not only to do what I came to do in the first place, I could also be able to spend most of the time with Guille, my daughter-to-be.

As I lay there, I thought of Guille and me together as a family. The more I meditated on the idea, the more I became scared of it. Could I really adopt Guille? Would Guille be able to adapt to an outside life? Would American children accept her in school and play? Was I too old for a child of that age? Where would we live? What do I know about raising a small child? I am a single male person. Will the courts let me have a child, no less a girl child? Who would I find to take care of her? What new things would await us? These thoughts were going through my mind like crazy.

I stopped myself and said, "Bob, God has brought you this far. I am quite sure he will bring you the rest of the way. Just don't expect it to be an easy road." With this, I leaned back in bed, still fully clothed, and shut my eyes.

But soon a different set of thoughts occupied me. Yes, I could go where I wanted, spend what I wanted, and see what I wanted worldwide. I had all the power and prestige for which a man could ever hope. Yet, in reality, I had nothing. My marriage had failed. I have two children whom I did not love. In fact, I had told both of them that I never wanted to see them ever again. To be honest, the first child I just could not stand. The second I actually hated. The day she was born there was a hurricane and the day became as dark as night. Five miles from the hospital, there was an earthquake. I should have read the signs of what was just born to me, what I actually think of as Satan's child. I remember those dark days and dark thoughts. I was alone and had no one with whom to share my thoughts of life. Why go on in this purgatory? Why not end it all? When I flew, I always had a subconscious hope that the plane would crash and that would be it. To sleep and never wake up was a thought that kept me going, but I was too much of a coward to take my own life. So from day to day, I just existed.

Now all that had changed. I was alive again. I looked forward to tomorrow and the idea of seeing Guille. I was eager to accept responsibility for a child that truly loved me and I loved her in return. What a feeling it was to be alive again and not wander the earth aimlessly. I was once more a man with a loving family. It was wonderful to listen to those words, "Daddy, Daddy, Daddy," that every man yearns to hear from a child who really means it and does not just say it for a tangible reward. This little girl desired only to have her love returned. God, what a feeling of contentment it was that spread over me as I drifted off to sleep. Now I knew that beautiful tomorrows would come and I would no longer wish for death to take me as I slept.

I looked toward the sky outside my window as I slowly shut my eyes and whispered, "Thank you, God, for what you have done. I hope that I will not let you down with the new life you have given to Guille and me."

Soon the next day was upon me. I woke and realized that I was still fully dressed. That was a first for me; I was a complete mess. I got undressed and took my shower. As I stood under the warm shower, I felt bad for Guille. While I had this luxury, the children at the Casa did not. Guille had to take a shower in cold water and in a room filled with other little girls. They only had one bar of soap, which they had to share. If she wanted to use the bathroom, she even had to ask for two sheets of paper from the Madre since the Madres kept the paper rolls under lock and key.

Why was I thinking of these things now? I quickly passed it off to the new life that Madre Maria, my angel, had given to me yesterday when she said, "I will do everything in my power to bring the two of you together." I was alive again. When I opened the drapes to my room, I saw it was a beautiful day. The sun was aglow and birds were in the air. Life was all about me and it was a good life. It was a great day to be alive.

I finished up and went down for breakfast, saying, "Good morning," to everyone I met. I bet they thought I was crazy. I felt like Mr. Scrooge when he woke up on Christmas morn after spending the evening with the three spirits. At breakfast, I even talked to the waiter, something I hadn't done for years. As I sat there, I reflected on yesterday when Guille was showing the madre all that she had learned. A smile crossed my face as I put the hotcakes into my mouth. I had ordered the hotcakes in honor of Guille and her recommendation from yesterday's lunch.

Finishing, I got up and left for the Casa to inform Madre Maria that all was set for her visit. While that was reason enough to get moving, I was honest with myself. I knew I was hurrying because my daughter-to-be was waiting for me.

My car seemed to have wings as I traveled down the road. Shortly before reaching the Casa, I stopped for a few moments. I just sat in the car and gazed at it. I wondered how people could live their entire lives in such a place, with its glass-tipped walls, never to see the real world just a few feet away. The walls looked so commanding and eerie to me now. Is this where my daughter lives? Soon I would have her in my arms, for she would be waiting for me. My car seemed to start up again on its own to take me down the last stretch of road toward the huge iron gates that encased my daughter, Guille.

After I brought the car to a halt, Guille was quick to open the door and give her usual greeting. Each time, the hugs and kisses seemed to get stronger. I got out of the car with Guille at my side and asked

Estella where Madre Maria was. I also reminded myself to ask Madre Maria to do something about Estella's ever-present nature, which was becoming increasingly unnecessary, or so I thought.

She directed me to the Madres' dining room and told me that the Madre was holding breakfast for their arrival. Guille and I, hand in hand, quickly hurried to the room. As we passed the children's eating area, I kept my eyes straight ahead. My dislike of that area had become so intense that I could not even stand looking at it.

Not having the same issues, Guille waved to the girls as we passed. I could feel by the pressure of her hand as we walked to the Madres' area that she wanted to stop. However, this was something that I just could not do for Guille. To this day, I will not enter that area when the children are eating if I can possibly help it.

Once in the Madres' section, I walked swiftly to Madre Maria and then to Madre Esmeralda to greet them. Madre Maria invited Guille and me to sit beside her. In addition, we were told that Guille would now be taking all her meals with the Madres. She would no longer have to eat in the children's area. She would also get to eat what the Madres ate. I seated Guille and then myself. By now, Guille had learned not to sit unless someone held her chair. I have come to regret this introduction to manners because, to this day, she will not sit at a table unless the waiter, the manager, or I hold her chair for her.

I soon started asking how the Madre slept and all the other goodies you must discuss before you get down to business. After they were out of the way, I proceeded to tell her that five days from now we would be on our way to Boston, flying first class, and that I had asked Dr. Adolph to meet us there. All of this conversation was being translated by Guille, who felt very important. The Madre was very excited about the trip and explained it to all the other nuns at the table. She was kind of proud that Guille was doing the translation. So was I.

Estella soon was finished her meal and left the area. I thought this would be a proper time to ask Madre Maria if I might be with Guille without Estella always being there. And that's just what I did. Madre Maria was prompt to answer my request. "Yes, I can see no reason why Estella has to always be with you now." She then asked Madre Esmeralda's advice on the subject.

The Madre looked very strangely at Guille when Madre Maria was not looking and responded, "Yes, I can see no reason at all." She then looked at Guille and asked, "Guille, can you see any reason?" That question had a funny ring to it, as if it was more than a simple question.

Guille looked funny and said, "No, I can see no reason. I can speak English now and know what to say." I wondered what she meant by "know what to say." She seemed to emphasize those particular words.

Madre Maria then looked at me and said, "Good, that's settled. Madre Esmeralda, please advise Estella that she is no longer needed to accompany Guille and Senor Nielsen when he is here or taking Guille out of the Casa for the day." Madre Esmeralda nodded obediently. I then asked the Madres if I might take Guille out after today's English class. They both agreed but warned me to have her back by eight in the evening since tomorrow was a school day.

After eating, Guille was fast to get ready to go to her newfound life, "The Outside World." She said her goodbyes to the Madres and off we went. This was the first time that we were to be alone. It was a good feeling. I could now discuss what I wanted without the fear of Estella always being there and listening. Guille spoke English very well now, as previously mentioned; all I had to do was watch my American colloquialisms.

As we exited the Casa, all the girls waved goodbye to her. She powered down the window with great delight and waved. We were now on our way. As we drove, I started to ask her questions. Why was

Blanca undressed in the Madre's office when the Americans were there for adoptions? Is this the normal procedure? Who were those strange people I saw a couple of months ago crossing the yard and going up to Estella's area of the Casa? Why do the girls always look tired on Mondays? My questions were coming at her fast. It was the wrong tactic. I should have realized that the questions would scare her and not have asked so many.

She only replied, "I don't know," accompanied by staring at the floor of the car. She would also try to change the subject all the time. In the years to come, I have found out that any time that Guille does not want to discuss something bad, she will always try to change the subject. It is a sure sign that something is wrong and should be pursued in a more delicate manner later.

I finally got the message and stopped asking her those types of questions. It was obvious that she did not want to discuss my questions, not that she just didn't know the answers. I then moved on to other subjects that were related to Guille and her friends.

The first place we went was the shopping plaza. By this time, Guille loved to shop and buy things, especially dresses, other clothes, and Barbie dolls (at one point, she possessed over 150 Barbie dolls, plus all that goes with them). After that, she took me to a house that was on the way to her school. There she showed me a dog that was in a fenced-in yard. She asked if she could have a dog when she was adopted and out of the Casa.

"Of course, you can. Any kind you want. I will buy you a book of all the kinds of dogs there are. Then you can just pick one and Daddy will get that kind for you."

She gave me a big hug and said, "Daddy, I love you so."

The outing went by swiftly and soon we returned to the hotel for supper. Guille ordered cherries with her meal. She had taken a liking to cherries with the stems on them. We always had to have them anywhere we went. The hotel put in an extra stock just for her so whenever we ate, there were always cherries on the table. When the supper was over, I returned her to the Casa. It was an early night because tomorrow was the trip to Boston.

Guille did want me to go and was prompt to tell me so. She was afraid that I would not return. While still in the car, she put her arms around me and looked up at me with the most sorrowful face I ever saw. "Daddy, you will come back? You will not ever leave me? I love you so. Promise you will come back, promise!" As she was saying those things, her eyes were full of tears. She had never acted like this when Estella was with us. This was something new and it took me back.

I responded, "Guille, there is nothing in this world that would or could keep me from coming back to you. You will soon be my daughter. How could a father leave his daughter?"

Boy, was that the wrong thing to say, as it gave her a punch line that floored me. I should have been smart enough to realize what the answer would be to that question. I no sooner got the question out of my mouth when the earth-shaking response came with a colossal flow of tears, "My other Daddy did, so why not you?"

Try to think of a quick answer to that little jewel. I had to reply quickly or else she would be the winner. I replied, "Guille, all daddies are not the same. I did not know your real daddy but I do know me, and I will return. That I promise not only to you but to God also." I put my arms around her and held her tightly as I rocked her back and forth in my arms. We must have been there for 15 minutes before I could calm her down. As soon as she was content, I dried her eyes and walked her to the courtyard outside of her dormitory. As we approached the hall leading to the dormitory, the giant Felipe stepped out and blocked my path. Upon seeing who it was, he stepped aside and retreated to his room.

I said good night to Guille at the door of the dormitory and told her that I would be back in four days. She kissed me and turned to enter the room. Then she ran back once more and kissed me again before returning to the door. I could see some of the girls waiting for her, waiting to hear what she did today in the big and wonderful world outside the high, sharp walls of their diminutive one.

By the time I got back to the hotel, it was late so I went right to bed. Along with the planned Boston trip in a few days, I had another business trip. I was scheduled to fly to India in the morning. It was going to be an exhausting week.

While in India, I had a little time on my hands. I always wanted to go to Tibet, so I took the opportunity. Once there, I wandered around the marketplace. That was one of my favorite pastimes when I traveled. I liked to inspect the culture of the country in which I was a guest. You will always find the real culture of a country in their market place.

As I strolled around, I found a shop off the beaten track that handled jade. It was a religious order of Tibetan monks who could sculpt jade into any animal that you so desired within 24 hours. I thought Guille might like an elephant carving on a gold chain to put around her neck, along with some new little diamond earrings.

I wanted the elephant to have its trunk held high. An elephant carving with its trunk held up is a sign of good luck, or so the superstition goes. You need that especially if the elephant is carved from jade, according to the story that accompanies jade when you buy it.

This shop had white jade, which I had never seen before this trip. I thought it was beautiful so I ordered an elephant carving made of white jade. One of the monks said, "If the person who wears it is warm-hearted, then in a couple of years, the stone will turn from white to blue."

I returned the next day and it was ready. It was beautiful. The monk had even slipped it on a gold chain for me. I had never seen anything so beautiful. It was a masterpiece of craftsmanship. I could hardly wait to give it to Guille.

That evening, I flew to Boston to insure that everything was set for the Madres' trip. The couple of days that I was there were very rewarding. I had everything arranged to my satisfaction. Then I was on my way back to the hotel in Tijuana.

The morning after I returned, I was at the Casa bright and early. The Madres and Estella were ready for their trip to Boston. Guille was standing beside them waiting to say goodbye to me. She did not look happy about the upcoming trip.

I stepped out of the car and said, "Guille, I have something for you." I then took the carving of the elephant and placed it around her neck, along with replacing her old earrings with the new diamond ones. After giving her the jewelry, I continued, "Guille, this elephant with his trunk held high is a sign of good luck. Wear it always and good luck will always be yours."

She lifted her hand, looked at it, and smiled brightly. She finally replied, "Oh, Daddy, I will never ever take it off. I love you." As the Madres and Estella piled into the car, Guille gave me a big hug and whispered in my ear, "Don't forget; you promised to return."

I smiled and rejoined, "I leave my heart with you here. Consequently, I must return." She gave me one more massive embrace before I had to get into the car. I waved goodbye to Guille through the open car window and then we were on our way to Boston.

We all arrived in Boston without much mishap. I rented a car and we went straight to the hotel. Upon arrival, the sisters from the school and Dr. Adolph were waiting for us. They invited the Madres to stay at their convent since one of the sisters spoke Spanish. I thought that a very good idea. This would give them time to talk and maybe help to convince the Madres that computers should be placed in the Casa. It turned out to work.

Doc, Estella, and I then headed to our hotel. Estella retired, claiming that she was tired from the trip. This was fine by me since it gave Dr. Adolph and me time to talk at the bar so I could fill him in on what was really happening. I did not have that much time on the phone when I discussed this trip with him. Soon Doc was filled in and agreed that I was on the right track. We decided to meet for breakfast the next morning and then go to the convent to pick up the sisters and Madres. I phoned Estella's room to tell her of the plans and she agreed.

The next morning after breakfast, we all proceeded to the convent to meet the nuns. After a short drive, we were at the school. Sister explained she had a long talk with the Madres last night and they were primed for what they were about to see today. Upon entering the school, we went to the computer room and spoke with the sister in charge. Soon the children arrived and the Madres were introduced. When the class started, all the visitors paid close attention. Class after class passed and the Madres never got bored. They enjoyed everything about it. They asked the children many questions through the translation of either Estella or Doc. After the class, the sisters brought everyone to the auditorium were the Sister Superior had arranged for a little show on their behalf. The Madres enjoyed that immensely. They clapped with great enthusiasm when it was over. The children that participated were very pleased at such a reception.

I took everyone to the best restaurant in the area to top off the day. That was my way of thanking the sisters for their time and effort.

Moreover, it gave me an opportunity to ask Madre Maria if she was convinced that it was okay to put computers in her school.

She looked at me and asked, "How come they are not in there now?" We all laughed.

I said, "I did one better; I have already ordered them so by the time you get back, they will be there. I hoped that you would like them and took a chance on you being as smart as I thought you were." We all laughed again and went on to eat a wonderful dinner.

The next morning we were on our way back to Mexico and the Casa after saying goodbye to Doc. He was too busy to return with us then, although he did plan on coming to the Casa to visit the Madre and Guille that Saturday.

Madre Maria said, "I will not be there; however, any time you want to visit me in Mexico City, I would be honored."

Upon returning to the Casa, guess who was past the gates and running up the road with excitement? The elephant that now hung around her neck swung from side to side as she ran. The little diamond earrings sparkled in the sunlight.

I stopped the car in the middle of the road and Guille opened the car door and jumped into my lap. She hugged me with all her might and kept screaming, "Daddy, Daddy, Daddy, you did come back like you promised! You did! You did! I love you so." She then embraced both Madres and returned quickly to my side, holding my hand very tightly.

Madre Esmeralda did not like the scene too much but Madre Maria leaned over to me and said, "You are a lucky man to have so much love given to you. Treat it well in the years to come." Then she leaned back with a big smile on her face.

Madre Esmeralda's eyes flashed angrily at Guille when Madre Maria was not looking. Guille saw this and quickly let go of my hand in fear. However, Madre Maria did catch the exchange after all and looked at Esmeralda with a look of "Wait until I get you back to the Casa. That child did not warrant such a look."

Standing by the gates as we drove past them was Jesus. He said, "Bob, I tried to stop her but I don't think a team of wild horses could have held her back."

Before I could reply, Madre Maria answered for me. "Blessed Jesus, it was a wonderful sight and you need not excuse yourself. If I was here, I would have suggested the child do just what she did. There's too much love in that child to be stifled now. To do so would cause great injury to her psychologically." Madre Maria never ceased to amaze me with her understanding.

After we parked the car and got out, Jesus said, "The computers are here. Do we use them or return them?"

With a look of pleasure, I turned to Madre Maria. She once more answered for me, "We use them." We all smiled and went to find a place to install them.

"I thought the classroom that you were using for the English class would work well," Jesus pronounced. We all agreed.

Guille was dying to see what was in all those boxes and could hardly wait to open them. Laughing at her, I said, "Tomorrow we start, not today. It is late now and we have to get some sleep. Don't worry; we will be back tomorrow."

She accepted my response and my goodbyes. Then she left for her sleeping quarters with Madre Maria, who was going to tuck the little girl in bed. As we left, Guille turned and waved goodbye with her free hand.

Success is mine, I thought, as I drove back to the hotel with Jesus. I was smiling ear to ear. Seeing my smile, Jesus said, "Tell me about the trip."

I explained to Jesus what had happened in Boston. He was all ears. This project by now had become somewhat important to him, as he, like me, had become very concerned about the children in the Casa. Even with his short time there, he said, "I have come to enjoy being with those children. They have something about them that draws you to them. Maybe it is because they appear to be so helpless, without parents or anyone to be concerned about them. I do not know what it is, but there is something about that place. It just makes you want to help. When you all were in Boston, I kept thinking of the Casa and the children, even while I was in Mexicali. It has become a haunting occurrence to me."

I exclaimed, "The feeling is mutual. Furthermore, Doc has the same mentality."

We arrived at the hotel and quickly went to the bar. I had been thinking of something as we were driving back and I wanted to discuss it with Jesus. After we were seated and our drinks were in hand, I remarked to Jesus, "Jesus, you seem as interested as I am in these children. I was thinking that if you could find the time to be the director of the Casa's computer school, it would be great. You have the teaching and director experience from the prekindergarten that you run in Mexicali. Plus, you want to learn more about working with computers.

"I would donate computers to your school in Mexicali after we are finished here in the Casa if you, in turn, run the school in the Casa. You could obtain teachers for the Casa right here in Tijuana, from the university. Here they have a computer science course plus a philosophy course. It would be ideal. You told me earlier that you have taught there, so you have all the 'ins' it needs to obtain the proper teachers. We could pay them, along with them receiving the knowledge of computer instructing."

Jesus looked at me and said, "I was hoping you would say just that and have already talked to the university here in Tijuana. They are all for it. All I need to do is to pick the students for the teachers."

During my years that I was to spend with him, Jesus always seemed to have the ability to read my mind. "Good," I answered, "Let's get going. This way, I can turn the entire thing over to you and still be here as a consultant."

I never dreamt I would do such a thing as to turn one of my projects over to someone else. Nevertheless, here I was doing it. It was a decision that was to play an important part in my future. Yes, my main objective of this move was to be able to spend more time with Guille without worrying about the school's progress. The time spent with Guille would insure that everything I had perceived in our relationship was genuine. I did not want to make a hasty decision about the adoption, as it was such an important step in both our lives. It was better to be sure of our feelings now rather than when it was too late.

I stated, "Okay, then it's settled. You run the school here and I will be your consultant. We will start tomorrow." We both stood up and clinked our glasses together in salute to the agreement we had just reached. In closing, I uttered, "I'm off to bed. Tomorrow will be a big day."

The next day was Saturday. During the morning, Jesus, Guille, and I were busy unwrapping computers in the classroom and setting them up. Guille and I made plans to stop by early afternoon so we could meet Doc at the hotel. This was the day that Doc was supposed to visit us for the weekend.

Unpacking with Guille was an interesting experience. The computers were nestled in protective bubble wrap, which soon became Guille's favorite toy. She loved to pop the bubbles with her fingers, especially in my ears when I was not looking.

She was also amazed by the computers. She was constantly asking what this was and what that was as we were unpacking them. Her eyes were wide with absolute disbelief of what she saw as we installed them. When we first turned them on to test them, she was terrified, because she thought they were possessed by the devil. Soon we convinced her to use the keyboard. After that, you could not get her away from them unless you turned off the power.

The other girls were not allowed in the room until we were finished with the installation. This made Guille a person of importance in the Casa, as all the other girls in the evening would ask her what was going on in that room. She played the situation for all it was worth. She was important now, and boy, did she know it. She played it for all it was worth.

Over the next couple of weeks, we were very busy unpacking and I was still teaching the English classes. Jesus was doing the same thing, along with the additional job of rounding up teachers for the project. Guille was all over the place helping, if you could call popping bubbles "helping."

CHAPTER EIGHTEEN

DOC ARRIVES AT THE CASA AND DOCTORS ARE NEEDED FOR GUILLE

The time came for Guille and me to stop unpacking and meet Doc at the hotel. Guille did not want to go, as she was having too much fun. She finally agreed but only after I told her she could take some of the bubble wrap with us.

Upon reaching the hotel, I was half-deaf from all the popping. We got out of the car and went into the lobby. Doc was not there yet. This gave Guille time to do one of her favorite pastimes, going up and down in the elevator. There were two elevators in the hotel. Guille would go up one and come down in the other. While she did this, I sat in the lobby and waited. Soon I saw an airport taxi driving up to the entrance of the hotel. I could see that Doc was in it. About the same time, Guille was getting off one elevator and starting to get on the other one.

"Guille," I yelled, "Doc is here."

She stopped and ran over to the entrance. She stood there with a wild and happy look on her face. When Doc got out of the taxi, Guille was all over him with her hugs and kisses.

Doc picked her up in his arms and said, "My, don't you look pretty, little lady," in English.

Without hesitation, Guille replied, also in English, "Thank you, I am so happy to see you again." Then she gave him another big hug and he held her a little tighter. I don't think he could put her down now even if he wanted; she was holding so tightly with her arms and her legs.

Still holding her, Doc said, "Bob, I see what you meant. She speaks English very well now. Likewise, she replies in English faster than normal for a child who has just learned a foreign tongue. You have done wonders with her."

"Thank you," I returned. "The credit goes to her. She is a good student. Even the Madres are surprised at her rapid understanding. Well, if you can untangle yourself from her, let's go inside and have some lunch. You must be hungry."

Doc tried to put her down but was unable. She had him in almost a death grip. Thus, the three of us proceeded into the dining room, Guille still wrapped in Doc's arms.

The manager said something to Guille as we entered. This was after Doc had to stop to let Guille give him the customary kiss.

Guille quickly replied, "Tres, por favor," and then gave him a laugh and a big smile. He laughed and smiled too. I asked Doc what was said as it was all spoken in Spanish.

Doc answered, "He asked Guille if the table would be for two or for three. Guille replied, 'Three, please.' The manager was being funny because Guille is in my arms. If she would she be sitting in my lap throughout lunch, we would not need a chair for her."

I smiled and remarked, "Lucky for you. She normally sits in my lap when we eat here. I have now become accustomed to it. Believe me; it took time." Doc smiled and we proceeded to our table for three.

Upon arriving there, Doc spoke to Guille in English. "Young lady, I would like to hold you all day if there were no one here. However, proper little ladies do not do this in public as they eat. See that other little girl sitting over there? She's on a chair. How about you doing the same?"

With that, Guille untangled herself from Doc and took her seat at the table, placing her feet under her on the chair as usual. She was so small that this was the only way she could see over the table. It was never more obvious to me than that moment why Doc was the leading child psychologist in America. He always handled situations with Guille with great understanding and concern.

The waiter came and we ordered, first Doc and then Guille. Guille ordered for me now that she knew what I liked. It was more than just humoring her since I could not yet read the Spanish menus. Doc watched as this ordering process took place. He turned to me and said, "You have quite a young lady here. She has changed so much since the last time I saw her. It is beyond belief. It only seems like yesterday that the both of you met. I can see by the way she looks at you that she loves you very much."

Guille was sitting next to me. I knew she wanted to get in my lap. If it was not for Doc's earlier comment, I was quite sure that is where she would be. Since she was not able to do so, she contrived a new "thing." She would sit there and hold my hand on the table while she looked around the room. She specifically watched the little girl to whom Doc had pointed. She was watching her with great attention just to see what she was doing. Then she would mimic it at our table.

As we waited for the food, Doc asked all sorts of questions about the two of us. He also spoke to Guille in English. Guille soon became bored with the conversation so she begged to ride the elevators as we talked and waited for the food.

I answered, "Sure, have fun, but every so often come back and see if we are ready to eat." She agreed and off she went. The hotel was very good about her doing that and never said anything about it. They liked her very much.

We now spoke about Madre Maria's permission to adopt Guille. Likewise, how I should go about it. Doc told me that I could count on his support as he thought I would be a good father for Guille and it was quite obvious that Guille wanted me as a father. He further added that now that she would be my responsibility, I should have a dentist and a physician examine her as soon as possible. He advised me that her teeth were in very bad condition. In addition, she was way too thin. He thought she must be loaded with parasites, as most Mexican children are.

After volunteering to inquire at the hotel desk of the names of two good doctors, one a dentist and the other a physician, he then continued, "Bob, what's really going on? You seemed a little upset when I spoke to you last week on the phone."

"Doc," I started, "do you remember what you said the last time you were here? Something about there being more than meets the eye going on in that Casa?"

"Yes," he responded.

"Well, the past couple of months since I have had the run of the Casa, I have seen some strange sights. I've seen the children abused, unexplained men, tired little girls on Monday, and other things."

Doc interrupted me, "Bob, I thought that would be the problem when I spoke to you on the phone. Yes, I tried to warn you the last time I saw you that you might see things like that. I expect as time goes by you will see worse. However, that warning was before you had a potential daughter in the Casa. I would now advise you to say nothing to anyone about anything you see until you get Guille out of there. If you cause trouble, Madre Esmeralda will ask you to leave and prevent you from adopting Guille. If you want and love that child, for God's sake, do not say anything to anyone, especially to me, as my code of ethics designate that I must report such incidents to the proper authorities. My suggestion is to get Guille out of there as fast as possible first. Then do what you think is best. Adoption is a long and hard road. I do not think they will do anything to Guille now that you are her protector and you donate rather heavily to the Casa."

I then added, "I have tried to ask Guille about some of the things I have seen and heard when we were alone but she wouldn't answer me."

"Good for her," he responded. "She's got more brains than you. She knows what would happen to her if you were to repeat anything that she said. Yes, she loves you very much. Trusting you, however, is a different story. It could take years before she will have enough trust to tell you what was going on there when you ask. She will then only tell you after she is absolutely sure that she will not be returned to the Casa. Even then, she might not say anything as it would be too embarrassing to have you think that she did those things."

Doc looked thoughtful and continued. "If she were to return after she told you, I'm quite sure it would spell her doom. She knows that, so don't push the subject with her. Let it drop for now. There's time for those questions later on if you want to pursue them. Right now, your main thought should be to have her teeth and physical condition taken care while you pursue the adoption. Enjoy her; don't make her afraid of seeing you because you will ask questions that she cannot answer now. I'm sure that when she is ready, she will do so. However, she will only tell you when she is ready, not now.

I know it may seem that I'm overreacting about this, but please, do as I say or else you will lose that child. That would be a disaster for both you and her. Take my advice under consideration, please."

I agreed with him and thanked him. I also felt kind of stupid for not realizing already what he had just said. However, he did put my mind at ease when he had mentioned that Guille would probably be safe now that I was her protector and donated to the Casa. I was still worried for the other girls, but my main concern right now was Guille.

I was sure something awful was going on in that place, but I did not want them to happen to Guille anymore. If my presence and money protected her, then I could put aside my fears. I would have to keep an eye open for anything that might seem strange with Guille and keep them shut for the rest of the girls. For the time being.

Lunch came just as Doc had finished his harangue. I went to the lobby to collect Guille, who by this time had pushed all the buttons in both elevators. She was standing there enjoying every minute of it. "Guille," I called out, "'it's time to eat. Please come and sit down." She promptly obliged and we went back to the dining room hand in hand. We had an enjoyable lunch with good food and a wonderful conversation. Doc complimented Guille on her table manners and the usage of her silverware. That made Guille very proud.

After lunch, we called the two recommended doctors we needed for Guille. Doc did the speaking. When he got off the phone, Doc announced that he had made appointments for today, one right now and the other in an hour. Without much time, we hurried on our way.

The dentist was the first stop. We arrived in his office and were quickly ushered into the examining room. Guille had never been in one of these places so the questions started. What was this? What was that? I do not know who was examining whom, Guille or the dentist. Upon completing the exam and answering ten thousand more questions from Guille, the dentist announced, "Two teeth need to be pulled and braces should be applied to her teeth as soon as possible." I arranged to have them done the following week.

Once finished there, we went to the other doctor. This doctor was to check on her physical health and why she was so thin. Upon arriving at the office, a young man greeted us. As we explained what we wanted, Guille was all ears, particularly the part where she was going to be examined. This did not sit too well with her since she had to get undressed down to her panties.

We clarified that only she and the doctor would be in the room in an attempt to put her at ease. Even that did not quell her fears. No way could any of us talk her into getting undressed. Finally, Doc negotiated a compromise. She would be allowed to keep not only her panties but also her undershirt. This took time to accomplish. She finally agreed to do it but you could see on her face that she did not like it.

Guille and the doctor went into the examining room. The walls of the room were not all the way to the ceiling so while she was in there, Doc and I could hear some of what was said. It went something like this, "Guille, please take your skirt off. Guille, you have to put your arms down. Guille, please take your hand away from there. I won't touch you there if you don't want me to. Guille, just lift the shirt up a little more so I can feel your stomach."

This type of conversation went on through the entire examination. Doc and I were both outside shaking our heads. Guille was really making that doctor practice his patience, along with his medical degree. Finally, they came out and Guille was clearly angry. She quickly ran to me and grasped my hand while glaring at the doctor.

Although he had not been able to examine her internally, the doctor said that, other than her having rickets and being extremely thin, she was in pretty good health. He also inquired if she had ever been to a doctor's office. He suspected, as Doc did, that she was loaded with parasites. He gave me three tubes and told me to have her place her stool in them each morning for three days. He then gave me the address of a place to bring them to be examined for any parasites.

We agreed and off we went back to the Casa. Doc wanted to see the Madre and the new computer room. He was also anxious to see and speak to Jesus, who was still there unpacking and installing computers. Guille was all for that. She wanted to get more bubble wrap.

CHAPTER NINETEEN

GUILLE GOES TO PRIVATE SCHOOL

Doc, Guille, and I arrived at the Casa and went straight to find Madre Esmeralda. We wanted to tell her about Guille's doctor visits. Doc also wanted to visit with the Madre. The Madre was happy to see Doc again and soon was talking in rapid-fire Spanish with him. I asked to be excused so Guille and I could see what Jesus was doing. I told Doc that we would be up in the computer room. Doc and the Madre waved us off so we went to find Jesus.

Jesus was working hard on the computer installations when we arrived. Guille quickly rounded up every piece of bubble wrap. I asked, "How are things going?"

Jesus replied, "Slow but sure." We talked and Guille popped. Soon the Madre and Doc arrived. Doc advised me that they had spoken more about the dentist and the stool samples and that the Madre agreed to supply them to me each morning for three days. We all talked while Guille popped her bubble wrap, though after a few minutes the Madre asked her to do it outside in the hall. As we spoke, the Madre examined the already installed computers with great delight. I think that she was happy with them now, especially since she was the only person in all of Mexico that would have such a set up.

I introduced Doc to Jesus and they seemed to get along with each other very well. I was not positive because they were speaking

Spanish, so I asked Guille, who was listening in on the conversation. She nodded her head to imply that they were getting along fine.

After a while, we all sat down and changed the topic to Guille and her outside schooling. The consensus was that she should be signed up for private school, as we had agreed to a long time ago. I agreed to do so after Doc left. When we finished our discussion about Guille's schooling, Doc asked the Madre if Guille could accompany us on an outing the next day.

The Madre agreed.

The next day Guille, Doc, and I spent all day just driving around Tijuana to look at the sights and buy things for Guille. We had a marvelous time. She did her happy little hop skip and jump most of the day, much to our amusement.

On Sunday evening, Doc was to leave but Guille did not want to let him go. She only did so after he swore to God that he would be her tío, her uncle, and that he would return. Finally, I was able to drive Doc to the airport.

Upon leaving, he reminded me once more not to get mixed up in the inner workings of the Casa. He then commented on Guille's advanced English skills, explaining that her thinking in English, while a very unusual occurrence, does occasionally happen if a child wants to communicate badly enough. He also added that he liked Jesus very much and thought he made a great addition to the team.

I thanked Doc for his time and advice and then watched him leave. Afterwards, I drove back to the hotel and went to bed. After all, the next day was to be spent with Guille again and I wanted to be rested. She could really wear you down. She was so full of life now that she had someone who cared for her.

Thus the days passed, and Jesus worked very hard getting the classroom set up. Eventually, everything was ready and classes began.

I stayed with them for about an hour each day. The rest of the time was spent with Guille exploring and doing things outside the great walls of the Casa. Guille learned to roller skate, eat hot dogs and hamburgers, and ice skate. She learned about movies, water fountains, how to behave and eat in fine restaurants, and many more things too numerous to mention. She was eight now; yet, in our world, she had essentially just been born and had to be taught everything a normal child is exposed to from infancy, things that you and our children take for everyday occurrences.

One fact that astounded me was that Guille did not know what year it was or even what a year was in general. In addition, she did not know what a day was, let alone the days of the week or what day it was. Her only awareness of time was based on the sun or if she had to go to school. When people referred to a day or night, Guille only knew sunup or sundown. For days, there were only school days and no school days, not Saturday, Sunday, or vacation days. Vacation days were always a mystery to her. They did not happen during the usual time she did not go to school (i.e., Saturday and Sunday), so instead, she accepted them as "funny" days. Nor did she know about summer recess from school, only that this was the time she just worked at the Casa all day rather than go to school. It just happened; she did not know why. Her calendar was the amount of time that she did work inside or outside the Casa. When I showed her a calendar, she asked all sorts of questions about it. She did not know such a thing even existed. Guille and I spent much time learning about time and calendar details.

And boy, does she know what vacations, weekends, and summer recesses are now. She has two calendars in her room and constantly refers to them each day. Her birthday is always the first entry placed on each new calendar.

We soon got the results of her stool sample. As we'd thought, she had every kind of parasite that you could imagine and then some. The doctor gave her a load of medicine to get rid of them. Not long after, she started to put on weight. She was no longer that skinny little girl. Likewise, her smile improved after her teeth were pulled and she got braces. She was so proud of those braces. She would show everyone whom she met her metal teeth.

The days flew by faster and faster. We had become very close to each other. We could almost read each other's minds; that's how close we were. We laughed and made plans for the future. She was always asking how families lived and what they did. We were becoming a father and daughter.

Much of the time was passed by Guille showing me her drawings. She loved to draw. All of her pictures were that of a family and the home in which they lived. We had so much fun with each other. It was a world that neither of us had ever known, as I never spent any time with my other children due to the trouble my wives would cause if I wanted to see them.

The project at the school was now very much in the back seat for me. With the world coming alive for Guille and me, I did not have much time for the school. Jesus was almost running it completely by himself anyway. And, might I add, doing a wonderful job.

By this time, Guille was speaking perfect English. In addition, her adaptation to the computer was very good. She was excelling in her methods of using it, much faster than the other girls were. I imagine that the "want" philosophy was present in that endeavor as well.

When her spring break approached, I asked the Madre if it was a good time to transfer Guille to private school. She agreed and suggested a Catholic school in Tijuana. But I had heard of a much better school in Tijuana so I suggested that school to the Madre. At that suggestion, her eyes flashed and she became quite upset. The only comment she made to my suggestion was that was where all the rich children go and it was not run by nuns.

Knowing the Madre very well by this time, I apologized and did not pursue the conversation of that school any further. When she offered to make the arrangements for Guille, I replied, "I can do it."

With her permission, I went to the school the Madre had suggested. The name of the school was El Progresso. By this time, I knew the streets of Tijuana so after I received the address, I thought it would be easy to find. I cheerfully went to enroll Guille in the next semester.

Knowing the streets of Tijuana wound up being no help at all. I promptly got lost and had to ask a taxicab to lead me there. Guille was learning English very fast. I, on the other hand, was learning Spanish very slowly. However, by this time, I could at least get my point across in Spanish. It took time, but I was able to ask the taxi driver for help.

Soon I was at the gates of a fine-looking school. I parked my car, got out, and walked into the front office. Upon arriving and speaking to the secretary, I discovered that almost no one spoke English, only one teacher, and she was busy in class. I, therefore, in my poor Spanish, stated that I would wait until the English-speaking teacher was finished with her class. I left my name and card with the secretary before going out into the hall to sit.

An hour later, a woman who was not a nun came up to me as I sat waiting in the hallway. She asked, "Are you Dr. Nielsen?"

"Yes," I answered very politely as I rose to shake her hand.

"Mrs. Gomez, the secretary, said you were speaking some strange language and she thought it might be English. Then you said something in Spanish that she did not understand. Is there anything that I might help you with? I am the English teacher here in the school."

She spoke English poorly, coupled with a heavy Spanish accent. I had a hard time understanding her. After exaggerating a look of not understanding, she repeated it. I took a guess that she was going to translate for me when I spoke to the director. For the first time in a while, I wished that I had Estella with me.

I took a chance and said in simple English that I wanted to speak to the director about enrolling a child in the school. She ushered me into a small office similar to the one that Madre Esmeralda had at the Casa. Before long, both she and I were standing in front of Madre Maria Elizabeth, the director, as the small sign on the desk read.

I requested Mrs. Gomez to ask the Madre what I had to do to get Guille into the school. Mrs. Gomez spoke to her for a while in Spanish. I assume that most of the conversation was the usual courtesies. After their discussion, Mrs. Gomez turned me and said, "There is no more room in the school and it is booked for the next three years." She then added, "The Madre is very sorry but she cannot accommodate the girl at this time. Maybe in four years from now."

I thanked her and left. I was able to find my way back to the Casa without the help of the taxi. Upon arriving there, I told the Madre that Guille could not go to her selected school. I did not really fight for it although I did not tell that to the Madre. I hoped that it would force the Madre to let me look into the school to which I really wanted to send Guille, "the rich school," as the Madre referred to it.

The Madre inquired, "Did you mention that Guille was from the Casa and I was the Madre who sent you there?"

"No, I did not think it was necessary."

The Madre then offered to try to get Guille into the school. When I agreed, she said that she would speak with the director at the school the next morning.

The following morning, the Madre met me, along with Guille, at my parking space in the Casa as I arrived. Guille, as usual, opened the door and pounced on me. "Daddy, Daddy, the Madre told me I was going to El Progresso school. Is that true?"

I looked at the Madre and she was all smiles. A sort of smile that said, "If you let me do these things, you will have no problems." I told Guille to ask the Madre how she was able to get around the school being full. Following a barrage of Spanish between the two of them, the answer came back from Guille. It went something like this, "The Madre said all she did was call Madre Director after you left yesterday and explained it was she, Madre Esmeralda, who desired the school for me.

"That's all that was needed to be said and it was done. It only took a few minutes to accomplish. The director thought I was an American child and the school is for Mexican children. Likewise, she did not know that it was Madre Esmeralda who wanted me to go there." Guille impressed upon me that the main thing that got her into the school was that Madre Esmeralda wanted it to take place. This was not the first time something like this happened. The Madre was very proud of the power that she had in Tijuana and loved to show it to me at every opportunity.

I had often spoken to Guille about going to a private school. She was looking forward to it. Her present public school was in a part of the town where the children had to walk about an hour to get there because the Mexican public school districts had no buses. That part of town was very poor and dangerous. American tourists would not dare to travel there. The windows of the public school were broken and the courtyard was strewn with debris and rubbish. It looked like it had not been cleaned in years. Outside the school at quitting time, one could even see Mexican pimps waiting for their girls.

The Mexican school system required all children to wear uniforms regardless if they went to a private or public school. Uniforms of this particular school were red and white, red pants or skirts and white blouses. The white was always hard to see since they were so dirty most of the time. Soap is expensive in Mexico and not to be wasted on things like school uniforms. I had seen those dirty uniforms many times, as I picked Guille up after school. I did this so she would not have to make that long hike back to the Casa.

When I did pick her up, it was sight to behold. She made quite a display of getting into the car, making sure that the girls and boys in the school saw her. These times she did not rush into the car, as she did when I went to the Casa; instead, slowly, ever so slowly, she would open the door, look around, and wave to the other children not from the Casa. By the time that she was in the car, a great many of the children had gathered around the car and Guille was showing them the power seats, windows, side mirrors, radio/tape player, and all other interesting gadgets inside her daddy's car. It also gave her an excuse to introduce me as her new father-to-be, her daddy. She was so proud of that fact and they were always the first words out of her mouth when I met any of her friends. She would introduce me and then hug me real tight.

She had often told me that her friends and the other children did not believe anyone would adopt such a thin and sickly girl as a daughter. Therefore, when the opportunity presented itself, she made no bones about taking advantage of the situation to introduce me. Whenever I told her in advance that I was to pick her up from school, there were always other children there waiting with her. She made sure of that by telling every one at school that her daddy was coming to pick her up.

She had also told them that she was going to attend a private school soon and wanted me to tell them as well. She wanted to prove that it was the truth and she was not just making up a story. The idea of a private school had to be explained to these children. They did not know what it meant nor did they know that these schools were in Tijuana. They all thought the only school in Tijuana was the one that they attended. I was dying to show her my preferred school, as that was the one I had seen from both the front and the inside.

I had not seen El Progresso until yesterday. And that was only really from the outside and the office area. I still had not seen the inside yet. This I was hoping to do soon. The Madre had promised me that she would take me back there this afternoon, along with Guille, to enroll her and pay the tuition.

As part of the private school tuition, a school bus would pick up Guille at the gates of the Casa and bring her to and from school. I had explained that to Guille when I told her about this new private school she would attend. She was amazed by the idea. To ride in a bus instead of walking to school was unthinkable. Guille had heard about such things from me but she had never seen one. Guille was really looking forward to that school bus.

Soon it was noon and the Madre, Guille, and I were in the car heading toward Guille's new school. Guille, as always, was playing with her toys, the power windows and seats. Up and down they went. I had often thought that if the car manufacturer wanted a testimony on window reliability, Guille could be the one to supply them with it. If they did not break under her usage, then they would never break for anyone else.

It didn't take long before we were at the front gates of Guille's new school. The director was there to greet us. This was not a coincidence. Madre Esmeralda had called prior to us leaving the Casa to make sure she would be there to greet us with all the respect that Madre Esmeralda had come to demand in Tijuana. Upon arriving, the women embraced and kissed each other softly on the cheek. Guille also kissed the director on the cheek, as not to do so would be an insult in Mexico to anyone whom a little girl was introduced, regardless if the child did not previously know him or her. Children must do this upon arriving or leaving the presence of any important man or woman.

Greetings were exchanged and soon we were on our way into the inner yard of the school. The inside consisted of a great yard enclosed by a high brick wall. Along the walls were the classrooms on two floors. The yard is a typical thing for a Mexican school, as the children are constantly marching to and from their classes and are on parade during recess. The marching is a requirement of the Mexican government. All schools teach the same subjects and have the same form of marching to and from classes. I have enjoyed watching this as the years went by in Mexico. It is a very pretty sight to watch.

We all inspected the classes and Guille spoke with some of the girls. There were no boys to speak to, since it was an all-girls school. She seemed to hit it off quite well with them. I was worried she would not do so because of being from the Casa. Mexican children are taught not to associate with such children. It is not considered proper because of their standing in the community. Mexicans are quite class conscious.

After we decided to send Guille to the school, I had a long talk with her about not being ashamed because she was an orphan. "After all, I picked you. I did not have to take what was given, as other parents have to do when they have a baby. Therefore, you are something special and do not ever forget it." I had told her this just in case the children went after her on that subject. There are times when children can be cruel. Even though I was worried about that, I hoped it would not arise since Guille had developed quite a bit of charm when it came to both adults and children of her own age.

As the Madre and I inspected the school, Guille went off and played with the other girls who were there. She even made a friend, a young lady named Veronica. She introduced us to her, me as her daddy and Madre Esmeralda as the Casa's Madre.

After the inspection, we went to the director's office to sign Guille up for the next term. When that was all finished, we had to round up Guille so she could get her new uniforms. The school colors here were blue and white. As Guille was trying them on, you could see how proud she was. She could hardly wait to take them back to the Casa to show all the other girls.

My thoughts drifted back to my first sighting of Guille. How thin, frail, and downtrodden she had been. Yet, now she stood there with an expression of self-confidence and a proud feeling that looked to say "At last, I am someone to be respected and admired."

Orphans in Mexico are spit on by the other children sometimes when they are out in public. This is to show them their position in society. The orphan children have come to expect this sort of treatment and soon get used to it. Therefore, they very seldom enjoy venturing far from the orphanage.

But no longer did Guille hold her head low and look towards the ground. She carried it quite high. The only exception to that was when she was in the presence of a Madre from the Casa. I was so proud of her. She stood there trying on uniforms with a wild look of happiness that only a child seems able to muster.

The months that followed in that school were marvelous for Guille. She soon made many friends. Veronica was always her best friend and I was to take her out many times with Guille when we went roller skating, shopping, and on other adventures. Guille often invited her friends from school to come with us when we went anywhere like that. Guille was very proud to have friends like them.

Although friends with these new girls, she still remained close with the girls at the Casa. I thought a problem might arise there due to jealousy on the part of the other girls in the Casa, but it never seemed to materialize. They were happy for Guille. This also gave them hope that someday this might happen for them. Likewise, they were learning about the world outside from Guille, as she was always telling them what she had discovered every time we came back from a venture outside. The Casa girls really looked forward to these events. They kept Guille up until all hours telling them about this and that.

Guille was now well-accepted in school by both the students and the teachers. She had high grades too. I still picked her up from school when I could. Although she liked the school bus, she preferred me picking her up so she could then show her new young friends the car. She would come running into my arms with a big kiss and hug with the same drama as she did at the public school.

She liked the school very much. She particularly liked the idea of being with girls who had money and things of value, not hand-me-downs like those that she used to wear. She once thought that everyone else in the world wore the same things. She was so happy with her newfound "normal" world.

CHAPTER TWENTY

GUILLE'S FIRST BIRTHDAY AND HER PAST LIFE

Months flew by like days. The classes at the Casa were well established and Jesus was doing a wonderful job. The children were learning at a rapid rate; we were all very proud of them. In the morning after their chores at the Casa were finished, they would line up outside the door of the school and wait until we opened up the doors. Then they would all run in to get the computer of their choice; being children, they had favorites. The teachers were also learning a lot about this new way of education and how culture causes a great difference in teaching methods.

Guille was the leader in these classes. She was excelling beyond our fondest dreams, far better than any child I had ever taught in America. In addition, she was acquiring knowledge of the outside world at the same rate of excellence. During my world travels, which I was still doing to a smaller extent, I was constantly referring to this wonderful orphaned child in Mexico whose name was Guillermina. She was learning so well and fast with this new way of acquiring a second language that soon a great many of the people who heard me talk about her would come to Mexico just to see her and talk to her.

However, when they came to visit and talk to her, they had a hard time pronouncing her nickname of Guille, let alone her full name of Guillermina. Thus, we all decided to call her "Gigi." It was easy to pronounce and soon became what she would answer to when called. We also started to refer to her as "The Gig."

In my talks around the world, I would always open up my talks with updates on how "The Gig" was doing. Soon everyone would ask about her. She had become quite a famous little girl in the world of intellectuals. Her adopted uncles and aunts (tíos and tías) number some of the most famous and prestigious people in the world in education and the government.

Gigi's confidence in me was becoming quite strong. She finally had started to believe that I would always be there and not disappear. We had developed a strong father-daughter relationship. Soon she was starting to tell me of her life as far as she could remember prior to coming to the Casa years ago.

The police had brought her to the Casa because they found her living on the streets. Before that, she had been with her father. The mother had left after he stabbed her with a knife. Her mother tried to take her with her but the father would not let her go. During the time with her mother and father, she remembers that they lived in a shack made of tin and wood. They all slept in one small bed in the center of the one-room shack. The only heat they had was a fire in the center of the shack by the bed. They also used this fire to cook their food.

She was very emphatic about not having enough food. Sometimes, they would go days without food. She remembers going to the garbage dump each day with her mother and looking through the garbage for something to bring home and eat. When they had some money, they would buy tortillas and crushed beans.

The streets where they lived were made of dirt. They had no water or bathroom in the shack. When they had to go to the bathroom, they would go outside in the streets. When they did bathe, they would do so in the town square's fountain late at night, along with the other people from where they lived. When they were finished bathing, they would use the same water to fill up water bottles to use for cooking and drinking.

They had a goat and a dog that she liked very much. She could not remember much about them, except that the dog had bitten her. She would always show me where he bit her when she would tell me about her past life. She also had a doll that was made out of rags. Her mother had made it for her.

Other memories were worse. She remembers her mother picking small white and red animals out of her hair. She also remembers the day that her father came home early and found her mother washing Gigi's hair to try to get rid of those animals. When the father saw that, he beat her mother for wasting the water.

She never wore shoes until she arrived at the Casa. She also had a big sister who had died and a baby sister that the mother took with her when she left. She had one dress and one pair of panties, though most of the time she only wore the panties. Sometimes she didn't even wear those; she would have to go out wearing nothing. She only wore the dress on special occasions.

She stayed with her father for a little bit after the mother left. Then one day, he brought her to the center of town, dropped her off there, and said that he would be back. She never saw him again. She waited for a long time before she understood that he would not be back but down deep in her heart, she still waited for him to come.

She survived for a while on her own. Men who she met in the streets would feed her and take her home with them for the evening to do "things" to and with her. Then in the morning, they would put her back on the streets. Each night, she would pray to God to have Papi return.

One day the police saw her on the streets and brought her to the Case when she said she had no home. Every time the doorbell rung at the Casa for the first year, she would run to the end of the girls' corridor and peer out to see if it was her father returning to take her home. (The Madres told me that part.)

The first day at the Casa, the Madres had to shave all the hair from her head and then put some sort of cream on it to get rid of the white and red animals that she had in her hair. She remembers that the cream they put on her head had burned when it was applied. She also remembers that she had to stay in bed for a couple of weeks, as she was not able to walk right.

She said, "The Madres told me later that I was not able to walk very well because I was so weak from malnutrition and hunger." However, she could not remember why she was really in bed, since she felt all right and could see nothing wrong at that time with how she used to crawl on all fours from place to place.

I had asked the Madre if these stories were true. She said, "I don't know anything about her previous life but I do remember that when she came to the Casa, she could not walk from starvation and rickets." In her opinion, Gigi would not have lived for much longer if she had not been brought to the Casa.

(Note of interest: If you could see Gigi's clothes and shoes closet now, you would think you were in a department store. She has a problem picking out what she wants to wear each day due to the sheer amount of clothes she owns. Each dress has to have a matching pair of shoes. Her underwear drawer bulges and barely shuts. Her room is abundant with dolls and stuffed animals. She has even taken over part of my closet for her clothes, as she had no more room in her own extra large closets.

Her governess thinks that I spoiled her; however, to this day, no one can talk me out of buying her things, nor will anybody ever. She has suffered so much in her short lifetime, more than most people have done in their entire lives. I feel that maybe I can make up for that suffering and horror she has gone through in this small fashion. I know I am wrong but I just can't help it.)

One day at the Casa I asked her when her birthday was. She looked at me and said, "What is a birthday?"

You could have knocked me over with a feather. What is a birthday? Not *when* is my birthday but *what* is a birthday? Then I comprehended my mistake. How could I be so dumb as not to realize that these children did not know anything about such an event? They never celebrate birthdays in the Casa. Therefore, they would have no reason to know what they were, let alone when. The only things that they were taught were what the Madres claimed to be right or wrong. Later I was to find out why this condition was an important factor to the existence of these girls and boys in the Casa.

Well now, it was time to stop and think. How do you explain to an eight-year-old child what a birthday is? You must first start with "birth." Gigi knew nothing about that and so we had to start from there. Then from that, you had to explain that everyone was born on a day. (Remember, Gigi had just been taught what a day was when I explained what a year and a calendar were.) Now she had to put them together and come up with the word birthday; not too easy for a child with this background.

While I was explaining that, I briefly had to mention sex and other sensitive topics. There were many words that Gigi was not taught and I had not come to learn in Spanish. Between Jesus and me, it took us about two full days to explain what a birthday is. With some glitches, I was finally able to explain that the day is always remembered and celebrated with a party because it was such a happy day.

Once that was explained, we discussed the party or fiesta. We now had to describe what took place and the extras, such as the cake, hats, and noisemakers. As we mentioned each of those articles, we had to explain what they were. Well that was enough for her. She wanted one of those birthday parties. However, then Gigi admitted that she did not know when her birthday was, or the year that she was born. She only said she was eight because the Madres told her to say that if someone asked her age. She did not really know what it meant.

I asked Madre Esmeralda when Guille's birthday was and she said that she had no idea, as these children don't usually come with a birth certificate. During this conversation (by this time I was speaking Spanish fairly well and did not require an interpreter), I found that about half of the Mexican people do not have birth certificates. They are often born in shanties instead of hospitals, and registering the birth took money that could be better spent elsewhere, like on food, clothing, and drink.

As we stood there, she said, "Wait a minute…when the police brought her here, they gave me a piece of paper that they found on her. Her father must have given it to her when he left her. It gave her name and age. Maybe from that, we can figure out what day she was born."

We went to her office and she opened up a drawer. Taking out some dusty files, the Madre said, "I know it's in here some place; give me some time and I will find it." After about 15 minutes, she exclaimed, "Here it is." She studied it looking for the date. As she did so, her eyes widened with great astonishment. She read it and then reread it. Finally, she announced, "What an error I have made all these years."

"'What? What?" I kept asking.

At first, she would only say, "How could this happen? How could this happen?" Eventually, she let me in on her surprise. "Roberto," she said,

"Guille is not eight years old but seven. She was born a year later than I thought. Her birthday is August 28th, ten days from now. Then she will be eight years old."

To us, that was a landslide discovery. However, to "The Gig," it meant nothing when we told her that she was one year younger than she thought. Time still had no real meaning for her and neither did age. Eight was the same as nine, ten, or eleven to her. "Old" was never explained; it was just a word to be used when asked, "How old are you?" So now, she would say seven instead of eight. At that time, she really did not understand why we were making such a fuss about saying seven instead of eight.

Soon, the words August the 28 *did* come to mean something to her but it was not the fact that it was her birthday. She still did not grasp the significance of the word, nor did she really understand "August" or the "28th." However, she knew that in ten days, we were going to have a fiesta for her. That she understood and became quite excited about it all.

Gigi and I now went about planning the fiesta. I wanted the best place in town for it, which I found to be a swanky country club. However, the club refused my request because I was not Mexican or a member. We came back and told the Madre about our disappointment. She promptly picked up the phone and in ten minutes, we had received permission to have the party there. Upon placing the phone down, she gave me that smirking grin again of "Why don't you ask me first about these things?"

Now that we had the place for the fiesta, we could start on the other items. The cake was ordered by Madre Esmeralda. Gigi and I took care of the entertainment. Piñatas were ordered and filled with candy and fruit. Gigi loved that job. We bought the biggest ones that we could find, even though she had no idea what you did with them. She just thought that they looked pretty. Gigi loved those piñatas. I had to explain what they were and what you put in them. Then what you did with them. Once she understood that, there was no stopping her. She wanted them at her party.

Everything was set and finally the day came. Gigi had a new party dress and off we all went to the club. The girls from the Casa, Veronica, and some other friends from school were all invited. The day went beautifully. Gigi looked so pretty in her new party dress. Everyone laughed and had a great time. Gigi learned how to blow out candles on the cake. She also drank punch and watched a ventriloquist with his dummy. That was the best part, she told me after the party, though she could not understand how he made the little person on his lap talk. After I tried a few attempts at clarifying it, she half-heartedly accepted my explanation. There were clowns all over the place. Gigi had so much fun, first looking at one thing and then looking at something else. Everyone congratulated her on her birthday, which made her feel special.

After the day was over and we were alone, she cuddled up to me on my lap. She looked up at me and said, "Daddy, I love birthdays. When can we have another one for me?"

I didn't answer for a while. I just held her a little bit tighter in my arms and rocked her softly. Finally, I said in reply to her question, "Soon, my daughter, very soon."

CHAPTER TWENTY-ONE

CIRCUS AND COMMENT "BORN FREE"

One day, Gigi came home from school and said Veronica had told her that a circus was coming to town. She did not want to tell Veronica that she did not know what one was so she came to me and asked. I explained that it was where wild animals, clowns, peanuts, cotton candy, and a whole bunch of other things were all under a single tent. With a wild expression, she begged, "Daddy, can we go? Can we go? Please, please can we go?"

"Sure," I replied. "We can go. Where is it and when?"

"I don't know. But, I know you will find out and then we can go, okay?" Gigi wildly declared.

"Okay, Daddy will find out all about it, happy?" I answered.

"Yes, Daddy, very happy, I can hardly wait. May we take some girls from school too?" she asked.

"You drive a hard bargain, little princess, but of course. Take who you want," was my response.

"Oh, Daddy, I can hardly wait to get to school tomorrow and tell the girls!" With that last remark, she threw her arms around me and gave me a big kiss on the cheek. Then she added, "By the way, what are peanuts? Just in case someone asks me if they will be there." When I explained that they were nuts in a shell, she looked confused. "What are nuts and a shell, Daddy?"

"Gigi, that's hard to describe. You will just have to wait and see when we get there." It was hard to describe something when even your definitions needed definitions.

"I can hardly wait," she repeated.

I think she was starting to learn how normal girls get things from their fathers. That little trick she had picked up as fast as summer lightning. She could say "Daddy" in such a way that I could not deny her anything. As the years passed, she got better at using that word. She has even added to it. Now she uses "Oh Daddy." That gets whatever she wants even more quickly from me, no matter how much I do not want to do what she asks sometimes.

The next day was spent finding out where this circus was. It seemed that I was now spending all my time with her and less and less time at the school in the Casa. I had become completely consumed with Gigi and her wants and problems. I was joyful beyond belief.

I thought she would explode with excitement before we made it to the circus. It was all she talked about prior to going, questions about this and questions about that: What is it like? What did you do? How long is it? What types of animals are there? What are tigers and lions?

The day finally arrived. I took the car and rounded up all her guests, both from the Casa and the school. There were eight in all. Thankfully, Estella came with me to handle the crowd.

At the circus grounds, there was corn on the cob with chili, cotton candy, and countless other things. To the children from school, this was old hat. However, to Gigi and the other children from the Casa, this was a first. Gigi loved the corn on the cob, and she especially loved the chili. She put gobs and gobs of it on the corn. This corn with the chili was one the greatest treats that she remembers of the day's events.

The funny thing is that today she cannot stand even being in the same room with the smell of that chili, much less eating it. I am the only one who eats it now. I got into the habit from always being with her. Not wanting to embarrass her for eating so much of it, I started to eat it too. Now I love it and she hates it.

Outside the circus tent, lions, tigers, and panthers walked around and around in their small cages. Gigi just stood there and stared at them as they paced around their small cage. Then finally she said, "Daddy, do they ever run free and play?"

"No," I answered. "That's the way they live their whole life. They live in that cage, except when they are inside entertaining us. After they are done, they are put back into their cage for the people to look at and maybe pet and throw peanuts to."

She looked at me and then back at the cage. She had a funny look on her face as we headed to the tent. When I inquired if there was anything wrong, she just shook her head.

Gigi and her friends had a phenomenal time that day, particularly the girls from the Casa. Soon the day was over and we took her friends back to their homes or the Casa. Then Gigi and I went to eat.

All throughout supper, she was quiet. Something was on her mind. I kept on asking her if anything was bothering her. Her reply was always the same, nothing was wrong. As a parent, you know when something is bothering your child and something was. I let it drop when it became obvious that she was not ready to tell me.

We finished our supper and were on our way back to the Casa. Just as we passed its huge wall and were in the courtyard, she looked at me and said in a very soft voice, "Daddy, you are putting me back into my cage for the evening. Is this where I am going to spend the rest of my life? Am I like the lion and other animals we saw today? Is this my cage? When the Americans come to feel sorry for us and give the Madre money, they also pet us on the top of the head. They give us food like we gave the peanuts to the lion today. We fight for the little they throw at us. Then we have to entertain them and make believe that we like it. We are told to do whatever they tell us to do. Daddy, am I like that lion?" she repeated. "Will I ever be free to play and run as I wish? Was I not born free like the other girls in the new school I now go to?" She added that last question wistfully and then waited for my reply.

Well, I finally found out what had been bothering her all day. She was smart enough to equate her life to that of the animals in the cages. As I sat there dumbfounded, I could not think of anything to tell her. What could I say? It was true. Her life *was* that of the lion we saw today. I never thought of it that way. She was in a cage and had to perform on cue for that little pat on the head the visitors would give her if she performed well. My God, she is smart. My voice was choked with emotion. Even if I had a quick answer to her question, I don't think I could have spoken.

I reached my arms out for her. She quickly came and embraced me, as I did her. I held her so tight that I thought I would squeeze her to death. Then on the other hand, she was doing the same to me.

"No, no, my little princess, the time is fast coming when your Daddy will no longer put you back in your 'cage.' You will run free as your friends from school do. No one will ever again pat you on your head and feed you candy for doing tricks for them. Soon, very soon, the cage door will swing open and you will never ever have to return." I said these words with tears streaming down my face.

Even now, as I write about this part of her life, I have to stop and wipe the tears from my eyes. This one moment, out of all the times I have been with 'The Gig' from start to present, stands out the most. It was the most emotional and heartrending time of all.

"Daddy, promise with all your heart that it is true and soon I will be free of my cage forever and never be put back again?" she entreated with heavy sobs and tears streaming down her face.

"I promise, Gigi, with all my heart and soul, it will take place and soon."

With that, she held me tighter and I did the same. We sat there awhile longer and just held each other without saying a word.

CHAPTER TWENTY-TWO

FIRST RESULTS OF PROJECT AND ESTELLA LEAVES

I left that evening resolved to secure Gigi's release as quickly as possible. I kept thinking about how profound Gigi's statement was. It really got to me. She was so perceptive to equate her circumstance of existence to that of a lion in a cage.

That evening I was to bring Gigi back much later than I did. However, due to her question of "returning her to her cage," I decided to return to the Casa earlier. I wanted to get back to the hotel to figure out what to do about releasing Gigi.

No one saw us as we walked to the girl's dormitory. The patio was empty and there was no one to be seen anywhere. I thought it strange but, then again, I had never been there at that hour.

When we entered the corridor that guarded the girls' area, Felipe stepped out and tried to stop us from proceeding any further. By this time I had become very influential in the Casa so I advised him in Spanish to "camine aparte" (step aside), as I was in no mood to deal with him this evening. And if he did not, I would advise the Madre of his actions. This was very unusual. He had not stopped me from entering the passage ever since Madre had told him that I could come and go as I pleased.

I looked at Gigi and she too was acting funny. She looked at me and said, "Daddy, let's go back to the hotel for some food; I'm hungry."

Gigi had just finished eating hot dogs, cotton candy, and other items at the circus and had said she was not hungry earlier when I asked if she wanted something to eat. This strange behavior only made me more interested in going down that hall. What did they not want me to see?

I stepped past Felipe, took the reluctant Gigi by the hand, and continued down the passage. Upon arriving at the door, I heard a lot of noise coming from the inside the dormitory. I opened the door and saw about six boys from the ages of sixteen to twenty in there with the girls. There was no Madre in sight. The older girls, from nine to twelve years old, were only dressed in pajama bottoms. The younger ones, from three to eight years old, were wearing nothing. They were all running around and a few of the boys were chasing them. The other boys were holding two or three of the girls on the beds and were playing with them. A little girl, about seven years old, was tied spread-eagle on top of one of the beds, completely naked.

Upon seeing me, they all stopped and looked at me. Furiously, I asked, "Qué el infierno son usted haciendo aquí?" (What the hell are you all doing here?) Then I told the boys to "consiga fuera de aquí y consiga fuera ayunar" (get out of here and get out fast). They all quickly ran past me and out the door. I looked at Gigi and asked, "Gig, what's going on here?"

Gigi looked at the ground and answered, "I don't know."

I then asked the girls the same question and none of them answered. They all just stood there motionless and stared at me.

I said to Gigi, "Go find Madre Esmeralda right now. I want to tell her what I just saw." Gigi promptly left to find the Madre. I then told the children who were wearing nothing to "consiga para lecho ayunar" (to get to bed immediately). They did so immediately. None of them said a word; they just did what I told them.

Soon Gigi returned with the Madre and I informed her of what I had seen. She told me that she and the other Madres had been in the church for their usual hours of prayers. She did not know what was going on but she would find out from Felipe and the girls, and she assured me that it would never happen again. She vowed that she was shocked over what I had just told her.

With that assurance, I kissed Gigi goodbye and left. I was absolutely staggered over what I had just witnessed. This made me want to acquire Gigi's release from the Casa all the sooner. If this was taking place, what else was going on that I didn't know about?

The next day, I promptly contacted a lawyer that was supposed to be an expert on adoptions in Mexico. He said that he would look into it and get back with me. I figured I would not tell Gigi what I had done because I wanted to be sure that the lawyer would come through. I did not want to get Gigi's hopes up until I was sure that things were proceeding correctly.

After the visit to the lawyer, I went to the Casa. Gigi was waiting at her usual spot. But, lo and behold, Estella was not.

Gigi greeted me in her usual fashion as I got out of the car. Then she said, "Madre told me that I do not have to have Estella with me anymore. I like that because I and the other girls do not like her."

It was the first time she had ever said something like that. I always had the sense that The Gig did not like Estella, but I never asked her about it. However, now that Estella was not there, Gigi volunteered the information.

I asked, "Why don't you like her?"

"I don't know; I just don't like her. Are you going to the computer class this morning?" Gigi replied.

When Gigi does not want to answer a question, as I said before, she will always provide you with a vague answer and then, in the same breath, change the subject. This was one of those moments. So, I figured, why pursue that question with her now? I can do it sometime in the future when she wasn't on guard. It could be that Gigi did not like her because Estella was always with us in the past, stifling Gigi's conversation with me. There could be a hundred normal reasons why a person did not like someone else. Anyway, I did not think it was important enough to push Gigi into answering.

Instead of pushing, I answered her vague question about class. "Yes, I am going to the class this morning. I want to see how all of you are doing. And I am going to ask the teachers how you are doing, too."

So, hand in hand, we walked to the class. Jesus and his teachers were there busily preparing for the morning session. We greeted each other and all gave The Gig a kiss on the cheek. She returned the gesture.

Shortly after, the class began and The Gig and the other girls quickly started their lessons. They all worked very well and loved the computers. Nothing was said of what had taken place last night. I decided not to mention anything about it to Jesus, since I was worried that the Madre would go through the roof if he said something about it to her.

All the teachers told me that The Gig was the best student of them all. She was acquiring knowledge at such a rapid rate. I was very proud of what she had accomplished in such a short time.

Even though most of my time was spent with Gigi, each Saturday evening, Jesus and I, along with his teachers, would meet at the hotel bar. While Gigi went up and down in the hotel elevators, the teachers and I would discuss what went on at the Casa's school each week. Jesus kept me quite informed. Putting him in charge was one of the best decisions I had ever made, although ever so often, I would still visit the class.

Gigi and the other girls now spoke almost perfect English. However, they would never answer questions concerning their lives at the Casa. Those they would always shrug off and change the subject.

While at the Casa, I would occasionally see new people visiting there. Then the next day, they would be gone. In addition, Jesus had told me that four or five of the girls who had started the class were no longer at the Casa. When he had asked where they were, the Madre told him that they had been adopted.

That always got to me. How could they adopt them so fast when, according to the lawyer, I had to wait six or eight months at the very least to adopt Gigi? Each time I considered saying something about this rapid adoption of the girls to the Madre, I would remember that Doc had advised me to stay out of the Casa's business. I did ask Gigi a few times, but she would always shrug her shoulders and say that she didn't know.

There were also those times that the girls would all get in the van and go to the park. Gigi never went even though she did say that she used to go before I came. A few times, I asked, "Why don't you go since I won't be here this weekend?"

She would reply extremely fast with an emphatic, "I just don't want to go there." She would always emphasize "there."

There was yet another mystery. The girls would occasionally go across the border to Marine Land or somewhere like that. Gigi did not want to go there either. She said that they never took her there anyway in the past and even if they offered to take her, she would not want to go. I thought that was strange.

When asked why not, she would reply, "I just don't want to go there." She would have the same tone and emphasis and then just leave it at that. I quickly learned to drop the subject.

The months now flew by and we were at the midterm grading period in the public and private schools that the girls were attending. Prior to the girls entering the Casa's computer class, they were tested in all subjects. Most, tested very low. The Mexican schools grade on a 1 to 10 level with 1 being the lowest and 10 the highest. All the girls' public school marks were 1s and 4s. This was also where they ended up when we independently tested them. Much to my regret, Gigi was a 5 when she was tested six months prior.

Although, we tested them in all subjects, we only taught them mathematics in the Casa's computer class. The girls did not do the normal drills or practice typing, as everyone else was teaching. Our concept was a different approach. The 'drill and kill' method, as most of us call it, is sure to lose the interest of a child very quickly. Once the interest is gone, the child's desire to learn is also gone. Therefore, our philosophy was based on taking advantage of the wants and interests of a child. That meant we had to develop new ideas. We did this with the help of one of Gigi's adopted uncles.

Dr. Seymour Papert, Gigi's tío, was the foremost authority worldwide in this new way of teaching with the computer, and a guru of modern education. People come from all over the world to listen to him when he lectures on the subject. We had done a lot of research together, Papert and I, when I was working in America on how to instruct children so they could learn not only about the computer, but about other subjects as well. We, IBM, also endowed his university, MIT, with a number of computers so we could do research with actual children.

Once the university had the computers for a while, we figured out which way we were heading. We then installed several computers in a public school in Boston. Thus, we were able to bring the think tank of the university into an actual environment of childhood learning.

The classes in Boston were very successful. Those children did extremely well. Now we were about to see how well these children of a different culture were doing in school after six months of working with our methods of combining computers with education.

The grades from the outside school were brought back to the Casa. We examined all their report cards and found they had all gone from 1s and 5s to 8s and 9s. Even though we did not work with them in anything but math, we found that the new method of teaching was spilling over to their other subjects as well. After looking at their report cards, we tested them again ourselves. We found their marks had gone up significantly. We were very happy and sat down to plan the next six months' campaign.

The school at the Casa was going very well now, even though I spent very little time there since I was always with Gigi. The other girls from the Casa now regularly came with us when they had nothing to do at the Casa. This was possible because they all now spoke very good English so we could all communicate.

Everyone at the Casa said that I was changing the lives of the girls and they started to tell me of some of their troubles at school and things like that. They really trusted me. Yet each time I brought up that incident of the boys in the dormitory, they would never answer and quickly changed the subject. Even Estella said that she knew nothing of it and that the Madre never told her what had happened that night. We saw very little of Estella during those days. She was always somewhere else.

Then one day Madre Esmeralda told me that Estella was leaving. You could have knocked me over with a feather. Estella had been at the Casa for 12 years. Why all of a sudden, without notice, would she leave? I promptly sought out Estella and asked why she was leaving. She never gave me any hint of her real reasons. She merely said that she was tired of the Casa and wanted a charge of scenery.

"Where will you go?" I queried.

"I don't know, maybe somewhere in South America. I could probably find a place to help in some other orphanage there."

Something that had always bothered me about all those years she had been at the Casa was that she had never received any salary. I tried to rationalize it. Why did she really need money? Her room, board, and clothing were supplied by the Casa.

Now, I had to wonder where she would get the money to fly to South America. That took a lot of money. It was really none of my business, so I did not ask. After all, maybe she had a rich aunt or uncle someplace. Anyway, two days later, she was gone. I wished her well and asked her to write every so often.

During these times, I kept asking my lawyer what he was doing about the adoption and his only reply was that he was working on it. In frustration, I once asked, "Other girls at the Casa are being quickly adopted. How come you can't do it that fast?"

He looked at me with an all-knowing expression and said, "That is the Madre's business. Why don't you ask her how those people do it? I'm doing it legally." Then he just left it at that.

I asked the Madre if she heard anything about the adoption paperwork for Gigi and she said, "No." One thing I had learned by this time was that you do not ever pressure Mexicans to do anything. They will do it in their own sweet time. If pressure is applied, they will take four times longer.

The lengthy adoption process was starting to bother me. On top of that stress, Gigi was now regularly asking when she was going to be my real daughter and leave the Casa. Every few weeks, I had to give her the same answer. "Soon, Gigi, Daddy is working on it very hard." She would smile, hug me, and then return to whatever she had been doing. I think she was taking it better than I was.

One day, to take her mind off the subject, I said, "Hey, how about a swim in the hotel's pool. You have never been swimming there."

She sorrowfully looked up at me and said, "Daddy, I have never been swimming. I don't know how."

"That's okay; Daddy will show you." With that, she jumped with joy and ran to the other girls to tell them tomorrow, her Daddy was going to take her swimming.

CHAPTER TWENTY-THREE

GIGI SWIMS

The next morning, Gigi and I left the Casa at ten. She had been looking forward to it since yesterday when I promised her that she could swim today. She was so excited that she did her happy little skip hop, on the way to the car.

It was going to be a busy day. First, we had to buy her a bathing suit. Then we needed a big towel, a tube to put around her so she would not drown, and, of course, some pool toys.

Gigi had never owned a bathing suit so this was going to be another new experience for her. Not only would this be her first time in a pool, it was also her first bathing suit. She made me promise that it would be a one-piece suit, not a two-piece, as she had seen some of the other little girls wearing at the hotel pool. She would have none of that. Gigi was proper and correct when it came to things like that. Regarding exposing her legs or anything about her body, she was extra proper and correct. At the time, I just thought it was due to her upbringing with the nuns.

As we left the Casa, she began asking me all sorts of questions about swimming pools. Was it cold? How do you drown? What is drowning?

What keeps you from doing that? How do you swim? Does it take long to learn? The questions were coming so fast that I could not finish answering one before she started the next.

We arrived at the shopping plaza just as the department store was opening. I always like to be there early, as the shops were always packed later in the day. The Mexicans do not buy much, but their favorite pastime is to take the family to a big store and just look and dream. At those hours, the stores become a mass of humanity. They push and shove much more than Americans. Why this is so, I have yet to find a reason.

We stood before the escalator and Gigi stepped on it quickly like a pro. I remembered that first awful escalator episode when I had to carry her up. No matter how familiar she got with them, she always had a fear that her foot would get stuck.

The expression on her face as those stairs carried her upward the first time had been priceless. Now she acted as if she had always been on them. Like most children her age, she never wanted to face the correct way on the escalator. Not only would she face downward when going up, but she would also try to walk down as the stairs went up. And, of course, if the stairs were going down, she would try to walk up.

As we reached our floor, I said, "Okay, Gigi, turn around and stop walking down. We are about to get off. If you don't look, you will fall." She promptly did as she was told and, once more, stepped off the stairs like a pro.

We went straight to the girls section. By this time, Gigi knew exactly where it was. The woman who usually waited on us came up and after the pleasantries, I said, "'We have come for a bathing suit. Can you help us?"

"Yes, come right this way, Senor Nielsen, and you too, Senorita Gigi."

Every time someone said that to Gigi, I felt a sensation of pride. It was only a short while ago that people like this woman would not have been seen talking to a poor little girl from the Casa. Now they treated this little miss with all the respect that they would have treated an older person or a young princess. If they only knew where Gigi lived! Everyone thought she was the daughter of "that rich American" and treated her with very high regard and respect.

At the bathing suit department, Gigi and the woman were soon involved in the mysterious selection process that goes on when a woman shops. She had developed a mind of her own when picking what clothes she wanted to wear. She was still nervous that the Madres would not like her choices, so there were still some of the Madres' thoughts in her selection criteria. Soon those fears would disappear, leaving her selections to be completely her own taste.

Of course, some things have not changed, despite the passage of time. To this day, you cannot get her into a two-piece bathing suit. She will not even look at them in a store. I love to tease her about it. When she is not looking, I'll pick up one of the two-piece suits. I then go over and say, "How about this one?"

Her reply is always the same: "Oh, Daddy, no way, you know that. Go put it back." Her face will then turn bright red with embarrassment.

But now, with the woman's help, Gigi soon had three bathing suits under her arm and headed for the dressing room to try them on. Half an hour later, she came out and handed me one. "This is the one I would like to have."

I replied, "Daddy did not see it. Are you sure it fits and everything?"

"Yes," she said firmly.

I left it at that. I was to find out later in the day why she did not volunteer to model it for me. I merely said, "Okay, let's go look for the rest of the swim things we need."

So off we went. For the next hour or so, we looked and purchased the other items she would need for her first dip in a pool. By the end of the shopping spree, she was beyond control with excitement and anticipation of the swim. All she talked about that morning was how it would feel. She had never even been in a bathtub, no less a pool, so it would be a real first of any kind of water completely surrounding her body.

On the trip to the hotel, she kept holding up the bathing suit and looking at it, as if it were some magical piece of clothing. It was bright orange and, of course, one piece. It had two shoulder straps that crossed in the back and a little skirt on the lower portion. It was very pretty and in good taste. One thing about Gigi: she has excellent taste in all sorts of dress. Where she had learned that, I hadn't the foggiest idea, but it was perfect. Everything always matches, right down to her socks.

Once in the hotel, I said, "Gigi, it's almost twelve. Are you hungry?"

"No, please, may we go to the room so I can put my suit on and swim?"

"Sounds good to me; let's go." We arrived at the room and she promptly went to the bathroom to put on the suit. After twenty minutes, Gigi came out of the bathroom. She had wrapped the bath towel around her like a sarong. Smiling, I said, "Gigi, let Daddy see your new bathing suit."

She gave me a strange look and stated, "No, it would not be proper."

"You have to be fooling. Everyone wears bathing suits at the pool. What are you going to do when we get downstairs?" When she didn't answer, I again asked, "Please, let Daddy see just once. Just so I can see if it fits okay."

She then very quickly opened up the towel and then shut it even faster.

"That looks very pretty. You'll be the prettiest little girl in the pool. Let's go down and see your admiring public." I laughed a little when I said it.

Boy, was that the wrong thing to say, because she promptly replied, "I don't want to swim now."

"Why not, you've been so eager to swim all day? Why change your mind now?"

"I don't know; I just don't feel like swimming now."

"If I said something wrong, I'm sorry."

The conversation went on like that for about an hour. I finally talked her into going to the pool with the towel wrapped tightly around her. She kept such a strong grip on her sarong-like towel that you would have thought it was pure gold.

When we arrived at the pool, we had a repeat of the entire conversation. She refused to get into the pool. She just wanted to sit there with the towel wrapped around her and watch the other girls in the pool. Soon Payola, her friend from the hotel, came over and asked Gigi to join her. They talked for a while and finally Gigi said, "Okay." Off the two kids went. Payola jumped in with no fear, as she knew how to swim quite well. However, Gigi stopped on the first step of the stairs in the pool with the towel still wrapped tightly around her.

Payola came over to reassure her. "It's not deep on this end. You can touch the bottom."

Gigi took another step into the pool, the towel still wrapped tightly around her.

Seeing this, I got up and said, "Are you going into the pool with the towel? It will get all wet."

She responded, "So?"

"Gigi, you are being silly. Give me the towel." I then went over to her, and grabbed the towel. Believe me, that was a struggle, as she fought very hard to keep it, but I won.

Now she stood there with one arm over her breasts and the other hand over her "privates." It was a sight to make any one laugh. I didn't, but it was difficult to mask my amusement. The problem was that she thought no one should see her wearing anything except her dress. She had never exposed herself this way before (as far as I knew at the time), but who would have thought that appearing in a bathing suit was exposing your body?

After talking to her, with some assistance from Payola's mother, Gigi finally took her hands away from her body and got into the pool. This had turned out to be a bigger job than I had expected, but soon she and Payola were walking all over on the shallow end of the pool. At first, she would still look around to see if anyone was looking at her. Then she would quickly grab for the towel to cover herself. However, with the help of Payola and her mother, she even got over that and became like a normal girl at the pool.

After a while, she came up to me with a new issue. Payola had told her that her things on her chest, referring to her nipples, showed when the bathing suit was wet.

I thought, "My God, there's nothing there. They are as flat as pancakes." But rather than argue with her, I said, "Daddy will buy you a new suit with special lining up there the next time we go shopping. Then no one will be able to see under the suit when it is wet."

She agreed and went back to swimming. Nevertheless, she was very careful when she got out of the pool that no one was looking "there."

By this point, Gigi and Payola were playing all around the pool. Gigi had to wear her inflated swim ring as she ran around, as I was afraid that she might fall in the water. Gigi did not mind that too much as she carried it up high. This way she could use the tube to hide her breasts from anyone whom she thought might be looking at her.

Soon they were jumping in the pool and splashing each other. Gigi looked like she had been in the water since the day she was born. The only tip off was she had that tube on her. She did not like it at all. She claimed that it cramped her style of swimming.

Gigi learned to swim very fast. I now call her my "water rat." She loves swimming and spending time at the pool with her friends. And one of the biggest problems that she had now was not the swimming, but rather the jade elephant necklace I had given her.
At age 9 and 23 still with her Elephant and nameplate

Gigi enjoyed putting the elephant in her mouth as she talked. This caused the chain that the elephant hung on to break. Just playing could do the same. The chain breaking was not as important as then finding the elephant, which was especially difficult in the pool.

After having to repair the chain three times, I finally had a special gold chain designed to alleviate the problem of her always breaking the necklace. Then we were faced with the elephant coming off the piece that held it to the necklace. The answer to that was to have the jeweler design an encasement in which to place the elephant. This encasement had a special clasp that attached to the chain. This whole enterprise of stopping Gigi from losing the elephant took much time and design. Yet somehow, someway, we always managed to find the elephant when it separated itself from the protection of the necklace—no matter where she lost it.

Once these little challenges were out of the way, we often went to the hotel to eat and swim. Gigi soon learned to avoid me when I got in the pool. This was because I was always "dunking" her and throwing her up in the air in the pool, which she disliked. She would stand by the edge of the pool and tell me how awful I was and to stop it. But I never did. To this day, I still do this to her when I get the chance. And she still gets out of the pool.

CHAPTER TWENTY-FOUR

SUSPICIONS GROW STRONGER

The day of that first swim, I brought my camera with me to record this monumental occasion—the day that Gigi first went swimming. I had hoped that years later we could look at the pictures and laugh.

I had seldom brought a camera to a pool because of fear of getting it wet or, even worse, losing it. Also, Gigi enjoyed playing with new things and liked to experiment with them to see how they operated. I did not want to put temptation of the camera in her path until she was accustomed to a few more objects of the outside world. A thing like a Polaroid camera would really fascinate her...or so I thought.

She had just finished swimming and was sitting at the table by the pool drinking a Coke when I showed it to her. "Look up, so I can take your picture." She looked up and gave me a strange grin. It was very wide and showed all her teeth, as if she were forcing a smile. I took the picture. The camera made a funny noise and then the picture started to emerge. I waited for Gigi to say something, but she was silent. In fact, she just went about finishing her Coke as if nothing had happened. She did not even want to see the picture.

That was strange. I would have expected her to be curious about the camera, especially after a picture "magically" appeared. It just wasn't like her to be quiet when exposed to a new gadget. I tossed it off with the rationale that she was probably tired from all that swimming and was too busy with her drink to be curious. She most likely would ask me about it later in the day, after she rested. At least that was the way I justified her lack of interest.

After she finished her drink, she went and lay on the grass on her side, looking at a book. Hoping to regain her attention now that she was relaxing, I said, "Let's take some more pictures, so we have a whole bunch of your first day swimming, okay?"

She nodded politely, as if to say "if that's what you want to do, then do it." This was not the Gigi I had come to know. She showed no excitement over this "new and marvelous" toy that I was using. It seemed to be "old hat" due to the 'Park' trips, to her. At this time in her life, when she encountered a new thing, she would always become very excited and ask all sorts of questions about it. She would also want to see how it worked or operated. This was so unlike her.

"Put the book down and smile and I will take some pictures."

Gigi put the book down and then promptly put one arm under her head. Then she lifted her top leg, placed the foot of the leg she had just raised on the knee of the leg that was still on the ground. Once again, she used that oddly fake smile.

I quickly told her to shut her legs. She did as I said and I took the picture.

Once that was done, I asked, "Why did you open your legs?"

She answered, "That's the way I did it before."

"What do you mean 'before'?"

She replied, "When the other men took our pictures. That's the way Estella always had us place our legs, if we are laying on our sides." The statement was said in a nonchalant manner, as if it were just the way you would take a picture when you were on your side. As if there were nothing wrong with it.

I looked around to see if anyone was within earshot, just to make sure no one had heard what she had said. Then I promptly said, "Gigi, let's go to the room because Daddy is getting sunburned." That was all I could think of at the time to get her someplace where I could pursue what she meant by her last statement. She had no problem with that suggestion, as I could see that she was getting a little burned also.

We took one of the Cokes on the table and went to my suite. We sat and chatted for a while in the living room as she drank her Coke. Finally, I felt the time was right to bring up the real reason we went inside—the remark about the men and pictures. I did not want to scare her. I decided to circle around to the subject very carefully. "Hey, let's take some more pictures. How about we do some of the poses the other men told you to do."
She agreed and put down her drink.

I then said, "Okay, I have the camera ready. Is this camera the same kind the other men had?" If so, that would explain why she had not been excited about it when I had taken the pictures outside.

"Yes, but they would then take the picture and put it in some other thing and a second picture would come out. Just like the one they just took. Do you have one of those too?"

"No," I said. She just looked and shrugged her shoulders, as if it didn't make any difference.

I lifted my camera and said, "What did they tell you do first?"

She just stood there for a moment, facing me with her hands stiffly held by her side. Her fingers were outstretched and pressed against her legs. That forced smile was on her face again. Not sure what to do, I took the picture.

She then struck a new pose, standing up facing me with her legs opened very wide. Once more, she waited for me to take a picture. After that, she sat down, leaned back, and opened her legs very wide with her head held back. The next pose was her legs crossed as she sat. Then she turned around and bent over so I could see her backside. The next was her on her side with one leg in the air. Then one standing by a chair with one of her legs on the back of the chair. Then one with her standing on her toes and holding her hair up in the back.

After a number of increasingly disturbing poses, she stood up and opened her legs. She put her fingers by her vagina and pulled it apart. As she was doing this, she casually said, "This is hard to do when you have something on."

With that remark, I almost dropped the camera. I quickly thought, "Bob, before you say anything, compose yourself so as not to frighten her. She doesn't realize that this is wrong." After taking a few calming breaths, I said, "What do you mean when you said, 'something on'?"

She innocently replied, "When we took the pictures before we never had on any clothes."

I had come into the room to find out about where and how she'd had pictures taken of her. Now I was faced with not only *that* question but also her remark of "We had no clothes on."

Before I could say something about her last statement, the word "we" hit me. "What do you mean by 'we'?"

"All the girls were there having their pictures taken."

"All the girls from where?" I asked.

"From the Casa."

You can imagine my dilemma. I didn't know where to start pursuing this line of questioning. Every question I asked led to another one. I was losing track of what question I was even asking. So I decided to stop with the picture taking farce and destroy the pictures I had takneb, sit down, and start to explore what was going on, all over again, from the beginning. I again wondered why the boys had been in their dormitory that night. My thoughts were bordering on panic. What I had to do was somehow have her start from the beginning of how this picture-taking episode with the men and what had happened there in the proper sequence, thereby, hopefully presenting some order to this predicament in which I now found myself.

I considered some of the things that I had to discover. How were these pictures taken? Who took them? Where were they taken? Who were the men? Did the Madres know anything about it? And what about the girls? Were all the girls undressed? How many girls were involved? And this was just for starters. How many more questions would come up as she started to unfold the entire affair? The problem now facing me was how to have her tell me this whole thing from start to finish. I had to proceed very carefully so as not to arouse her suspicions of any wrongdoing on her part. I knew that if Gigi suspected she had done something wrong, she would promptly stop discussing the subject.

The part that really upset me was that this was my Gigi who presented herself as so prim and proper. The little girl who was raised by nuns from the age of four. A girl who was too embarrassed to show herself at the pool. A girl who was too modest to show her legs. "My God, what is going on here?" I thought. "There is more than meets the eye with this little girl."

The biggest problem of my life was now facing me. All my previous trials now seemed trivial. How could I find out what was going on with this little girl and why she was so paradoxical in her actions, along with trying to find out more about the Casa? By now, I was sure that whatever was going on with the pictures had to do with the other strange happenings I had seen in the Casa.

I could see that Gigi was getting nervous about my questions. To put her mind at ease, I said, "Oops, no more film in the camera, I'll buy some more tomorrow and we can start again where we left off today, okay?"

"Okay," she replied before asking if she could turn on the TV.

"That's a great idea. There might be some cartoons on? Why don't you see?" It was a perfect way to keep her occupied while I collected my thoughts on how to proceed with the situation.

My speculations wandered as I sat there watching her flipping the TV dial trying to find her cartoons. I thought, "Look at her: nine years old, a child. A baby. How could people take pictures of a little baby like that? What kind of men are they? If I could put my hands on them for just a minute, what would I do? What I was thinking I would do to them, I don't even think I was capable of doing. What part of this were the actions of the Madres and the Casa? What the hell had taken place with this girl? What did she still have left to tell me?

Finally, she found some cartoons. Soon she was engrossed in the show, sitting there laughing and watching them intently. God, she was such a small, frail child—not much meat on her and so very skinny. Why would anyone want to take pictures of her wearing nothing?

My mind now went back to wondering why she would undress in front of men and let them take pictures of her naked when she was so embarrassed if her dress went above her knees when she sat down in public. How did that fit with her not even wanting to come out of the bathroom with her bathing suit on, worried I would see her without any clothes? Or how she feared that men would see her that way at the pool?

Why would a little child act so modest in some ways but then think nothing of being completely naked and having men take pictures of her? Did she not know why they were taking the pictures? Was she trying to throw me off the scent that she would do something like that? Knowing the way that I felt about modesty (I had always told her to pull her dress down, shut her knees when she sat, and similar things), she might have thought I would get mad. Was she afraid that if I got mad at her, I might abandon her?

No, those thoughts were too advanced for her. There must be some other reason. All I had to do was put my mind to the situation and I hoped I could come up with a plausible answer to this whole mess. I needed a starting point to find out what was going on at the Casa with Gigi and the other girls. Rambling all over the place when I started talking to her would get me nowhere.

From the short time that I had been at the Casa, I could see that when the Madres said something to the girls, they would do it without hesitation or question. It was almost as if God himself were giving the orders. These children at the Casa had no minds of their own. They were not taught to think for themselves. If anything, they were taught to have no thoughts of their own and no feelings. They were trained to do what the Madres said. If the Madres said that it was good, then it was good. If the Madres said that it was bad, then it was bad. They were kept under strict control while at the Casa and taught not to be seen outside of their play area of the Casa without the proper dress. So, if you were to go along with these thoughts, you would come up with the following conclusion:

If the Madres said that it was proper to have those types of pictures taken, either with clothes or naked, then Gigi would think there was nothing wrong with it. On the other hand, if the Madres were to tell them to act and dress modestly in the outer part of the Casa or in public, they would do that too, not worrying about why the actions were so different and paradoxical.

So if Gigi could be her real self, she would be shy and embarrassed to expose any part of her body. But if told that it was wrong to feel that way by the Madres, then Gigi would accept that it was wrong. If anyone were to ask them to do something like what I just did with the picture taking, they would respond the way that they had been programmed: It was correct and proper to do so, yet only for that particular purpose and not anything else, or whatever the Madre so declared.

Yet, when with me, Gigi felt she could be herself. When I had gotten involved in this picture-taking episode, it had stuck a chord and she had unconsciously reverted to the commands of the Madres, somewhat like a trigger word being said after being hypnotized. Even now, this causes issues for Gigi. She sometimes has trouble making her own decisions of what is right and what is wrong without double-checking with me first.

With this chain of logic, I now felt that I had a starting point to continue the discussion at a later point. I had determined that the Madres were part of this whole picture-taking thing.

"Gigi," I started, "it's almost time to get back to the Casa. You better get your bathing suit off and start getting dressed. There's always tomorrow for a swim."

She got up and turned off the TV without question. Then, as she headed towards the bathroom to get dressed, I said, "Gigi, who were the other girls with you when you took those pictures?"

"All the big girls at the Casa. There were eight of us: Maria Celer, Maria, and the rest of the girls between six and eleven."

"Oh," I said, and continued. "Was it fun when you went there?"

"No, not much, all we did was take pictures; we could not play any games or watch TV, just take pictures. I was so tired when I got back to the Casa."

"How long were you there?"

"Most of the day, and the room was cold and wet."

"Were there a lot of men there?"

"At first, there was only Estella and one man. By the end of the day, there were many men," she replied.

"What did you do when all the men were there?" I quickly inquired, still trying to sound casual.

"They all wanted us to do the same poses we were doing when only Estella and the man were there. Some of the men asked us to kiss the other girls when they took the pictures. Ugh, that part I did not really like. We had to kiss them all over and not just on the mouth. Some of the men tied us up in all sorts of positions before they took some of the pictures. That part hurt. Then they did other things with us," she replied.

I did not pursue where "all over" was or what were "the other things." That I could imagine for myself from the way she spoke. And something else she said was much more important: Estella. Estella was almost like a Madre to the children. They responded to her almost as they did to the Madres. "When did Estella take you all there?"

"When she took us out for the day. Sometimes she would leave a girl there and not bring her back until the next day."

"Did the Madres say that it was okay for the girl to stay?" I asked.

"I don't know, but I guess it was. The Madres never said anything about the girl not being with us when we returned."

I now saw why Estella had left the Casa so fast and without warning. Gigi and I were becoming friendly and she could now speak fairly good English. Estella knew it would only be a matter of time before Gigi blurted this whole mess out to me, including the part that Estella played in it. This would also explain where Estella was getting the money to finance her leaving. Some "rich aunt or uncle" was really these men.

By this time, I had lost my cool and said, "Do you realize what the men do with those pictures? They put them in books and then sell them all over the world. These are bad people who should be put in jail. When you took these pictures, was that all you did? Did you go to bed or did anything else with these men?" I just about screamed at her. I was so damned mad that I could not hold back my emotions any longer.

Gigi looked at me with a terrified expression on her face and said, "That was all I did, just those pictures." She started to cry, and between sobs, she said, "I did not think it was bad or that I was doing anything wrong. Estella said we should do it, and that that was what we were in the Casa for. Please don't be mad at me. I have not done that since you have been here. They do not take me now."

"Daddy is not mad at you. It is the men and Estella who I am mad at—"

She interrupted me. "Please, don't tell anyone I told you. If they tell the Madres, I would not be able to see you again. Please, oh please, do not tell Estella or the Madres that I told you. Please!"

By this time, I realized that I had scared her, just what I'd wanted to avoid. I stopped the questioning and just held her, repeating, "Daddy is not mad at you." Then, to make sure, I added, "And now that you know it is bad, never do it again."

"Daddy, I won't, I promise."

I continued holding her for quite some time until she regained her composure. Then I had to take her back to the Casa and the hell she went through there. All I could think of now was *What else is there? What more have I yet to learn?*

CHAPTER TWENTY-FIVE

CONCEALMENT DISCLOSED AND TEARS FLOW

When I took her back to the Casa that evening, Gigi was still a little bit shaken, but at least her eyes were not too red. The Madres would have been sure to say something otherwise.

The next time I saw Gigi, I did not say anything further on the subject of the pictures. I did not want to frighten her any more than I had at the pool and we had plenty of other things to discuss. Her questions about life were now becoming staggering and quite profound. All I could think of was how smart she was and how aware she was becoming of the life outside the great foreboding walls of the Casa.

I had almost forgotten the picture-taking episode. I had driven the thoughts from my mind by rationalizing that the events had all happened before I arrived. I was also quite sure it would never happen again to her, as long as I kept coming to the Casa. I could do nothing about the past without getting Gigi or me in serious trouble with the Madres, so I trained myself to stop thinking about it.

I had another motive for not wanting to push the subject. Like many children, the more you pushed a subject that Gigi did not want to recount, the more reluctant she was to discuss it with you, especially a topic as touchy as this one. I was just thankful she had enough confidence and trust in me to divulge this one picture episode. But I knew she had more to relate by the way that she had answered my questions. When children are ready and the time is right in their mind, they will tell you. I hoped that her future revelations did not lead to any more difficult questions and horrible answers.

Ever since I had asked if anything else had happened that day, Gigi had been acting strange. She just did not seem like the old "Gig." She did not laugh very much now. When she did laugh, it often seemed forced. She never skipped that funny way anymore, either. She became very quiet most of the time. She had all the signs that something was really bothering her.

Her expression and attitude now were as if she wanted to get something off her mind but could not figure how. I felt sorry for her and kept asking if anything was bothering her. The answer was always the same: "No."

In defense of what I am about to describe, if that is at all possible, you must understand some of the Mexican way of life. To the average Mexican, children and family are the most important things in their life. Mexican parents will do everything in this world to protect their children.

Yet, Mexico also has an extreme poverty problem. Many of the people have babies because they do not know how to prevent it, or it is too expensive to prevent. Some even look at having babies as a blessing, as they are marketable. Perhaps these sort of thoughts go back to the times of the Aztecs. Back in those times, girl babies, and women were held in no regard at all. Many were sacrificed to their

Gods or used by the priests as they so desired. Though the ancient culture is gone, perhaps some of the attitudes remain.

Thus, some parents may sell their baby or even give it to people to "use" however they wanted. They feel they can always have more babies and promptly do so. It's a fast way to make money and lots of it. These types of people see children as no more than pieces of flesh to be bartered and done with as they wish. Repugnant as it may seem to us, it is for some a way of life—one of the many things that need to be changed if Mexico is ever to join the rest of the world. And thank God, this sort of mentality is no longer as widespread as it was in the past due to very strong efforts of the present day Mexican government to prevent it.

Orphanages must get the support of the church, the city or town in which they reside, or the government. Even today, these agencies do nothing to support the orphanages. They are often left on their own to come up with money. The children there must eat and be tended but with no real means to do so. While contributions from generous people account for much of the orphanages' income, the usage of some of the children in their care is their way of obtaining constant revenue. The children under the nuns' supervision have no parents, no one to watch out for them. There is no real motherly feeling present. These children are the perfect victims for deranged minds.

These institutions also teach the children to do as they are told and to never question authority. They only know right from wrong if the people in charge tell them what is right and what is wrong. The children have no contact with the outside world to assist them in their judgment or to protect them.

This "no contact" philosophy is a must if these children are to be used as quite a few of them are used in Mexico. The usage not only consists of child prostitution, but also of other abuses, such as child labor. Many of the upper class families in Mexico employ children as live-in servants starting at the age of eleven. (One was offered to

as live-in servants starting at the age of eleven. (One was offered to me, which I of course turned down.) This is considered an acceptable practice, as it is a large resource of cheap labor. This too must be stopped if child abuse in Mexico is ever to be brought under control. Yet, the people who employ these children are powerful and rich, so the hope of having something done about it is almost nil.

The children in the orphanages, as Gigi related to me, "are trained from early childhood that it is their obligation and expected function to be sold into one of these two practices." Consequently, they anticipate that this will be their future. They see nothing wrong with doing things with men while in the orphanages at early ages and when serving as servants; they are expected to do without question whatever the man of the house wants them to do, both in the house and in bed.

These children are little more than robots to do with as you desire. Essentially, the only difference between these robots and mechanical robots are that they are flesh and blood. Feelings are not part of their life. Normal children learn to feel sorrow, pain, pleasure, want, happiness, and all the other emotions as they grow to adulthood. However, many of the children in these orphanages will never truly feel these things. These were the biggest obstacles that Gigi had to face when finally set free from the hell in which she had lived. To this day, she has not fully acquired the essentials to express herself as a normal child would.

If I were to write in the orphanage management's defense, it would sound like this: "To sacrifice a few for the sake of the many, is that not really the best thing to do in the long run?" My answer to that is "It could be, if all else fails." My only problem and concern would be if I were part of the 'few' selected.

In any event, a week later at the hotel, as we were coincidentally watching the TV show *Father Knows Best*, Gigi looked up at me and said, "Daddy, would you promise never to tell anyone a secret if I told you one?"

"Sure, Princess, if you tell me not to say anything, Daddy would never say it to a soul unless we talked it over first. Just like I didn't say anything about those pictures, anything you tell me is our business."

Gigi replied, "You also promise you will not be mad at me?"

"Cross my heart and hope to die."

"Oh, Daddy, sometimes you can be so corny."

With that remark, I thought, "*Just think: one year ago, she could not even speak English. Now she is using Americanisms all the time when she talks and she is somehow picking up a Brooklyn accent.*"

She started talking. "Do you remember before when we were talking about those pictures the men took of me and you asked me if anything else ever happened?"

I interrupted her. "What do you mean by 'anything else happened'?"

She replied, "You know with other men or women, like when they took those pictures of me and the other girls? When we talked about it then, you got real mad."

"I was not mad at you; I was mad, yes, but at the people who took the pictures, not you. It wasn't your fault. I thought I had made that clear."

She looked at me with those big Bambi eyes filled with tears. She continued, "Oh. I thought you were mad at me, so when you asked me if anything else like that happened, I lied to you. You have often said that you do not like people who lie. So when I did not tell the truth about it then, I was afraid to tell you the rest later."

"What made you change your mind now, Princess?" I asked very cautiously.

"The TV show that we just watched where the little girl in the show told everything to her daddy. I wanted to be the same as her."

I hugged her and said, "Go ahead, Princess, and from now on, tell me anything if it bothers you to the point that this must have. Okay?"

"Okay, I promise," she said and then gave a big hug in return.

"Well, what's the big secret that I can never tell?"

She came over to me and sat on my lap before continuing. "I did do other things with men, boys, and women besides just taking pictures. Girls from the other orphanages were there doing the same things. We all did. When we went into one of the places where we did those things, other girls from different orphanages were always in there and coming out of the place. Inside the houses, I could see into some of the other waiting rooms on the first floor as we walked to our waiting roam. These rooms always had girls our ages and sometimes even younger than us, about three or four years old, waiting to go upstairs into one the rooms that where up there. Sometimes, I could hear them crying and screaming in the rooms next to our room upstairs."

"Also, there were times the boys would come to the Casa in the evening and do things with us in the dormitories. You remember the night you came to the Casa and saw those boys in there? That was one of the times. They were not expecting us to return so early and the next morning I got in a lot of trouble and was punished and spanked for allowing you to take me back earlier than you said you would."

"When we first went, we asked why we were going to these places. The Madres and Estella told us that was why we were in the orphanages. We were supposed to please the men and boys and do what they wanted. We did not really think it was that wrong since all the girls were doing it. We always knew when we were going by the way we were told to get dressed in the morning. If we were going to a house or a cantina that day, they told us not to wear slips, just our underwear, blouse, and a skirt. The big girls, like Maria Celer and Maria, had to wear bras, because they have 'hills' on their chests. If we were going to a cantina, we had to wear makeup and special short underwear. If we were going to a house, we did not wear makeup. They would also give us a pill just before we went, to make us feel better about all of it."

Shocked, I said, "Gigi, when did you have the chance to do all this? You are always at the Casa."

"When we had no school in the summer and when we went to the park with Estella on Saturdays. But since you have been here, I have not gone with them, I swear. I stay at the Casa when they go now. Estella and the Madres have also told me not to say anything to you about this."

"I have not seen any girls leave while I was there."

"No, they only go now when you are not there. Since we started with the classes, they very seldom go to the houses now. When they do go, they go without me. They take one of the new girls in my place," answered Gigi.

"Well, princess, when you did go, what took place?"

She continued with her tale. "Well, I started going when I was five years old. Then Estella would take us to a house or a cantina where it happened. During the summer, we would leave the Casa in the pickup truck at six in the morning with just Estella and not get back until eight or nine that evening."

I said, "But when Felipe drove and left you all at the park on Saturdays, he always brought the pickup back to the Casa and then picked you up later."

"That was when we went to the house by the park. You know all those houses across the street? We would walk there."

"Oh, I forgot about those houses. I thought you went somewhere else. But they are still a long walk from the park."

Gigi produced a small smile and said, "Yes, they are a long way. We were always tired when we arrived there. During the summer, we went to houses and the cantina that were not by the park. Those houses were very far away and took us an hour or so to get there. Estella drove us then."

"Did the other girls always go too?"

She said, "Yes, there were always eight of us."

"Just like when you took the pictures?"

"Yes," she answered.

"Well, just start the story with what you did at the houses. Then you can tell me about what happened at the cantinas."

She agreed and continued. "There was Maria Celer, Loraina, Elizabeth, Suzanna, Blanca, Naria, Carmelite, and me. We went all the time."

"All of the big girls?"

Gigi said, "Yes, the ones between five and eleven years old. Sometimes, only the three to four year olds went with Estella. When they came back, we asked what they did. They said they just went to the park and played. We knew they were lying because their eyes were red and they walked funny and always took a shower when they came back, but they never told us what they really did. I expect they were afraid that they would get a beating if we told one of the Madres."

"How often did you go?" I asked

"Every Saturday during the school year and every day during the summer since I was five years old."

After a moment of silence as I digested that, I said, "Well, start from the beginning and tell me exactly what happened when you went there the first time. You said that you were tired when you arrived there. Then what happened?"

She continued. "We all walked into the house. We were all expecting a party that first time. After that, we knew better. We knew why we were there and what we had to do. We walked into one of the living rooms that were on the first floor and there was a man there. Most of the time there would be a man or sometimes a man and a woman waiting there. Although, there were many times when there was a man there with a bunch of boys."

I asked, "About how old were the boys?"

"From seven to fourteen."

"Oh, that's interesting. Please go on with the story," I said. At this point, you could conjure up what was going through my mind. I was not going to blow up this time. I knew that if I did, it would stop her as it did months before when we were talking about the picture-taking episode. Then she would never tell me anything. So I had to bite my tongue.

"When the man saw Estella and us, he came over and said something to Estella. Then Estella told us to sit by the wall in the living room and not to talk. After we did that, the man and Estella went out to the hall and talked. When Estella and the man were finished talking in the hall, they came back into the room. Estella told us to line up by the wall while the man looked at us. Then the man told Estella if we were okay or not. Sometimes we were all wanted; other times, only a few of us. If he did not want all of us, he would pick the ones he wanted. The rest would wait in the car until the ones he picked were finished. Then the man would give Estella a lot of money."

As I was listening to this story, I was too shocked to say anything. When she was about halfway through the story, I wanted to believe that she was making it all up. But what she was saying could only be learned if you heard it somewhere, or read it…or experienced it. Gigi never had access to such fictions or books so it had to be true. (I later verified it all with two of the other children that had participated and came to trust me not to say anything.)

I was not only becoming sick over all of this but also so goddamned mad trying to figure out what to do about it. I now understood the day I had looked through the window in the Madre's office when I went to say goodbye and seen those people inspecting Blanca. It also explain why Gigi and Estella had those strange expressions when I came back after seeing that. They had known what was going on in there.

I could not tell any of the Madres because it looked like they were all in on it. And I could not go to the police or the social workers, as either they were on the Madres' payroll or they wouldn't believe a gringo against their most holy Madre. Who would believe a Madre could head up a child pornography and prostitution racket in Tijuana, especially if it was Madre Esmeralda? Even if I did say something, I was sure the children would not back up the story. They were afraid of their very lives, let alone jail, which is where they were told they would go if they said anything.

I could not think straight. The main thought at that moment was to hide my inner feelings from Gigi, as that would really upset her. My only real thought was that I somehow had to get Gigi out of that hellhole. Once I got her out, then I could worry about the rest of the girls at the Casa.

One factor that kept popping up in my thoughts as I looked at this little crying child was how right Doc had been on his feelings regarding concealment. I could not even tell him he had been correct in his fear, because he might contact the authorities, as the law requires. Who would have thought a thing like this could occur at a place run by nuns? I was also afraid that Doc wouldn't believe it either, and then who would back it up? Not the kids, they were too scared.

The only thing I could think of was to supply Madre Maria with sufficient hints about the situation and then let her take it from there. I didn't have the feeling that Madre Maria had any part or knowledge of what was taking place at the Casa. At least, I hoped not. If she did and I said something, I was a dead goose and so was Gigi.

At first, I didn't think that the children would ever tell anyone, but maybe they would tell Madre Maria. They all loved and trusted her. Now the problem faced me on how to get Madre Maria to investigate the Casa without saying too much to her.

I must have held Gigi for about an hour as she sobbed and begged, "Please, don't tell anyone and don't be mad at me. I really did not think I was doing wrong, as all the girls do it in the orphanages. Please, please, please."

CHAPTER TWENTY-SIX

MORE CONCEALMENT

I continued to hold Gigi for quite some time, rocking her in my arms. I spoke to her in a very soft voice, assuring her that I was not mad at her and, in fact, I was extremely proud of her for recounting to me those awful days. I also kept reassuring her that I would never tell a soul. Her greatest concern was that I might speak to the Madres or tell someone else and it would get back to the Madres. If this happened, she insisted that she would be badly beaten and never be able to see me again. She was shaking like a leaf in a tornado as she clung to me.

At this moment, I think she was having second thoughts about what she had just told me. Yet, I still sensed there was more going on than what I had just heard from Gigi. She was still hiding something even more terrifying. I felt like I was just touching the tip of the iceberg.

I had hopefully convinced her that I would not tell. The biggest thing I had going for me was that I had never said anything about the picture-taking episode that she had told me about previously. With that fact, I convinced her that I would not tell this story either.

Soon she was well enough to go back to the Casa. At the Casa, I was greeted by Madre Esmeralda as I stepped out of the car. Gigi looked at me and then the Madre. Gigi's eyes said all there was to say. "Please, Daddy, please do not let on that I told you."

I was very pleasant to the Madre outwardly, but on the inside, I wanted to put my hands around that rotten neck of hers and choke her with all my might. The hatred I had for her now had reached such a peak that I had a hard time restraining myself. I don't ever remember feeling such hate for one person as I now held for the woman who stood before me. I even hated calling her "Madre." If it were not for Gigi still being in her clutches, I would have told her off with words that would have made the devil blush.

As I was contemplating these thoughts, she smiled at us and asked if we had a good time swimming.

"Yes, we had a wonderful time. Gigi is a good swimmer now. She looks like she has been swimming all her life."

Gigi sort of relaxed as she heard this conversation. I imagined this was because of the way I was speaking to the Madre, whom I now just thought of as "Esmeralda," nothing motherly about her. It put Gigi's mind to rest somewhat that I would not say anything. Gigi kept looking at my face as I conversed with "that woman" for a sign of my displeasure with her. She knew that Esmeralda would be looking for any hint of a problem. Then after I left, Gigi would be put through the third degree by Esmeralda to find out what was wrong with me. So I was very careful not to let on that anything was wrong. Believe me, it was one of the hardest jobs I have ever done.

I walked Gigi to the dormitory and gave her a really big hug and whispered, "Don't worry, little princess, Daddy will never tell anyone. Okay?"

She gave me a hug and replied, "I believe you, Daddy."

The next day, I went to my lawyer and insisted that he proceed faster with Gigi's adoption. He said that he would, but with the way he said it, I had no faith that he would actually do so. Because of this lack of faith, I did not say why I wanted this big push on the adoption. By this time, I had grown not to like him. I believed that he too was on Esmeralda's payroll.

I figured out why they were not pushing for the adoption. Since I had been there, I had personally donated over twenty five thousand dollars to the Casa for its reconstruction and the welfare of the children. This was in addition to the computer school that Esmeralda was so proud of. She most likely thought that if Gigi were to go, so would all of those advantages. Plus, there was the worry that if Gigi was not under her control, Gigi might say something now that she spoke English so well. With what Gigi had been telling me these past days, I expected that part must really worry Esmeralda most of all.

Other girls from the Casa were adopted, but I'm quite sure their "adoptions" were not for the reason normal people adopt children. Those poor children were trapped into continuing elsewhere what they had been doing in the Casa. Mexican border towns are famous for this type of "entertainment," so Esmeralda had no concern over those girls saying anything to anyone, no matter where the children were. But Gigi being adopted by me was a different story. I was considered a "goody two shoes," as Gigi had recently informed me.

But Esmeralda hadn't expected that Madre Maria would speak to me about the adoption. In addition, I don't think she expected Madre Maria to speak so strongly for it. In fact, when Madre Maria had spoken to me about me adopting Gigi, Esmeralda had been very upset over it. This made me think that Madre Maria might be the answer to this whole disgusting situation.

Something had to be done and done quickly. Knowing what I did now, I did not think that I could keep up the act of being myself with that woman for any length of time. I was in a quandary. For one of the very few times in my life, I did not know what to do. Even with my own family, I had figured out a path and then walked away along it.

Now Gigi, that's a different story. All that was worthwhile in this world was wrapped up in that little child. No way, no how, could I walk away from this situation. Gigi was my daughter whether I had the papers to prove it or not. I would solve the situation by hook or by crook. Gigi had to be brought out of their clutches and fast. At the same time, she had to be consigned to a place of safety before someone realized that she had told me what went on in that hellhole that they called a "Casa."

I even thought of setting out a "contract" on Esmeralda. It is an easy thing to do in Mexico. Then again, whom could I get that wasn't already on Esmeralda's payroll or hadn't received a child from her? I decided to go back to the hotel and get a good night's sleep. I always think better after a good rest.

I got in bed and tossed and turned over and over again. I thought about how small and fragile this little girl was. How could any man do that to a girl, let alone this little pitiful looking child? There are such sick minds in this world. Who could advise me? I couldn't think of anyone to tell. Even if I did, who would believe me? Gigi would deny the entire story, as she was so frightened by the repercussions. My thoughts were running rampant, and my good night's sleep never materialized. The next morning, I was even more tired than I had been the night before.

Until I could figure out what to do, I had to be cool, as if nothing happened. That meant I had to be at the Casa at eight this morning, my usual time of arrival. I was up and out of the hotel swiftly. I did not even stop for breakfast. I was not really hungry anyway. Like most people, I can't eat when I am this upset over something.

Gigi was there waiting for me with her usual happy greeting when I parked my car. She acted as if nothing had happened yesterday at all. I tried to act the same way. As I stood there, I saw some of the girls were getting in the bus to go somewhere.

"Where are the girls going?"

"Across the border to Marine Land," Gigi answered.

"Oh, that's nice." I counted them as they got on the bus. Twelve girls left that morning. Later that night, only nine returned. Three were missing—three whom I never saw again.

I was determined to find out what was happening with these children in what was supposed to be a place of God. I knew some people in the shady part of Tijuana who trusted me. This was due to my having helped their families once or twice with money. Likewise, these people also worked at the Casa for food. I figured they could pay me back by either telling me what was going on at the Casa or finding out for me.

I targeted one man whom I had helped quite a bit. He had been working in the Casa for many years. I contacted him one night and persuaded him to tell me what was happening at the Casa by paying him a huge sum of money, along with a promise of sworn secrecy.

His answers were not too explicit. They did not tell me what was happening to the children after they crossed the border, because he never went with Estella when she crossed. However, his answers did resolve most of the events that were taking place at the Casa. I spent about four hours with him as he told me what he knew. When he was finished, I thanked him very much and then gave him his money before returning to the Casa.

On my drive to the Casa, I remembered something that happened one day while I was at the Casa. This memory probably surfaced due to what I had just heard. That day, I had seen a man and a woman in the Casa's courtyard. The man was Asian and the woman looked like a barmaid. At the time, I had pointed them out to Gigi as we stood there and asked who they were. Gigi had told me that they were taking Maria Celer out for the day.

That evening, Jesus had come to the hotel and said, "I was at the window of the computer room and saw Maria Celer when she came back to the Casa after her visit. She was covered with blood and cut all over. Do you know anything about this?"

"No," I had answered. "It's a surprise to me. I will speak to Madre about it." I had figured I could say something to Esmeralda on this subject because I could legitimately add that Jesus had told me so as to not arouse her suspicions. So the next morning, I had asked Esmeralda about Maria Celer. She replied that she fell when she was outside and that was all. She was quite upset with me for asking. I had told her that Jesus had asked me and I was just getting the answer for him. I had done my best to act as if I personally did not care. I had also taken the opportunity to throw her off guard by adding, "Madre, you know whatever you do in my mind is correct no matter what it is. I love you very much." I had barely been able to choke out the words. Then I had volunteered to supply the Casa with an icebox, stove, and freezer for her outdated kitchen. Plus stocking it up with whatever food she so desired.

That had really done the trick. Because after that she had given me a little hug and said, "Roberto, I know that, and I trust you to keep whatever goes on here to yourself. And, of course, thank you so much for your generous donation."

Jesus, however, had been on the outs with Madre Esmeralda ever since then, but because of the computers and the children's increasing learning, she could say and do little.

Now that Gigi trusted me enough to tell me her secrets, I asked her about Maria Celer. She told me that the man and woman wanted her to do things that she did not want to do. They did not give her the pill beforehand so she did not feel like doing "it." None of them would do "it" if it weren't for the pill. So they beat Maria Celer until she did "it" for the people.

My friend's story rested heavily on my mind for days. It was too much for me to believe. I had to confirm his information. The next day, I took Gigi on a visit to the hotel for a swim and lunch. While we were poolside eating our lunch, I said, "Gigi, why didn't you tell me everything?"

She stopped and looked all around. "Daddy, I do not know what you are talking about."

After much cajoling, she finally said, "Daddy, they would kill me as they did the last girl who said something. But I will tell you about it all. I swear."

"Okay, tell what you know. This time tell me everything."

For an hour or so, I sat there and listened to almost the same tale that the informant had told me a few days ago. I also asked Gigi about the children after they crossed the border because the informant hadn't had the answer to that part of the story. Gigi filled in those blanks, much to my dismay. Along with the abuse, she spoke of men with guns and drugs.

Well that answered the last part of the puzzle about the disappearing girls.

It was organized crime, the cartels. That was the only reasonable answer. Who else could be involved in drugs to this extent? This was millions of dollars in business each year. The drugs and the killing of a girl must be the work of professionals. Who else has that kind of a network but organized crime?

With this information, it made it all the more necessary that I get Gigi out of there fast. I could now also expect interference from the drug people. They would not want the information that Gigi had just told me to be publicized. She was a witness to it all, one who might just talk. No wonder Esmeralda was so dead set against my speedily adopting her.

As I sat there, I kept thinking about Doc and his warning that I might see and hear things that would shock me at the Casa. He had pleaded with me not to get involved with Gigi. But I don't think he ever thought it would be this bad.

Upon telling me all of this, Gigi was a nervous wreck. She had finally told me everything. It took a great deal of love and trust on her part to do so. I was thus very proud of my daughter-to-be, and I told her so.

CHAPTER TWENTY-SEVEN

MADRE MARIA INVESTIGATES

After a while, Gigi calmed down from her anxiety over telling me the whole story. I then returned her to the Casa with a pact between us never to tell the Madres what she had just told me. I said my said farewells to The Gig and then returned to the hotel to think some more on the situation that had presented itself to me in the last couple of days. I had the information that the informant and Gigi had given me. Along with what The Gig had told me about Maria Celer, this all made it necessary that I get Gigi out of there.

I had gotten an idea as I stood in the Casa talking to Gigi. I had been right about the lawyer. Now maybe I was right about Madre Maria. I had to find some reason to go to her headquarters in Mexico City. Not for just a day' that was easy. If my hunches were right about Madre Maria, I would need time there to have her take action and get The Gig out of Tijuana.

Gigi would never be safe in Tijuana as long as Esmeralda was there and alive. Esmeralda had a lot of influence over certain people, probably due to those pictures that Estella had taken of the girls with the men and presumably given to Esmeralda afterwards. The bishop was also in the palm of her hand. Knowing the bishop, I didn't have to think long on how Esmeralda controlled him. The bishop was an all-too-frequent visitor to the Casa of Esmeralda and spent much time with the children—especially the girls.

I still had the feeling that Madre Maria was not mixed up in all of this. Nor did she have any knowledge of her great friend Esmeralda's rackets. Then and there, I decided to go with my hunch. If I were wrong, both Gigi and I would be in serious trouble. But Madre Maria was the one who genuinely thought I should adopt Gigi, so logically, she would not be mixed up in these affairs.

My company, as I said before, was a worldwide company. So, I got on the phone and scheduled a meeting with the president of the Mexican operation. The next day, I was off to Mexico City. I had told Jesus and Gigi I would be gone a couple of weeks. However, I did not tell them where I was going, in case the plan fell through. I arrived in Mexico City and set up my own headquarters at Rosa, a hotel in the American zone. I then promptly went to see the president of my company in Mexico.

He was a gray-haired man in his late fifties who spoke English very well. He was tall and sported a small mustache. He was not too fat but not too thin, just right in weight. It was an unusual appearance for a Mexican man in his position. After a brief time with him, I could see he was an advocate for early schooling. He really wanted to do something for the children of Mexico. During this period of my career, the executive management team in my company was interested in doing something for the children of the world. This president was no exception.

We talked a long time on the subject. He was very interested in the work we were doing in Tijuana. Much to my surprise, he was not upset that we were there without his knowledge. At the end of the conversation, he called in one of his people and assigned me to work with him to bring the project to Mexico City while still letting it continue in Tijuana.

I was ecstatic; I had gotten what I came for: a reason to be in both places whenever I needed to be. Not only in both places, but also for the time I thought necessary to get the job done in either place. I left his office and returned to the hotel. That evening, I celebrated. I was on my way.

Now I had to determine if Madre Maria was mixed up in Esmeralda's crimes. If not, how was I to get her to investigate? Then how was I to get The Gig out of there and beyond Esmeralda's foul and vindictive clutches? Where would Gigi live? There was much reason for concern. Nevertheless, at this moment of triumph, I did not worry about the results too much. I had accomplished the first step. The first step is always the hardest in any plan, especial mine. It was so complicated and complex, with two lives being held in the balance.

While in the hotel, I was trying to think ahead. If Gigi were to come to Mexico City, where would she live while I found my own temporary quarters? I considered my hotel. It was a Spanish-speaking hotel and not too many Americans were there. Being a Mexican hotel, the children of the guests all spoke Spanish, which would give Gigi some playmates. It would be ideal for a couple of refugees, so I inquired at the desk if they had any suites with two bedrooms. When told there were some available, I asked to inspect them. I was taken to the top floor to examine them. The suites were beautiful with large living rooms, two baths, and bedrooms with a big terrace overlooking the city.

I had overcome one more hurdle. I had found a place for us to stay if The Gig were to come to Mexico City. "This is my day," I thought. "God must be with my venture."

The following day, I went to the office. There I once more met the man who was to assist me, Senor Gomez, in setting up something for the children here as we had in Tijuana. My thoughts for setting up a computer school were to find a Casa here in Mexico to repeat what we had done at Esmeralda's Casa. My plan was to have the computers in one of the Casas that Madre Maria oversaw. Upon discussing the matter with Senor Gomez, I was quickly advised that the president had already picked two schools that he would like to see be the recipients of such a project. One was Green Gates and the other was the Merci.

"I thought we would do the same as in Tijuana and put the computers in an orphanage," I asked.

"The president thought we had gotten enough from that aspect of the study. Now we should try the project with better schools because the parents of those students have money to buy computers," Gomez answered.

I could not argue with what he said; it made good business sense. The only problem was that it stopped the next part of my plan, the part where I was able to be with Madre Maria all the time if the computers were in her Casa in Mexico City. Being there, I could have slowly suggested to her that something was going on in the Casa at Tijuana.

So with that idea of meeting Madre Maria thwarted, I had to come up with something else. It's lucky, though that I had gone along with the president's suggestion, as I was to find out later that one of the schools selected was where the president's daughter was enrolled. The other school selected was where the vice president's child was registered. This was to prove useful in the future.

Gomez and I contacted the schools and visited them to inspect the grounds. Both schools were beautiful. They were attended by the children of the very wealthy of Mexico, the ambassadors, high government, and foreign businessmen. The classes, grounds, and teachers were of the highest grade—nothing like any of the schools in Tijuana. Even the "rich" school in Tijuana was nothing more than a run-down public school when compared to these schools. After the tour of each school, we discussed our project with the people in charge.

This was all confusing to Gigi. She had never left her particular area of Tijuana. No other landscape existed for her. She knew nothing of Mexico City. In fact, she knew nothing, except for what I had been showing her, namely the hotel and the Plaza. We had never really discussed other places than Tijuana, so how could I be anywhere but in Tijuana? If there, why was I not with her? And why was I talking to her on this strange object? She knew that I sometimes went some place but she thought it was there in Tijuana, because I always came back in a couple of days. She could not comprehend that I was hundreds or thousands of miles away. Then again, she did not understand the word "miles."

It was becoming more and more understandable to me why these children were being kept in total ignorance and isolation from the world. This way they could be used for anything the Madres so desired without any conjecture on their part that something was right or wrong. Even if they dared think for themselves, they didn't know if there was some place to run to or escape. They were slaves to the Madres' desires, and were human flesh to be used and bartered without any questions on their part.

Soon Gigi got accustomed to me phoning and talked longer with me. She still did not really understand what was happening. The only thing she knew was Daddy was talking and she was talking to him. She somewhat forgot her concerns about this strange object she had in her hand because Daddy said that he would explain the entire thing to her when he saw her again. That was enough for her.

In the mornings, I would spend my time with the selected schools' teachers, instructing them on the new educational method. In the afternoons, I would visit Madre Maria in her Casa—it only being polite since I was in the area after all. This was my new plan and it seemed to be working well.

During this part of the venture, every other weekend, I would fly to Tijuana to be with Gigi. I did this for about two months. I was getting to know Madre Maria very well by this time. We were becoming extremely close friends. I also had the opportunity to visit more of her Casas that were in Mexico City.

When I was convinced that Madre Maria was not part of Esmeralda's intrigue, I commenced with the next step: introducing the idea of something going on at the Tijuana Casa. I would say, "Madre, who are all those strange men I see living in the Casa in Tijuana? I do not see them here in your Casas. Your children seem so much happier and not as tired looking as the ones in Tijuana." Words similar to those I would somehow slip into our conversations.

Each answer from Madre Maria to my questions and statements were always the same: "I did not know."

One evening at supper, Madre Maria brought a new companion to supper with us. It was a young Madre about 28 years old. Her name was Dolores. She was extremely pretty and very knowledgeable about what was happening in the rest of the world. We talked that evening on many subjects. At the close of the evening, Madre Maria announced to me that Madre Dolores was going to Tijuana to help Esmeralda in the Casa for about six months

Thus, Madre Maria had gotten the hints. Madre Dolores was now going to check on what I had been suggesting these past couple of months. Madre did not specifically say that, but I could draw conclusions from the questions Madre Dolores asked me as we ate. They mostly concerned the Tijuana Casa. Her main theme of questioning was my opinion of the Tijuana Casa in comparison to the Casas I had visited here in Mexico City. I anticipated that Madre Dolores would keep in close contact with Madre Maria once she was in Tijuana.

Madre Dolores left the next day. In the weeks that followed, Madre Maria confirmed why my theories about why Madre Dolores was in Tijuana. Madre Maria would ask me if I knew this or that about the Tijuana Casa, details that Madre Dolores had been telling her over the phone. Along with that, she asked if I knew why Esmeralda would keep Madre Dolores in isolation and not let her be alone with any of the girls.

I felt this was my opening. 'The next night at supper, I discussed what Gigi had told me about her and the other girls. Madre Maria turned white with anger and shock. She knew I had been hinting at something these past months about the Casa in Tijuana but never in her worst nightmares did she think this.

Madre Maria sat there for about an hour at the supper table. Not eating or talking, just staring into open space. Every so often, she would look at the pictures of the girls. She kept staring at the one of Gigi and then looking at me. She only spoke once. "God, forgive me; I did not know anything about this. You have got to believe me."

Soon she completely broke her silence and said in a commanding voice, "Roberto, tell Guillermina on your next visit to trust Madre Dolores and if she feels anything is wrong or she might be in danger, to contact Madre Dolores immediately. I will likewise instruct Madre Dolores to keep a close and protecting eye on Guillermina without making Madre Esmeralda suspicious. The most important thing we need to do now is to get that child out of there as fast as possible so I can take action. If...*when* I take the action that I am planning, it will surely endanger Gigi's life. Madre Esmeralda will know who told on her." Madre Maria also added that Madre Esmeralda probably knew why Madre Dolores was there and that Madre Esmeralda would never consent to me adopting Guillermina.

Madre Maria then stated that she would introduce me tomorrow to someone whom she trusted and believed would help me. She promptly advised me that she was no longer hungry and wanted return to the Casa to phone this man. She wanted him to come to the Casa that evening to discuss her plan to save Gigi and eventually the other girls.

I paid the bill and then took the Madre to her Casa. Before returning to my hotel, I stopped at a small church and thanked God for allowing my decision to be correct about Madre Maria.

CHAPTER TWENTY-EIGHT

JOSE LOUIS AND MADRE MARIA'S RESCUE PLAN

I went to the Mexico City Casa the next afternoon. Madre Maria escorted me into her little living room that all these Casas seemed to have. There seated in the armchair was a man. He was tall, slender, well built, and rather good looking. On his upper lip was a finely kept small mustache and his hair was the typical cold, raven black. His face indicated that he was a man with great knowledge. Wearing a fine business suit, he appeared to be a professional man in his early forties. Beside the chair was an attaché case. I presumed it was his.

As I entered the room, he rose from his chair and extended his hand, introducing himself as Jose Louis Gonzalez, the lawyer for all the Casas in all of Mexico. "Madre Maria has been telling me about the situation in Tijuana and a little girl named Guillermina. The Madre states that you and the child are very much attached to each other. Likewise, she believes you are a fine man and the two of you belong together. Now if what she says is true about that particular Casa, then I agree with her. We have got to find some way to get that child out of there before any further action can be taken to elevate the situation for the other girls. I think we have a plan if you are willing to go along with it."

I quickly replied, "Anything that would get Gigi out of that place, I would go along with."

Gonzalez nodded and then continued. "We have one serious problem. This is the month of February and Madre Maria will be replaced at the end of April. Every ten years, the Madre general is replaced with a new elected Madre. This insures that the order does not stagnate under one Madre's control. It's a good idea in theory. However, in this particular situation, it is not too good for us.

"This is Madre Maria's tenth year as Madre general. The Madre who is slated to replace Madre Maria is a very good friend of Madre Esmeralda. Therefore, whatever must be done to get you and Gigi together legally so Esmeralda cannot touch you has got to be done by this April. That's not much time. We will have to work long hours and fast. Are you willing to do this?"

"As I said before, anything you say has to be done, I will do."

He smiled. Then he came over to me and gave me that big Mexican hug that shows they really like you. "You are everything the Madre said you were and then some. It will be a pleasure to undertake this impossible task with you two," Jose Louis pronounced. "Well then, with that out of the way and everyone understanding the predicament, let's get started."

"The first thing Madre Maria and I feel is of a necessity is to get Guillermina to Mexico City. We can place her into one of the Casas under Madre Maria's direct control and then transfer her to a place of secrecy. This way we can watch Guillermina so nothing happens to her, and can have access to her twenty-four hours a day. Likewise, it would put Guillermina under the protection of the state of Mexico, where my practice is. I have many contacts here that we might need if Madre Esmeralda tries anything."

"In addition, we need Guillermina here to have her testify in favor of the adoption. Judges, state and government lawyers, police, and government officials will have to speak to her during the procedures. And there are various papers that we need her to sign. Plus, we have got to find a way to submit a birth certificate for her into the records before we even start the procedures. There's a lot of work to do and not much time to do it in."

"If we can have Guillermina here with Madre Esmeralda's permission, that is all the better. Her permission for adoption, though, will not be necessary if Guillermina is transferred to one of the Casas here in Mexico City. At that point, permission can be given by Madre Maria. The first and toughest job will be to get Guillermina here without arousing Madre's Esmeralda's suspicions that we think anything is wrong. She is already suspicions because of Madre Dolores' presence in Tijuana. Once we try to place jurisdiction over Guillermina in Madre Maria's hands, then Madre Esmeralda will surely be aware of what is taking place."

"At that time, she will do everything in her power to stop us. We can stall her just by the fact that she must obey the Madre general. The only recourse she has then is to go someone higher in authority, the bishop. The relationship between Madre Esmeralda and the bishop is well known. His intervention will supersede Madre Maria's authority. He most likely will order Madre Maria to return Guillermina back to Tijuana. I do not have an answer yet for that if it is to take place, but one bridge at a time. The difficulty of this first bridge will set the pace for the decisions that follow. I do not want to plan too far in advance in case things change."

"Now, let us discuss how we will get Guillermina here in Mexico City and under Madre Maria's authority. The Madre and I have a plan. It goes like this: Madre Esmeralda likes to travel. She also has not been to Mexico City in a long time. She has a lot of friends here that she would like to see. Therefore, you will to return to Tijuana to see Guillermina as usual. While there, suggest to Madre Esmeralda that she and Guillermina should come to Mexico City next weekend for vacation. We think she would go along with that and it shouldn't arouse her suspicions as to what we are up to. How does that sound?"

"Sounds like a good plan so far," I answered.

"Good," Jose Louis replied. "Once they are here, Madre Maria will suggest that Guillermina remain behind when the weekend is finished for a physical because she looks so thin. Then Madre Maria will say, 'When Guillermina is finished with the physical, which ought to take two days, she will then be returned to the Tijuana Casa.' Madre Esmeralda won't like it, but she will have to agree. She will not be able to do anything about it until the two days are up."

"I expect Madre Esmeralda will then call and ask where Guillermina is. At that time, we can say the doctor wants to take more tests. I believe we can stall her for about a week. That's about as much time as I need to complete the paperwork needed to have Guillermina transferred under the authority of Madre Maria. Then the only recourse Madre Esmeralda will have are her friend the bishop and the cartels."

"She cannot afford to let Guillermina reach friendly hands that might expose her and the other people's actions. Esmeralda, in my mind, will never go along with you adopting her. That would be self-destructive for her. Because of your relationship with Guillermina, she is bound to tell you what has happened to her once she is no longer afraid of being returned to Esmeralda's hands. Also with Guillermina gone, Madre Esmeralda will lose your contributions, which I understand from Madre Maria have been substantial."

"This is a dangerous plan. We could all end up with a kidnapping charge hanging over us. And maybe even worse from her friends if it is not done properly. Bob—may I call you Bob?"

"By all means. May I call you Jose Louis?" I responded.

"Yes, of course," Jose Louis said. "Let's start this plan this weekend. You should go up to Tijuana on Wednesday of this week so you can get Madre Esmeralda to agree to come to Mexico City this weekend, okay?"

"No problem," I quickly replied.

It was now five in the evening. Time for supper. Jose Louis asked if he and a friend might accompany myself, the Madre, and her companion for supper.

"I would enjoy that very much," I answered.

Then Madre Maria interrupted and said me that her companion that evening would be Madre Antonio. She and Jose Louis had discussed Madre Antonio prior to our meeting. The Madre also added that she had informed Madre Antonio of the plan and she was willing to go along with it.

Madre Antonio would be the Madre in charge of the Casa in which Gigi would be placed when she came to Mexico City. This was necessary, as Madre Maria could not be at the Casa all the time due to her duties as Madre general. Madre Antonio would be there all the time to protect Gigi, 24 hours a day.

Jose Louis entered back into the conversation at this point. He informed us that his friend who would be accompanying us to supper was a judge in Mexico City—the judge who would be handling Gigi's adoption when it was ready.

I thought to myself, "I only told Madre Maria last night about the situation in Tijuana and look at what has been done in this short time. This woman is unbelievable. So is Jose Louis."

Madre Maria got up and left the room. She returned shortly with Madre Antonio and introduced us. Madre Antonio was a tall, middle-aged woman with well-kept hair styled much like Madre Maria's. It was not pulled back into a bun as the Madres did at the Tijuana Casa. She likewise stood straight as an arrow. Her face and attitude reminded me strongly of Madre Maria. A glow of saintliness surrounded her entire being. Her eyes were warm and comforting, a woman you could trust. Like Madre Maria, however, she spoke no English. Jose Louis had to interpret the conversation.

Once the introduction and pleasantries were out of the way, Jose Louis suggested that we leave. Since the judge was meeting us at the restaurant, we all got up and headed for the car. Within a few minutes, we were at the restaurant. Upon entering, we were greeted by Jose Louis's friend, Judge Rodriguez. The judge was built like Jose Louis. The only real difference was that he was much smaller in stature. He, like the Madres, spoke no English.

We all proceeded behind the captain to our table. Madre was speaking to Rodriquez as we were being seated. I did not understand what they were saying, as they were speaking quite fast in Spanish. After we were all seated, Jose Louis ordered for us all. "This will permit us more time to discuss the plan we are about to undertake," he declared.

The food Jose Louis ordered was agreeable to everyone except me. The food was totally Mexican. One thing I have never gotten to enjoy is Mexican food. When asked if I wanted what Jose Louis had ordered, I replied, "Yes, it one of my favorite dishes." I did not want to say anything negative, as it might insult Jose Louis and his friend the judge, so I just acted as if I ate it all the time. That was a job within itself.

Jose Louis informed us that he'd told the judge about my interest in adopting Gigi and that the procedure seemed to be taking way too long. He was prompt to add in English that he had not mentioned anything about the girls and the way they were being abused. If he were to have done so, then the judge would have gone straight to the police and Gigi would be in serious jeopardy. Jose Louis had just told the judge that this would be a normal adoption procedure and that he wanted him to meet me. This way the judge could get to know me as a person.

The evening lasted into the wee hours of the morning. The judge asked me many questions concerning everything from soup to nuts via Jose Louis's translation. I was a nervous wreck. I was afraid I might say or do the wrong thing.

Finally, the time came for us to leave. I paid the bill and we all stood to go.

The judge came over to me and put his arms tightly around me. "Roberto, you are a fine man and I will do everything in my power to see that this little girl is placed in your home."

We all walked to our cars and said our goodbyes. I walked with the two Madres, and Jose Louis walked with the judge. He was speaking to the judge in Spanish so I was not able to listen to the conversation. However, I was quite sure they were discussing my case. Jose Louis, as I was to find out later, was not a man to let grass grow under his feet. The judge departed first and then the rest of us climbed into my car.

During the drive back to the Casa, Jose Louis told me that he had been speaking to the judge about my case, but he would not tell me exactly what was said. "Don't worry; he likes you very much. I set up a meeting with him in two weeks to get the first papers for the adoption reviewed. I also explained the urgency due to Madre Maria leaving at the end of April." With that, he added, "Bob, it's up to you now to get Guillermina down here. We are all counting on you." He then spoke to the Madre in Spanish to tell her what he just said. The Madre agreed with him and told me that she knew if anyone could do it, it would be me.

I dropped them all off at the Casa, as Jose Louis wanted to speak some more to Madre Maria about the plans to make sure everything was set on both their ends. We said our goodnights, and then I drove back to the hotel.

Once in my room, I sat in an armchair for a while. My head was in a spin. The plan was in place within such a short time. Now everything was up to me. In this human game of chess, the next move was mine.

I thought, "What happens if I cannot talk Madre into coming to Mexico City? What happens if she gets suspicious? What happens if she will not leave Tijuana without Gigi?" These were just some of the thoughts that I had as I sat there. Many more whirled and danced in my mind. Thus, once again, I drifted off into a very restless sleep.

CHAPTER
TWENTY-NINE

THE RESCUE

I awoke the next morning still in my armchair. My back was sore from it but I took my shower and that seemed to pep me up. Just as I was about to leave the room for breakfast, the phone rang. It was Diane, my secretary. She warned me that there was about to be a reorganization within the company and that I should return to Texas to protect our interests. She added that this was due to the old chairman of the board's retiring and a new one taking over. The new one was, essentially, a bastard who did not think being in the field of education was worthwhile.

I told her that there was no way I could do that now. She and my boss, Tom, would have to do it for me. I regretted this very much, as I owed a lot to Tom and my upper management, but there was nothing more important to me now than the plan to save Gigi.

Tom got on the phone and pleaded with me to return. He insisted that I was the only one that had the information and ability to speak on the subject convincingly, as I had always sold the project in the past. He didn't think that they would listen to anyone else. I said, "Tom, I love you as a brother. Any other time but this, I would die for you. However, this takes precedence."

He replied, "Bob, I understand. The only thing is that the new reorganization will put the opposition back in place here. Then our project in education will come to an end. As you know, these people don't give two damns for the kids. Just their wallets. You have heard them say, 'I don't give a damn for those kids. They don't buy computers.' What will you do when they come into power?"

"Tom," I answered, "I will cross that bridge when I come to it. Just have faith that something is going on that means life or death for Gigi. Otherwise, I would return."

Tom replied, "Okay, I have known you a long time and have faith that what you are doing is the right thing. I wish you luck. Keep in touch so I know where you are. That way I can at least keep you up to date on what is taking place back here."

I agreed and hung up. I thought, "It not only rains but it pours. What's next?" As far as the office went, that was a blow. I knew if I did not return, then my company would never enter into the field of education. The entire project and about 20 management people, the entire management chain all the way to the top, would be gone, along with over 308 people associated with the project. I knew it and knew it quite well. This was because all the opposition had just been waiting for their chance to get rid of this expensive section of our company. Now that the new chairman of the board had been elected, they would have the authority to cancel our project. I knew all these things, and yet nothing was going to sway me from the Madre's plan.

I pushed those thoughts from my mind and went to breakfast. I had a lot to do. Change plane reservations to Tijuana. Get reservations for three coming back to Mexico City. What happens if there were no seats on either flight? The entire plan would be shot. I had to pack my stuff. Change hotel reservations from the Hotel Lucerna in Tijuana. Decide on how I would approach Esmeralda. How would I explain the plan to Gigi? I needed Jesus' help. How would I explain all this to him? With these thoughts, I did not have time for the protection of my future. The Gig came first and foremost in my mind.

The airlines advised me that they could accommodate my requests for tickets on all the required days. That was one uncertainty out of the way. If all the others were as easy as that, I would be home free. Then I called the hotel in Tijuana to change my reservations there. They too cooperated and granted my desires. They were booked, but they did like Gigi so very much. They always bent over backwards on any of my requests involving Gigi. They enjoyed seeing her at the hotel.

I then called Jesus and told him to meet me in the hotel that Wednesday evening as I had something important to discuss with him. I added that I did not have the time to tell him anything on the phone now other than it concerned Gigi. He agreed. The rest of the day was spent wrapping up the work that had piled up in my hotel room from the office. In all honesty, though, I did not get much done as my mind kept voyaging back to Gigi and the plan.

Wednesday was fast upon me after one more restless night. I quickly got dressed and left for the airport. Shortly, I was arriving at the Tijuana airport. I deplaned and pushed my way through the always-present mass of humanity that seems to crowd the airports and stores in Mexico. I rented my car and I was on my way to the hotel, then to the Casa.

I had not told anyone in the Casa that I would be coming early except Jesus. I did not want to put them on their guard and I wanted to be there to watch their faces when they found out about my rescheduled arrival. I registered at the hotel and dropped my bags off. I then proceeded from there to the Casa. For some reason, the great walls that surrounded the Casa looked bigger to me that day than they ever did before.

I drove to the colossal gates and sounded my horn. Felipe was quick to appear and opened up the great gates as if they were nothing. I could hardly move them when I tried such a feat. I then proceeded to my parking space. No one was in sight. I inquired from Felipe where they all were. Felipe told me that they were in church so I just sat on the fender on the car and waited for them. The church was on the other side of the inner courtyard, opposite of where I parked. Church soon ended and the children started to march out in rows of twos. The boys were first, then the girls.

When the girls started to come out, I could see by their faces that they were surprised that Gigi's daddy was here early this week. I could also see they were passing the word back to Gigi, who was at the end of the line, that her daddy was here. By the time she was outside, I could tell by her expression that she had gotten word. Gigi wildly broke ranks and came running down the stairs to me in complete disregard of procedure, all the time screaming "Daddy, Daddy." She fell as she jumped the stairs of the church leading to the inner yard in her rush to come to me. But she quickly got up and continued her wild dash to my arms.

I knelt and opened my arms for her attack. I also braced my back against the fender of the car. This was because I was sure she was going to come into my arms at 90 miles an hour. Once in my arms, she wrapped herself around me with arms and legs and just squeezed with all her might.

While this was all taking place, I could see Esmeralda on the top of the church stairs. She was smiling at me and waving. She seemed to be enjoying what was taking place. For a moment there, I almost forgot what kind of a person she was. I think she could deceive the very Devil himself if she put her mind to it.

"You are early with this visit. You do not come until the day before the school is ended for two days," Gigi exclaimed.

This was her way of telling when I would come or not. My visits weren't on Friday afternoon, but the day just before she did not go back to school for two days. She knew she went five days to school and then had two days off. Then she had to wait five days again before her daddy would return. Her calendar was not the weeks or dates, just the days of school and no school. Even though I had taught Gigi what days and months were, she was still not sure of them.

"Daddy came early this week because he has to ask Madre Esmeralda something. I think you will like it too," I answered.

"What? Oh, what is it, Daddy? Tell me, tell me, please, please," she pleaded.

"I have to ask the Madre first and then if she says okay, Daddy will tell you, okay?" I laughingly replied.

With that, she unwrapped herself from me and started across the inner yard towards Esmeralda, who was walking to greet me. Gigi grasped her by the hand to hurry Esmeralda across the yard to me and the "something" I was to ask her.

Due to my interest in her and my donations to the Casa, Gigi was starting to throw her weight around in the Casa. She was smart enough to realize that Esmeralda liked me and that if she pleased Esmeralda, she got more things from me. Gigi learned very quickly to adapt to a situation that was in her favor. She does that even now. She has a way to get things from me like no one else could. Many orphans have that particular trait. I expect it is acquired by the children to survive by getting just a little more than the other children vying for attention in an orphanage.

Esmeralda was soon next to me. I placed a kiss on her cheek and she the same to mine. "Roberto, I did not expect you until this Friday. What brings you here so early?" Esmeralda inquired, with Gigi doing the translation when I got stuck on certain words.

"Well, Madre," I replied, "when I was in Mexico City, I had the chance to visit with Madre Maria. During those visits, a lot of the Madres asked me how you were. So I thought that it would be nice if I could take you to Mexico City this weekend and you could be with them. If you wish, we could have a party for your friends in a nice restaurant of your choosing. You would be the guest of honor. How does that sound?"

During the time I had been at the Casa, I had discovered that Esmeralda liked fine things and restaurants, so I knew this would get her attention. I continued without waiting for a reply. "I asked Madre Maria if it was all right if you came. She thought it was a great idea as she misses you also. And if it is all right with you, maybe we could bring Gigi along too."

Esmeralda looked at me and said nothing, just stared into empty space. She was thinking. I could see her mind going a mile a minute as Gigi pleaded with her to go. Shortly, Esmeralda broke her meditation. A huge smile appeared on her face and she said, "That is a wonderful idea. I was just thinking of the things I had to do this weekend, but I can get the other Madres to do those. The ones they cannot do, I'll just put off to Monday or Tuesday. First, I must call Madre Maria to make sure she agrees with the visit."

So off we all went to call Madre Maria. As we walked to the place where Esmeralda office was to phone, Gigi was doing her happy little hop skip. "Goody, oh goody," Gigi said. Then she asked, "Where and what is Mexico City?"

"It is a far off place with big buildings and we have to get there by plane."
Gigi had seen pictures of planes but had never really understood what they did. So as Esmeralda was phoning, I tried to explain to Gigi about airports, planes, tall buildings, streets, the lots and lots of cars

that were there, and even city smog. Each explanation led to ten more questions. Gigi was alive with excitement by now. She was hugging me and kissing me on the cheek with every explanation that I delivered to her.

Esmeralda finally hung up the phone and with great pleasure said that Madre Maria had verified the invitation and that all the other Madres would be thrilled. Esmeralda was very excited over the prospect of seeing her old friends and going to Mexico City.

The trap was sprung and Esmeralda had fallen for it. Not only fallen for it, she could hardly wait to get into it. I had accomplished what I had set out to do. The only thing left now was to make sure nothing happened to upset the apple cart between now and the day we left. That was just two days away. During that time, I had my job cut out for me. I had to explain the plan to Jesus and Gigi. I'd speak to Jesus this evening. That would be easy. Explaining it to Gigi would be the tricky part.

The hour was now late so I bid goodbye to all. Gigi came with me all the way to the street, where she waved as I drove away, one of the new privileges that were granted to only her due to our association. It was a privilege that she took great pride in, as she was the only child in the Casa that could go anywhere near those gates, let alone go on the street outside of them. Until this time, that freedom was unheard of.

Upon entering the lobby of the hotel, I spied Jesus sitting in his usual chair. He got up and proceeded towards me. We both embraced. "What the hell is going on? You sounded so mysterious over the phone," he said.

I looked at him and replied, "Let's go into the bar. It will take some time to explain it to you. It has a lot to do with what you saw when you told me about Maria Celer being all bloody. I do not want to go into why and what happened there. You would not believe me even if

I did. So, please, accept that there was a reason for what you saw and it was not pleasant. The problem is that Gigi might be put in the same situation. Therefore, Madre Maria and I have a plan to get Gigi out of the Casa and take her to Mexico City to Madre Maria's Casa. I need your help to do so. Will you help?"

"Of course, Bob, but I wish you would tell me why."

"Jesus, please take my word that it is of a necessity. If Madre Maria is in on it, then it must be all right. Don't you agree?"

"Well if you put it that way, then I must agree. Tell me what I have to do."

"I will take Gigi out tomorrow for a visit. I will explain to her then that she is leaving and going to Mexico City. During that time, the Madres will be in church. What you must do is go into the children's dormitory while they are in church with the Madres. Felipe will let you past, as the girls won't be in there. Gigi keeps all of her "treasures" in a shoebox under her bed. I need you to get them and bring them to me here at the hotel. If she were to bring them to Mexico City just for a weekend, Esmeralda would get wise to something being up. Gigi's treasures mean a lot to her. I do not want to leave them behind when we go. Will you do me that favor? Also you must never tell anyone of this conversation, especially Esmeralda, agreed?"

"Agreed, Bob. I hope to God that you know what you are doing. You could be accused of kidnapping," Jesus warned.

"Yes, but those are the chances we take. We have a lawyer in Mexico City that has agreed to the plan. In addition, we have some officials of the government prepared to take action if anything happens. Don't worry; with God's help, we will pull it off. Let's not discuss it any further as I don't want you to be in a position to know anything more, just in case the plan blows up. Then you can in all truthfulness plead you knew nothing about what was going on, okay?"

Jesus agreed. We then discussed the computer school at the Casa and how it was going. Shortly thereafter, we said our goodbyes. Jesus went home and I retired to my room for sleep. I was tired, as I had a nerve-racking day. The next day, I was at the Casa bright and early. Gigi was waiting for me as usual. I asked Esmeralda if I could take her out for the morning for a shopping spree. She agreed and off we went.

I took Gigi into the shopping plaza and parked. As she started to get out, I said, "Gig, wait a while. Daddy has something to tell you. Madre Maria and I have decided you should live with her in Mexico City. When you are there, Daddy will adopt you so we can be with each other forever. Would you like that?"

"Yes, oh yes, Daddy, I would want that more than anything," she said as she threw her arms around me and hugged me tightly.

"The only thing is you must not tell the Madre about this. She thinks the visit to Mexico City will only be for the weekend. We are going to trick her because she would never agree to me adopting you. So we have to do it this way. Just like Daddy promised never to tell anyone what you told me a couple of months ago, I am asking you never to tell anyone what I am now saying to you. Don't even tell any of the girls. Today, Jesus is getting your treasures from under your bed. Because if the Madre were to see you take those, she would wonder why. So you don't have to worry about them. Do you agree with everything Daddy said and do you really truly want to come?"

Gigi looked at me with tears in her eyes and said, "Yes, yes, very much. It is what we have been talking about for a long time. I will finally have a family and a daddy that I love so very much. Daddy, I am the happiest girl in the world right now. I am going to have a real daddy and not just a make-believe one. Oh, Daddy, I love you so."

We sat there for a while until Gigi stopped crying. I wiped her eyes and waited a little more until the redness in them went away. When her eyes looked okay, we got out of the car and then went shopping for the long journey that she was about to experience.

It seemed like we bought out all the stores that day. She needed shoes, dresses, slips, pants, a suitcase, and many more things for her stay in Mexico City. I would bring most of it back to the hotel and then tell Esmeralda that the extra bag was mine if she asked. Doing it that way would allow Gigi just to pack a small bag at the Casa to bring with her. Gigi's traveling bag was nothing but a small paper shopping bag. She never even had that until we started shopping months ago. Now she saved all those bags under her bed. They were part of her treasures that Jesus was collecting today.

We finished shopping and I brought Gigi back to the Casa. Arriving there, we saw Jesus at the computer school window. He looked out and gave me a sign that he had completed his task and would bring Gigi's things to the hotel that evening.

Gigi and I went looking for Esmeralda to tell her we were back. I had reminded Gigi before getting out of the car about not telling anyone what we were planning, though it probably wasn't necessary. Upon seeing Esmeralda, we stopped and talked to her about tomorrow when we were to leave. She was excited about seeing Madre Maria and her friends. She told me that Gigi and she would be ready at 8:00 the next morning for me to pick them up to go to the airport. I agreed and gave Gigi a hug and a kiss goodbye before leaving for the hotel to await Jesus.

Jesus was watching for me to leave and soon followed me to the hotel. There he gave me all of Gigi's "treasures": one small broken doll, handmade dresses for the doll, five rocks that we had gotten one day on the beach, eight paper bags, five hair ribbons, and a deflated balloon that she had from her birthday party. To Gigi, these were her sole possessions, to be protected with her very life if necessary.

I thanked Jesus and gently packed them in the suitcase that we had bought today. I packed them in the bag as if they were diamonds and rubies. To her, they were.

Jesus and I spoke for a couple of hours. He mainly lectured me on whether I knew what I was doing. I listened attentively, but nothing and no one could talk me out of the plan. After a while, we both said our goodbyes. As he left, he turned to me and said, "Next time I see you, it will be in Mexico City. God go with you and The Gig. I love the both of you."

A
t eight the next morning, I was at the Casa. Esmeralda and Gigi were waiting, Esmeralda with her suitcase and Gigi with her small paper shopping bag filled with her good clothes. They both got in the car. Gigi kissed me and then sat in the back, relinquishing her front seat to Esmeralda.

"Next stop Mexico City," I said cheerfully.

We arrived at the airport and I turned in the car. Esmeralda and I both held onto Gigi's hands. Gigi's eyes were all over the place. She could not stop looking here then there. Each look produced ten questions. She was stunned at the managed chaos of the airport.

The hour approached for us to get on the plane. Gigi got on without any trouble, although she certainly took her time. She was very suspicious of this thing she was entering. Once inside and seated, the questions started again. Everything Gigi saw prompted an explanation.

Soon we were taking off. Now there was a sight to behold. Gigi was so scared. She clung to me so tightly I could hardly breathe. She wanted to get in the seat with me so she could hold on better. I told her the stewardess would get mad so she reluctantly gave up that feat. She closed her eyes and held her breath as long as she could. Then she took a new breath and held that. This went on for the entire two-hour flight.

Once in the air, we enticed her to look out the window at the clouds and ground. One fast look was all she needed and back she flew into my arms, never to let go until we reached Mexico City. She would not even let go when the food was served, so the both of us decided not to eat on the plane that day. Esmeralda just watched. She had tried to comfort Gigi at first, but Gigi would have none it.

We finally arrived in Mexico City. We unraveled Gigi from me and deplaned. The first thing Gigi did was to go to the bathroom. She'd had to go on the plane but she wouldn't even think about releasing her grasp on me long enough to go. She just kept crossing and re-crossing her legs for most of the trip.

From the airport, we went to the Hotel Rosa. The trip was once more filled with Gigi looking this way and then that way. I had never seen her so excited. Even during her first trip outside the great wall of the Casa to Tijuana, she was not this excited.

We arrived at the hotel and the bellboy went to take the bags. Esmeralda and I gave him our bags. When he went for Gigi's paper bag, Gigi would not let him have it. I finally persuaded her that he just wanted to carry it for her, not take it for himself. However, all throughout the check-in procedure at the front desk, she kept one eye on me and the other on the bellboy and her paper bag. She just did not trust him out of her eyesight.

Gigi loved our suite. She jumped on the beds and furniture. After that adventure, she went out to the balcony that overlooked the city. She had never seen anything like it. She would point to anything that caught her eye and have me tell her what it was. This went on for an hour. Esmeralda unpacked during this episode on the balcony.

Once our unpacking and sightseeing were complete, we called Madre Maria to tell her we had arrived safely. Then we arranged to meet that evening for dinner.

Gigi and I left to go downstairs and look around while Esmeralda took a brief nap. She was tired from the trip. Gigi's idea of looking around consisted mainly of riding elevators. I sat in the lobby as she went up and down in them. After about two hours, we came back to the room, got Esmeralda, and then went to the Casa to meet Madre Maria and her current companion, Madre Antonio.

We made our introductions and Esmeralda met Jose Louis, whom Madre Maria had asked to join us for supper. I later found out that she had invited him to verify that Gigi wanted to be adopted by me.

Supper went well. The next two days went well also. Esmeralda stayed with the Madres in the Casa during the day while Gigi and I went all over town. Gigi would not stop going. She just went and went. I was exhausted every evening by the time that we got back to the hotel.

Soon the day for returning to Tijuana was upon us. During our stay, Madre Maria had very slyly slipped in comments every so often on how sickly and tired Gigi looked. So when the day arrived to leave, she was able to suggest that Gigi stay behind for a complete physical by the Casa's doctor without it sounding contrived. I "volunteered" to stay an extra two days to bring her back to Tijuana. Esmeralda did not like the idea but finally agreed to it and returned to Tijuana alone.

The plan was going according to schedule. Now we were on our way to the next step. The rescue was successful so far. The Gig was free of Esmeralda, for the time being.

CHAPTER THIRTY

SAFETY AND PROTECTION

Gigi was now in the hands of Madre Maria. Gigi and the new Madre, Madre Antonio, hit it off at first sight. Gigi liked her very much. They talked a while in Spanish and then Gigi looked at me.

"Daddy, will I ever go back to Tijuana and the Casa"?

"No, never, Gig," I answered.

Madre Maria and Jose Louis, who was also there, confirmed what I said. Gigi watched their expressions to make sure everyone agreed. Gigi accepted what we said, but her eyes said that she still did not believe it.

Madre Antonio took Gigi to her new temporary quarters. It was a small room outside the girls' dormitory. The room had one small window and religious paintings on the walls. There was also a small bureau and desk. A closet at one end completed the room. Even though it was small, the room made Gigi very happy. She never had a room of her own before in all her life. I then took her secret suitcase and helped her unpack. Each piece was taken out of the suitcase and very gingerly placed in a drawer or the closet. She was very tidy, something that would change after a year or so of being free, much to my displeasure.

Madre Antonio then introduced her to some of the other girls there at the Casa while Madre Maria, Jose Louis, and I went to Madre Maria's living room to plan our next move. Jose Louis opened the conversation. "Luck has been with us so far. Let's hope it stays."

Madre Maria interrupted and in a funny tone of voice said, "Jose Louis, luck might be the answer. However, I have an unusual feeling that it goes further than that. Maybe, just maybe, God had a little to do with it. Then again, we will see what happens as we continue with the adoption procedure."

Jose Louis and I looked at each other with apologetic expressions. The Madre continued. "I think this would be the time to go to our chapel and thank the person who really permitted Guillermina to come to us."
We both humbly agreed and proceeded to the chapel behind Madre Maria.

While in the chapel, a strange occurrence took place that we all witnessed. As we knelt there praying, a light appeared, surrounding the statue of Mary, the mother of God. The lifelike statue of Mary was the centerpiece of the altar. At the base of Mary were three tiny, lifelike children. All were girls. They were dressed in rather torn and tattered dresses with no shoes upon their feet. Two of the children were sitting and one was standing. The children that were sitting appeared about four or five years of age. The child that was standing was about eight or nine years old. All the children were gazing up towards the face of Mary. At the children's feet were rose bushes.

The light that we were now observing first appeared dimly, but as we prayed, it got brighter and brighter until it filled the room with a frightening glow. The standing child at the base of Mary seemed to take on a brighter brilliance than did the sitting children. Around this child's head there seemed to appear a halo. Then from the corners of her eyes emerged minute droplets of water that seemed like tears. The room became warmer with each increase of illumination.

Jose Louis and I stared at each other as this was taking place. We could not believe it. We were looking all around to see where the light could be originating. We saw nothing that could explain it. Even if we were able to explain the light, I had no idea how to explain the tears in the standing child's eyes. Madre Maria took no notice of the luminous energy or the child's eyes. She just kept on praying harder than ever. The more she prayed, the brighter the light, the warmer the room, and the more tears appeared.

After the Madre finished praying, the light disappeared and the child's tears stopped. She then stood up and pronounced again, "Maybe, just maybe, He did have something to do with Guillermina's coming." Madre Maria never conveyed the impression that nothing took place out of the ordinary, although Jose Louis and I both went to the statue and felt the child's eyes before exiting the chapel. They were still wet from the tears that were flowing during the Madre's prayers. As we did so, we looked at each other with looks of disbelief.

To this day, Jose Louis and I have never said anything to each other about what took place that day in the chapel and I don't think we ever will. However, from that day on, Jose Louis was absolutely dedicated to helping us to the point that he stopped all his other work to put his full effort into Gigi and this situation. I never asked why.

We left and returned to the small living room. Jose Louis and I were speechless. We just sat there staring at each other in wonderment. Madre Maria broke the trance. "Jose Louis, what do we do now?" Jose Louis did not answer immediately. It took him a moment to compose himself and then he replied, "Madre, the next step is to get a birth certificate into the Hall of Records here in Mexico City. You, Madre Antonio, and myself have got to go to the hall and swear in front of the judge that Guillermina was born in Tijuana on a certain day and year. We think we know the year but have no idea of the exact day so go ahead and pick one."

I interrupted and said, "We have already done that when she had her party in Tijuana. It's August the twenty-eighth."

Jose Louis added. "Guillermina can stay here in the Casa temporarily for about a week. Then when Esmeralda becomes aware of what we have done, Guillermina will have to be moved to a place of secrecy known only to us three."

The next day, we all went to the Hall of Records and spoke to some of Jose Louis' friends there. Many questions were asked of the Madres and Gigi. The results of the meeting were good. A birth certificate was placed into the records; Gigi could now prove she had been born, that she existed.

The next step was to have her meet the judge and the attorneys of the state of Mexico. This was important, as they had to ask her questions about her willingness to be adopted and other matters pertaining to the adoption. The Madres were going to answer some questions also.

Gigi met with them all and was very positive about being adopted by me. They were concerned that I was a single man. They said that this would be the hardest factor of all to overcome. I would have to have letters from very important people in the world to substantiate my character, since Mexico City had never granted such an unusual adoption before. I informed them that I could obtain the proper references. The meeting there also went well.

The next two days flew past. We were very busy going here and then there with Jose Louis to meet people who would take part in this unusual adoption. Jose Louis wanted them to get to know The Gig and me personally. He knew that if they could meet us, along with reading the letters, they would believe that this adoption was truly in the best interest of the child.

When the two days were up, the expected phone call came from Esmeralda. Madre Maria told her what we had planned, and the doctor needing more time to examine Gigi. Once more Esmeralda accepted it. However, this time she delivered an ultimatum to Madre Maria. Guillermina was to be back in Tijuana by next week or Madre Maria would be in serious trouble.

This demand came as quite a blow to Madre Maria. You do not talk that way to the Madre general. When you become a nun, you take three vows: poverty, chastity, and obedience. Esmeralda had just in no uncertain terms disobeyed the third. Thus, Esmeralda must have had a good idea of her own ill-begotten power to speak that way to Madre General Maria.

The next move was up to me. I had to secure the letters. The officials of the state of Mexico all concurred that I was a proper person to adopt Gigi and Gigi was in full accord with the adoption.

During the next week, I was very busy contacting people for the necessary letters of recommendation. During that time, Gigi played at the Casa most of the day with the younger girls while the older ones were at school. Madre Antonio told us that Gigi would pray every night never to be returned to Tijuana. She prayed to stay here with her daddy forever.

Gigi could not attend school during this time. We could not afford to apply for a school because Gigi's school transcripts would have to be sent from Tijuana. The school officials in Tijuana were very good friends of Esmeralda. They would be sure to inform her of such a request from Madre Maria or from any school in Mexico City that requested the same. Schooling for Gigi was important but we all agreed that it was not important enough to blow the plan.

I had thought all I needed were letters from the appropriate people. Thus, that was all I got, and by special delivery. When I presented them to Jose Louis, he told me that they were no good because they had to be approved and verified by the Mexican consul of the country in which the person was a citizen. I also needed my own certified birth certificate.

This was all news to me. I had barely enough time just to get the letters here in the first place. What he now wanted, I could not do within the time restraints of the week. I had blown the week on getting these now useless letters.

Jose Louis, Madre Maria, and myself now met again to discuss the next step, as we had run out of time.

"How long will it take to get the right papers?" Jose Louis asked.

"About two to three weeks, if I am lucky."

Jose Louis looked worried and said, "That's too long. Madre Esmeralda will be on us and we would be too far into April when Madre Maria has to resign her post. Then it would be impossible for the adoption due to the new Madre general being a close friend of Madre Esmeralda.

"Okay, first things first," he said. "First we must find some way to get Guillermina to safety. The first place they would look for her would be in one of the Casas. We have to move her out of here right now. I have already spoken to my wife in case this situation came up. She has agreed to take Guillermina to live with our family until we can get the final adoption papers finished. I have three girls around Guillermina's age. They are eight, nine, and eleven years old. If she came to live with us, this would serve a dual purpose. First, she would be safe and they would not think to look for her there. Second, she would be to allow her to live with a normal family before the adoption. She would also be able to go to school. I have a good friend in the school my girls attend. She will accept Guillermina for a while without the transcript from her current school. She would also get accustomed to being free with normal girls around her to teach her things that little girls do in a normal world. This is the best way to get her temporarily out of Esmeralda's reach."

"Next, I will have to make arrangements with the authorities to expedite the adoption before the end of April when Madre Maria will be relieved of command. After we receive permission from the state of Mexico, we must then get the Republic of Mexico to permit the adoption. These are two separate governments. First the state and then Mexico. These cases usually take four to six months to do. We only have three *weeks* to get it done. God has got to be on our side or else all is lost."

With this statement, Madre Maria added, "Jose Louis, do not worry; He *is* on our side. He will make it happen, just wait and see."

"Madre, I hope you are right or else we are all in for it."

I sat there and shook like a bowl of jelly. I kid you not; I was terrified of what would happen to Gigi if she were to be returned to Esmeralda. They would get out of her what she had told me. Then her life would not be worth a plug nickel—nor would mine. I knew too much. With no witness except Gigi, my testimony would be unsubstantiated and useless in the court. I was old and had no reason to live except for Gigi, but her life was just starting. Chills ran up and down my body as Jose Louis spoke.

We all agreed; the first thing was to remove Gigi from the Casa. Telling her was my job. Then Madre Maria would draw up the legal papers allowing her to stay in Jose Louis' house temporarily. This was not unusual. They had done it before with other children so there was no problem there. After Gigi was safe, I would get the necessary papers. Jose Louis would grease the wheels in both governments and Madre Maria would fend off Esmeralda as long as possible.

We then broke up to attend our appointed tasks. I went to Gigi, who was playing with some of her new friends in the Casa's courtyard as she waited for me to finish. I went down with Jose Louis standing close by to take her.

I called her over and said, "Gigi, you are going to leave the Casa now to live with Jose Louis for a while. Then you will come with me forever. The reason you will be staying with Jose Louis is because he has three daughters your age. Plus, you can go to school with his girls. This way you will not lose any more school then you already have. His girls will teach you how to live in the new world you are about to enter, okay?"

She listened to what I had to say and then said, "Daddy, I do not understand. But if you say that it is right and what you want me to do, then I will do it." This was one time that the Casa's strict obedience paid off to the good. Gigi went and said goodbye to Madre Antonio and Madre Maria. Then she collected her clothes from her small room and returned to the courtyard. "I am ready, Daddy."

We left for Jose Louis's house in the suburbs of Mexico City.

Upon arriving at his home, Maru, Jose Louis's wife, and his girls were waiting for us. Jose Louis had phoned them prior to us leaving the Casa. They all greeted Gigi with hugs and kisses. We then went to the girls' bedroom to get Gigi settled. Within minutes after putting her things in the room, Gigi was out in the yard playing with the girls. She had settled in without any problems.

Maru told us that she had already contacted the school and everything was arranged for Gigi to start school tomorrow with the girls. The first step of the new plan went smoothly. The next step for me was the papers. I still had no idea how I was to do that within time. But before I thought of that, I wanted to make sure Gigi was safe and happy in her new life and fortress.

Jose Louis encouraged me to get started on my phone calls to the states and wherever else I need to call and due to get those papers. Once more, he reiterated that there was not much time and still much to accomplish. He, in turn, would go to Mexico City and start talking to people about Gigi.

I said my goodbyes to Gigi and Maru and off I went to my hotel to start the next important step in the plan. At least I was able to leave for my duties with the sensation that Gigi was well protected and safe for the time being.

CHAPTER THIRTY-ONE

ADOPTION AT LAST

After a brief drive back to the city, I arrived at my hotel. I had a phone message from my secretary, Diane, waiting for me. I promptly placed a call to her and she said that things were happening hot and heavy with the new reorganization. It looked like we were soon to be out of business with our early education effort. That, of course, meant I would be reassigned to a different job.

I said, "I agree, things do look bad. However, I just do not have time to worry about that now. Things down here are blowing up, but please keep in touch so I know what's going on up there." I thanked her and got on to the more important thing, adopting The Gig.

The first call was to Doc. I told him the letter he had sent me was not correct. He had to do it all over again and then get the Mexican consulate in New York to sign it and give Doc a special piece of paper that verified that this was Doc's letter.

Doc is an important man in New York and he had a tremendous work schedule. Even so, he was quick to drop everything and proceed to get the necessary documents for the adoption once he heard about our new predicament. I also asked him to get a certified copy of my birth certificate from the New York Board of Health that Jose Louis had said I needed for the adoption. He agreed to do that likewise. Not only did I have to have those things, I told Doc that these documents had to be here yesterday so to get them to me ASAP.

After that, I made two similar phone calls to the people who were supplying the same documents. They both responded by saying they would drop everything they were doing and get right to it. These people knew The Gig very well. They had visited with her many times in the Casa. They not only knew her, but they also loved her very much. Each and every one of them would go way out on a limb for her. Though they knew her, they knew nothing of my recent discoveries of what was taking place in the Casa. Nor was I ever expecting to tell them

All I could do now was wait. I had done all I could for the adoption until I got the paperwork from those people.

The next day, Doc called and said he could not get my birth certificate until I sent him a notarized letter stating that I had given him permission to secure it. One more hitch in the plan. I quickly arranged to secure the letter and sent it off to him by special delivery. Three more days would now be lost.

During that week, Jose Louis was entertaining many of the public officials who would be necessary in the adoption procedure. I was present at most of these meetings. Jose Louis thought this was important to help them really get to know me. With being single, I had a tough row to hoe if I were to adopt Gigi. As I had previously mentioned, adoption to single American men had never been done before in Mexico. I would not only need letters from very important and outstanding persons but much support from the Mexican public officials.

Some days, we would have two or three meetings that started early in the morning and did not end until the wee hours of the next. I also attended parties of the officials' children along with Gigi. This gave the officials and their families a chance to know Guillermina. At each party, she was very well received by the adults and the children. The parties also gave Gigi a chance to learn more about life. The parents would comment on how proper and nice Guillermina was. They thought that she would be a joy to have in any one's family. They would all wish me well on my endeavor.

At Jose Louis' house with his girls and at school, Gigi was acquiring more and more information about the new world she was about to enter. One of the things she was getting acquainted with was the way that children expressed themselves when they wanted something. The word "want," as I had mentioned before, was foreign to Gigi. It was taking time to adjust, as a lot of the children in school were taking advantage of her good nature.

Gigi would not express herself. Nor would she exercise her rights. She would always do what the kids told her to do and never gave any thought as to whether it was right or wrong. She just accepted it was right if they said it was.

One day, I asked where her schoolbooks were.

"I do not know," she said.

"You did not know? Didn't you see the other children had books?"

"Yes," she answered.

"Well don't you think you ought to have the same?"

"Yes, I think so," she exclaimed.

"You think so. What kind of an answer is that?"

"No one told me to get them."

"Gigi, no one is going to tell you to get them. You must ask for them. You cannot study without them. The days of you being told what to do and what to say are over. Now you must ask or tell someone if you want something, understand?"

"Daddy, I don't know what to say," she replied. Tears were coming to her eyes because I had raised my voice to her. As she stood there with her head and eyes fastened to the ground, I promptly realized I was handling this whole matter of the books incorrectly. Once again, I had forgotten Gigi's background. I then said in a soft forgiving voice, "Daddy will go to school tomorrow and show you how to ask for them, okay? It's not a problem."

She raised her head a little and with a sobbing, pitiful voice said, "Thank you, Daddy." Then she came to my arms that were held wide to comfort the tears that were now streaming down her face due to my mishandling of the situation.

This was a lesson I would never forget when I was to speak to Gigi in the future on situations similar to this. I had to speak in a low tone and not raise my voice or risk bringing tears to her eyes. I'm not sure who felt worse over the matter, her or me, but I think it was me. I could have cut my tongue out that day if I only had a knife. Needless to say, she got her books the next day.

Jose Louis' daughters were caught a couple of times by Maru doing the same type of things to her, taking advantage of her good nature. This soon stopped as each time they were caught doing it, they got some zumba, or spanking, for it.

All in all, Gigi was settling in with her new surroundings and friends very well. Time, I thought, would take care of the rest. She was learning so much. How to ride a bike. How to operate a radio and record player. What TV and McDonald's were. What Saturdays and Sundays were. She even had a better idea of what time was. She still could not tell time with any accuracy, but she was working on it very hard.

She was also acquiring a taste for food other than beans and tortillas, except for pizza. I thought that every child liked pizza, but for some reason, she did not and still doesn't. She grew to enjoy hamburgers, French fries, and a Coke or milkshake at McDonald's. Also hot dogs with chili—she really liked those.

Jose Louis' girls played with dolls. Gigi liked those as well. She wanted one but she would never ask for it. Every time I went to visit her, she would show me one of the dolls that Maru's girls had and say, "Gee, I wish I could have one like this." I am sucker for that comment. Thus, the next day she would have one.

The best part of Gigi living with Jose Louis' family was that Gigi was differentiating the way of existence in a family versus the way of the Casa. She learned how a family all sat down for supper and the way they would participate in family activities together. She was gaining knowledge of these and many other similar family details. They were being unknowingly assimilated by Gigi by osmosis.

During this time, Gigi and I did many things together. I had completely forgotten to worry about my job and my work there in Mexico City. We went to the zoo, plays, the circus, and many other events. Every time we went out, her questions got shorter. She was starting to accept her new environment, although many events were still new. The one thing she was really learning was that life was not just all work, and that there was a tomorrow. She now was looking forward to her tomorrows and what they would bring.

She was so very happy. She was now doing her little hop, skip, and jump routine every time I saw her. The only problem she had now was wondering when Daddy would come and live with her all the time. Then she wanted to know where we would live. After living with Jose Louis's family in a house, she wanted a house of her own. She always would ask me what her room would look like and if she could have a dog, another new obsession. The word "house" no longer held the terror for her as it did when she was in Tijuana and Estella would order the girls to prepare for going to one.

The week went by swiftly. As expected, Esmeralda called Madre Maria and asked to have Gigi returned to Tijuana and her jurisdiction. We could no longer put off the inevitable. Madre Maria informed her that Guillermina was not to be returned to Tijuana and she was to stay here under her scrutiny.

With that, Esmeralda went through the roof. Jose Louis and I were standing by the phone when Madre Maria informed her of her decision and we could hear every word. Esmeralda screamed and shouted like a madwoman. She delivered all sorts of threats to Madre Maria, even threatening to have Madre Maria done away with.

Madre Maria was a soft-spoken, gentle, and easygoing person. She took this indignity for much longer than either Jose Louis or I would have. But eventually this gentle woman blew her own top. She, in no uncertain terms, informed Esmeralda who the Madre general was and how dare she go against her vows of obedience.

This did not stop Esmeralda. She continued her tirade.

Finally, Madre Maria hung up on her after stating, "Guillermina is staying here, and you will do as I say." She also added that she was not finished with Madre Esmeralda even after this matter of Guillermina was completed. Many more matters had come to her attention than just the welfare of this one particular child.

After Madre Maria hung up the phone, her face was red with anger. Madre Antonio was summoned and informed of the conversation that had just taken place. She was speechless over what she was told about Esmeralda's conversation. Madre Maria then issued orders that no one was to disclose the whereabouts of Guillermina except herself. She turned to Jose Louis and said in a commanding tone, "Jose Louis, protect and watch that child with all urgency. Let no one near her that you do not know. Esmeralda has threatened to do away with her if she is not returned and she has people who could do it. That child must not be hurt in any way. Guillermina's safety is in your hands now." She then went to the chapel with Madre Antonio to pray both for Esmeralda and for forgiveness for the anger that she now held within her heart.

Jose Louis and I left. I returned to my hotel to see how the correspondence was progressing from my friends and Jose Louis returned to his house. That evening, I called Gigi around 8:50, as I usually did each evening before retiring. There was no answer. I called again at 9:50, still no answer. I was starting to get worried. I called at 11:00 and again no answer.

By this time, I was really worried. I got into my car and drove to Jose Louis' house. The house was dark. I rang the door and got no response. I then went back to the hotel. I called Madre Maria from my room. She was not there either. Nor was Madre Antonio.

What the hell was going on? I panicked. I could not call the police, as they only spoke Spanish and I still was not the greatest with the Spanish language. All I could do was to wait restlessly. Finally, at 6:50 a.m., the phone rang. It was Jose Louis.

"Where the hell were you and everyone last evening?" I snapped.

Jose Louis replied, "Bob, everything is all right now but we had a rough night. I did not call you, as I knew you would worry and you could be of no real help in this situation. I removed my own family to a friend's house for safety.

"After she and Mother Maria had spoken, Madre Esmeralda called the bishop who had authority over Madre Maria. He called Madre Maria and ordered her to return Guillermina to Tijuana. Madre Maria then called me. I, in turn, called the chief of police in Mexico City. He requested Guillermina to come to the police station immediately to tell him why she did not want to return to Tijuana. Guillermina then went to the station and told the chief some of the things that were going on up there. After hearing those events, the chief issued an order to place Guillermina under the protection of the government of Mexico and the police in Mexico City.

"She was to be removed from the protection of the Casa's authorities and permanently placed in a safe house. The police chief recommended the house where Gigi was now staying. Then I had to get a judge out of bed to have the order legalized. After that, we had to deliver the order to the bishop. The order states that if any effort is commenced to remove or harm Guillermina from the protection of the police, then that person or persons would be libel to arrest and legal proceedings. The bishop was furious but had no other recourse other than to obey it."

"We then took Guillermina back to my house from where I am now calling. She was exhausted and is at present fast asleep. You would have been proud of the way she acted and behaved last night. You have some girl there."

He continued. "It was rough, but we now have time. Esmeralda is stopped for the moment, but I do not think she is finished. She will try something else. Even though we bought some time, we must act swiftly for the adoption. One of the biggest things we have going for us is the support of Madre Maria and Madre Antonio. When they are replaced in two weeks, the chances of getting Guillermina are nil."

I agreed and said, "Give me a call when Gigi wakes up so I can come out and see her." After a few more minutes of discussion, he got off the phone so he could get some sleep and I followed suit.

At about 4:00 that afternoon, Maru called and informed me that Gigi was up and asking for me. I hung up and started heading for their house. I arrived and Gigi flew into my arms. She was so afraid that she would be sent back to the Casa and Esmeralda. Likewise, she was terrified of what had taken place last night.

Jose Louis, Maru, and I spent most of the remaining afternoon trying to convince her that she would never be sent back to Tijuana and the evil Esmeralda. She finally said she accepted it, but I do not think she really believed it in her heart. I spent the rest of the day there. I also spent the night in Jose Louis's house, sleeping on the couch with the very frightened Gigi in my arms.

Within the next couple of days, I had all the paperwork necessary for the adoption on my end. Jose Louis spent many more hours running all over the place to get things set up for the adoption. Soon all the proper paperwork had arrived, due to my friends working night and day to secure them. Finally, within the time restraints that Jose Louis had placed upon me to secure all the necessary papers, Guillermina and I were standing in front of the judge in the adoption court. After three grueling, nervous hours, the adoption was granted, both in the state of Mexico and the Republic of Mexico.

The letters of reference from my friends overcame any objections the court might have had about a single man adopting a little girl. The people whom I asked to write the references were some of the most famous and powerful people in the world and well known in the country of Mexico. Not only were they well known, but they were also well respected as to their qualifications to judge a person's character. In addition, many of the people in the court who had to pass judgment on the adoption had gotten to know Gigi and me in the days gone by, thanks to Jose Louis' efforts. They too supplied an opinion to the adoption procedures. And, of course, a letter from the Vatican helped a little. (I had installed a computer system in the Vatican years ago.)

Now she could call me "Daddy" and we had the papers to prove it. She could also leave Jose Louis' house and come live with me at the hotel until we could find a place to live. That she understood. She was coming to live with her daddy now and we were going to start looking for a house.

As we discussed it, she quickly added, "And a dog too, Daddy!"

"Yes, my daughter, any kind you want. Just name it and Daddy will get it for you."

I now had Gigi as my real daughter, along with a passport for her and all the necessary papers to tell the world she was legally mine. Madre Maria, Madre Antonio, Jose Louis, and Maru were beside themselves with joy as we exited the courtroom. Gigi did not understand the whole thing, but she did understand that she had a new name to use for the rest of her life.

CHAPTER THIRTY-TWO

THE ADVENT OF THE ROSE

After the court procedures, Madre Maria, Madre Antonio, Jose Louis, Maru, Gigi, and I all went to the best restaurant in Mexico City to celebrate. We had been there in the past to entertain some of the people who wanted to meet The Gig and me. The captain knew Gigi quite well, as she has a way of capturing the hearts of all who meet her. He was happy to see her again and showed her all the consideration of a young lady.

Gigi promptly informed the captain that she had a new name and he made a big fuss over it. This went over big with Gigi. All of us just took a back seat as all the waiters and employees came over to congratulate her on her new daddy and name. They even gave her a small cake with her new name on it for dessert.

For just this occasion, I'd had a jeweler create a gold necklace with a little gold placard that hung on the chain. On the placard was inscribed Gigi's new name: Guillermina Nielsen. The design was very unusual. The jeweler did an outstanding job. This placard now adorned Gigi's neck, along with the ever-present elephant necklace that had been placed there years earlier.

These two chains were the first of many gold chains or necklaces that Gigi has come to possess. The others are put on and taken off at her desire, but no one in this world besides God could get Gigi to take off her elephant or name necklaces. Those two pieces of jewelry have become part of her whole being, never to be removed in her lifetime. In fact, I think Gigi would even give God a hard time if he told her to remove them.

We stayed there at the restaurant commemorating Gigi's new identity until late in the evening. We could see Gigi was becoming tired so soon all agreed to leave and return to the hotel to put her to bed. Then we would carry on the celebration at the hotel.

Gigi and I were the first to alight from the car at the entrance to the hotel. The others were close behind us. Just as we were about to enter the hotel, a little girl stepped out from the shadows. The night was cold, as most nights were in Mexico. This little girl had nothing on but a flimsy tattered dress, much too short for her age. She was about eight or nine years old. She had no shoes and her hair was in total disarray. It looked as if it hadn't been washed for about two or three months. Her face was pale and shallow, and her body was frail and very thin.

Her big brown eyes were sunk deep into her face, yet a strange glow seemed to emanate from them, as if there was a fire within them. A brilliant light surrounded her entire body. Even though the night was nippy, this child seemed not to show any signs of being cold. On the contrary, she appeared to be very warm. But those weren't the strangest thing about this little girl. She looked very much like the little child that had been standing at the feet of the statue of Mary in the Madre's chapel months ago during that strange time when the Madres, Jose Louis, and I had been praying for Gigi's safety.

In her small, frail hand, she held a single tightly closed rosebud. She walked up to Gigi and me, said nothing, but held her hand up towards us with the rosebud in it, as if to offer it to us. Gigi looked at me, her eyes begging me to buy it so the child would be able to retire for the evening. I got the message and Gigi and I tried to purchase the single rosebud.

The little flower girl nodded and gave us a small smile, but refused the money. She gave Gigi the rose and said, "God bless." Then she curtsied and walked away.

Gigi now held the rose in her hand as we waited for the rest of the party to join us at the entrance to the hotel. The rosebud appeared to gleam. I had never seen a rose like it before.

Soon all the party was inside the hotel. Maru saw the rose in Gigi's hand and asked Gigi where she got it.

Gigi replied, "From the little girl outside as we entered."

Maru said, "What little girl? We were right behind you and saw no one but you and your daddy. You all were standing by the entrance in a corner when we got out of the car. You were talking but we saw no one else with you."

Maru looked at the rest of the party for agreement. They all nodded in agreement. Only Madre Maria's face showed an expression of belief at our explanation of the rose's appearance.

Maru continued, "When we had reached you that was when we saw the rose."

I tried to convince them that a little girl had been there with the rose but all of them, except Madre Maria, looked at me as if I were crazy, so I promptly changed the subject. That was four years ago, and the rose is still in Gigi's possession in a vase at the head of her bed.

When Madre Maria comes to visit us, as she does quite often, she never hesitates to go to Gigi's room and stand by the rose in silence to stare at its ever-present beauty. Two years ago, the Madre placed a rosary at the foot of the vase that contains the now-dead rose. Many times, she has asked us to leave the room so she may be alone with the rose that has become as important to her as it is to Gigi and me.

Gigi and I know there was a girl and we secured the rose from her. Maru and the others always swore there was no girl. However, the only question that they still cannot answer is where we got the strange flower.

The adoption did not fix everything. Three days after the adoption, a car tried to run us over in the street outside our hotel. Once, a car tried to run us off the road as we were driving. One day, as we were walking on the street Mexico City, I was wounded by a bullet fired from a passing car. Jose Louis chalked all this up to Esmeralda's friends. Esmeralda had stopped trying to get Gigi back to Tijuana legally, as she and the bishop were afraid of the police. But she had not stopped trying to silence Gigi from disclosing what she, unbeknownst to Esmeralda, had already disclosed. During this time, I had also heard via Jesus that my informant from the Tijuana Casa had met with a fatal car accident, which makes my heart heavy when I think of it and of how good he was to us.

The new Madre general was appointed as expected. She and the bishop took no time to get back at the two Madres who had participated in the release of Gigi. Madre Maria and Madre Antonio were promptly transferred to some remote place in Mexico to serve their penance for what they had done to the bishop for the sake of a child.

Gigi's claims never surfaced due to the bishop not believing Madre Maria and Madre Antonio, or so he claimed. Nor would he believe Gigi or myself. In fact, he did not even want to see or talk to us. He refused to take any action and forbade the Madres from discussing the matter with anyone. Although I have no proof, I strongly believe from what I had witnessed in the Casa that the bishop was in on what was going on in the Casa and took his share of the profits.

Madre Maria and Madre Antonio did not care what punishment was delivered to them. They believed that what they did for the sake of a child would eventually be judged by God and not the bishop. On judgment day, they felt that God would deliver to them the rightful praise or punishment for their actions.

They and Jose Louis warned me to stay out of Tijuana. We could never safely return there. Esmeralda was all-powerful and just waiting for us to return to get her revenge.

So Gigi was now living in the hotel with me. She was fast becoming the hit of the hotel personnel, much like she had been in Tijuana. School was coming along wonderfully and she was meeting people in my office in Mexico. She was just in seventh heaven. She was so ecstatic over having a real family of her own that she had to introduce her daddy to everyone she met.

Every day, we would go out and look for a house to rent. I now had the job of finding her a governess—a nana as they are called in Spanish—and a permanent school. I also knew I had to protect her from future attempts on her life. Both Jose Louis and I knew Guadeloupe had not given up.

There was no end to my "to do" list. I still had to find a dog for her. Plus, we were planning a big adoption party for her in one of the finest hotels in Mexico City. My job was cut out for me. My troubles back in the office had to be resolved, but I had no time for that now.

Even though it was hectic, I enjoyed every minute of the time I spent with Gigi, as I too now had a real family. Gigi might not be of my blood. However, in my mind, blood does not make a family. Love for each other makes a family. And we had plenty of that.

Each evening, as I put her to bed and tucked her in, I would stand over her little body and think how wonderful God had been to me to give me my daughter. Gigi would look up at me, as she lay in bed ready to sleep, and raise her arms in an open embrace. "Daddy, I love you." Then she would slowly shut her eyes and drift off to sleep with her fellow angels.

As I stood there that first night in the hotel watching her sleep, I thought about the last goal I still need to accomplish, as if the past events were not enough. This forgotten child would learn to live in her newfound world. She would learn to live and play—things that normal children have known since birth. It would be a colossal job but I was sure that with the help of God, both my beloved Gigi and I would accomplish it some way or another. She has a spirit and way about her that I had never seen before in any child in all my world travels. She is a living angel, in both thought and action.

So many problems and situations still lay before us. However, I knew that this child was the "chosen one." The protection and guidance from above would always be there as it pertained to the welfare and wellbeing of Miss Guillermina E. Nielsen.

When God spoke to Moses, it is written that He said, "It is those who have suffered greatly that shall be first in my thoughts and deeds." Surely, this little child in her short years on earth has fulfilled those requirements and then some.

But this is not the end of Gigi's tale. It is only the beginning.

EPILOGUE

Gigi knew nothing of what was going on for her protection against the still irate Esmeralda. The chief of police in Mexico City had two plainclothes men always following us or standing guard outside our hotel room when we were there. Though Gigi was very much at home in the hotel, Jose Louis suggested that I live close to him and Maru, just in case anything happened with Esmeralda or I needed something. I thought his idea was good, so most of our house hunting was confined to his immediate area.

By this time, Gigi was speaking almost perfect English. With this ability under her belt, she was constantly asking what this was, what that was, and all about my life. I, in turn, was explaining everything. Likewise, I was asking many questions about her life as far as she could remember.

The telephone in our room was a great joy to Gigi. She was always calling room service for something. In reality, she really did not want the food, just the adventure of speaking to someone on that little "thing" we call a phone.

The time was passing rapidly and Gigi was getting impatient. She started to ask about when she was going to get a dog as I had promised. So we went out and bought some books with pictures of all the different types of dogs.

All of my life, I had always owned Dobermans. Thus, as we flipped the pages of the dog book, somehow the Doberman page regularly appeared under her scrutiny. Gigi eventually scolded me for it.

"Daddy, you are doing that on purpose. You think I should have that kind of dog. I like them but they are too big. I would like a real small dog at first. Something I can hold and love."

Those comments reminded me of her previous years with no love. Why shouldn't she feel that way? What a dummy I was not to realize it.

We quickly started to look at the small dogs in the book. Finally, she found a dog she would like to have. It was a Maltese. If I disliked any dog, it was a Maltese. Yet I had promised her any dog she wanted, and this was apparently the dog. If that was not enough, I had to find this type of purebred dog in Mexico.

Gigi suggested we look in the papers where they advertise. I agreed but there were never ads in the paper here in Mexico about dogs, let alone for a Maltese. However, she was insistent so I bought a paper and we looked. Lo and behold, there was a single ad in the paper for a dog. And this only dog was a Maltese. So off we went and now Gigi had her dog—a Maltese that she named Princess. These miracles always seemed to happen when Gigi was in trouble or wanted something and, they still do.

And one evening, Jose Louis called and informed me that Madre Esmeralda had had a fatal heart attack.

"She was in perfect health; how could that have happened?" I asked.

"What difference does it make? It happened! Now you and your precious Gigi can now be free and no longer worry about the 'problem,' as it seems to have taken care of itself."

To this day, I know that Jose Louis had a part in making sure that Gigi and I could live freely. He is quite a guy.